Corporate Compliance and Conformity

Traditionally, control in organizations is concerned with top-down approaches, where executives attempt to direct their employees' attention, behaviors, and performance to align with the organization's goals and objectives. This book takes a new approach by turning the problem of control upside down as it focuses on control of executives who find white-collar crime convenient. The bottom-up approach to executive compliance focuses on organizational measures to make white-collar crime less convenient for potential offenders.

Rather than focusing on the regulatory formalities and staged procedures of compliance and audits, the book emphasizes the organizational challenges involved in compliance work when trusted corporate officials exhibit deviant behavior, refining, and advancing knowledge in this field by reference to contemporary international case studies and associated original evaluative research. The themes and cases covered are carefully selected to provide the reader with an insight into professional conduct and procedural practice – the organization of corporate compliance success, failure, and corruption – with the theory of convenience placed at the fore. It is the bottom-up approach by application of convenience theory that makes the proposed book unique compared to other books on corporate compliance.

This book is a valuable resource for scholars and upper-level students researching and studying in the areas of business administration, organizational behavior, corporate and white-collar crime, as well as business ethics and auditing.

Petter Gottschalk is Professor in the Department of Leadership and Organizational Behaviour at BI Norwegian Business School in Oslo, Norway. Before joining academics, he held several chief executive officer positions in business enterprises. He received his education in Germany (Technical University of Berlin), United States (Dartmouth College and Massachusetts Institute of Technology), and United Kingdom (Henley Management College). Dr. Gottschalk has published extensively his research on knowledge management, police investigations, fraud examinations, white-collar crime, convenience theory, and corporate investigations.

Routledge Advances in Management and Business Studies

The Corporation of the Future
Edited by Stuart Orr and Paul Hunter

Organizational Management and the COVID-19 Crisis
Security and Risk Management Dilemmas
Edited by Wioletta Sylwia Wereda, Jacek Woźniak and Justyna Stochaj

Digital Entrepreneurship and the Global Economy
Edited by J. Mark Munoz

Cross-cultural Knowledge Management
Cultural Influences in China and Brazil
Jacky Hong and Jorge Muniz Jr.

Human Resource Management and Internal Marketing
Teena Mishra

Human Resources Management in Multinational Companies
A Central European Perspective
Marzena Stor

Corporate Culture and Globalization
Ideology and Identity in a Global Fashion Retailer
Yi Zhu

Corporate Compliance and Conformity
A Convenience Theory Approach to Executive Deviance
Petter Gottschalk

For more information about this series, please visit: www.routledge.com/Routledge-Advances-in-Management-and-Business-Studies/book-series/SE0305

Corporate Compliance and Conformity

A Convenience Theory Approach to Executive Deviance

Petter Gottschalk

Routledge
Taylor & Francis Group
LONDON AND NEW YORK

First published 2023
by Routledge
4 Park Square, Milton Park, Abingdon, Oxon OX14 4RN

and by Routledge
605 Third Avenue, New York, NY 10158

Routledge is an imprint of the Taylor & Francis Group, an informa business

British Library Cataloguing-in-Publication Data
A catalogue record for this book is available from the British Library

ISBN: 978-1-032-45908-0 (hbk)
ISBN: 978-1-032-45914-1 (pbk)
ISBN: 978-1-003-37924-9 (ebk)

DOI: 10.4324/9781003379249

Typeset in Bembo
by Apex CoVantage, LLC

Contents

Introduction

Compliance refers to meeting legal and other formal obligations, while conformity refers to meeting and potentially exceeding societal and other informal norms and obligations (Durand et al., 2019: 300):

> [W]e posit that conformity characterizes voluntary actions that constitute a response to social and normative expectations not (yet) codified in standards and law, while compliance relates to formal mandatory regulations that typically enact only minimal conditions of institutional acceptability.

Compliance refers to accepting by obeying the formal laws, rules, regulations, and guidelines in force within the jurisdiction. By meeting legal obligations, compliant organizations obtain a legal license to operate. Conformity refers to the informal norms, values, expectations, and opinions observable within the society. By meeting or exceeding societal expectations, conforming organizations obtain a social license to operate. While compliance is typically an obligatory corporate practice, conformity is typically a voluntary practice.

Traditionally, control in organizations is concerned with top-down approaches, where executives attempt to direct their employees' attention, behaviors, and performance to align with the organization's goals and objectives. This book takes a new approach by turning the problem of control upside down as it focuses on control of executives who find white-collar crime convenient. The bottom-up approach to executive compliance and conformity applied in this book focuses on organizational measures to make white-collar crime less convenient for potential offenders (Haines et al., 2022). Generally, the bottom-up perspective "highlights local, on-the-ground variations in practice, value or belief and the more-or-less strategic improvisation of rank-and-file institutional inhabitants as the locus of higher-order institutional change" (Ghaffari et al., 2022: 1710).

Yet another novel approach is introduced in this book by the social license to operate. It is a matter of countering corporate power through social control. The social license is predominantly centered on social permission by stakeholders for business activity where the media, social movements, and citizen

DOI: 10.4324/9781003379249-1

watchdogs exert pressure, demand change, and bring enterprises to account (Sale, 2021).

Rather than focusing on the regulatory formalities and staged procedures of compliance and audits, this book emphasizes the organizational challenges involved in compliance and conformity work when trusted corporate officials exhibit deviant behavior, refining, and advancing knowledge in this field by reference to contemporary international case studies and associated original evaluative research. The themes and cases are carefully selected to provide the reader with an insight into professional conduct and procedural practice – the organization of corporate compliance and conformity against failure, fraud, and corruption – with the theory of convenience placed at the fore. It is the bottom-up approach by application of convenience theory and the challenges from the social license to operate that contribute to the book's uniqueness.

The importance of the bottom-up approach lies in the failure of traditional approaches to prevention and detection of executive deviance. At the top of organizations, trust rather than control is the main attitude toward other privileged individuals. Not surprisingly then, deviance is more convenient at the top than further down in the organization. When scandals emerge after detection of executive wrongdoing, people tend to be surprised as scandals reach newsmaking criminology. The bottom-up approach can be efficient and effective to prevent and detect white-collar crime, as skepticism of management actions creates a motivation to correct the situation. People in the organization want to preserve and improve the reputation and survival of the business and avoid organizational mourning after organizational collapse (Crosina and Pratt, 2019).

Bottom-up approaches and requirements for the social license are discussed in Chapters 8 and 7, respectively, in this book. These two chapters are core in the second part of the book that addresses compliance control. Chapter 9 discusses how auditors can disturb crime convenience for white-collar offenders. Important elements in auditors' disturbance of financial motives are goal and bonus reviews, of organizational opportunities are status ignorance and forensic accounting, and of personal willingness are transparency and professional skepticism.

After detection and investigation, white-collar defendants end up in court where the prosecution and the defense present different stories in the form of narratives to convince the judge. Chapter 10 discusses the performance of prosecutors and defense lawyers in the courtroom that is sometimes compared to a theater scene.

Sometimes when there is rumor of wrongdoing in organizations, corporate investigators are hired to conduct internal fraud examinations to reconstruct past events and sequences of events. This is the topic in Chapter 11, where a sample of fraud investigation reports is reviewed. The following and final chapter, Chapter 12, discusses alternative policing of financial crime by corporate investigators in Australia, Canada, the Netherlands, Norway, and the United Kingdom.

While the second part of this book is concerned with various measures as described earlier, the first part of the book presents crime convenience by white-collar offenders, where Chapter 1 discusses various issues related to convenience orientation, compliance issues, and conformity problems. Chapter 2 applies convenience theory for profiling of white-collar offenders. Chapters 3, 4, and 5 present international case studies related to corruption in sports, economic crime in the fishing industry, and non-compliance during the COVID-19 pandemic. The final chapter, Chapter 6, in the first part of this book addresses the stigma effect versus the competition effect, where it is an interesting research issue whether competitors lose or gain when an industry peer is hit by a scandal such as white-collar and corporate crime.

References

Crosina, E. and Pratt, M.G. (2019). Toward a model of organizational mourning: The case of former Lehman Brothers bankers, *Academy of Management Journal*, 62 (1), 66–98.

Durand, R., Hawn, O. and Ioannou, I. (2019). Willing and able: A general model of organizational responses to normative pressures, *Academy of Management Review*, 44 (2), 299–320.

Ghaffari, M., Svystunova, L. and Jarvis, L. (2022). Cracking the box or stretching its walls? Exploiting institutional plasticity in Iranian creative advertising, *Human Relations*, 75 (9), 1707–1740.

Haines, F., Bice, S., Einfeld, C. and Sullivan, H. (2022). Countering corporate power through social control: What does a social licence offer? *The British Journal of Criminology*, 62, 184–199.

Sale, H.A. (2021). The corporate purpose of social license. *Sothern California Law Review*, 94 (4), 785–842.

Part I

Crime Convenience

1 Compliance-Conformity-Convenience

The main perspective in this book is concerned with lack of compliance and conformity as a result of convenience among executives and other trusted and privileged individuals. The extent of convenience orientation varies among members of the elite in society, where convenience orientation refers to the value that individuals and organizations place on actions with inherent characteristics of saving time and effort as well as avoiding strain and pain. Convenience orientation can be considered a value-like construct that influences behavior and decision-making. Mai and Olsen (2016) measured convenience orientation in terms of a desire to spend as little time as possible on the task, in terms of an attitude that the less effort needed the better, as well as in terms of a consideration that it is a waste of time to spend long hours on the task. Convenience orientation toward illegal actions increases as negative attitudes toward legal actions increase. The basic elements in convenience orientation are the individual attitudes toward the saving of time, effort, and discomfort in the planning, action, and achievement of goals. Generally, convenience orientation is the degree to which an individual or a group of individuals are inclined to save time and effort to reach goals.

Convenience orientation refers to a person's or persons' general preference for convenient maneuvers. A convenience-oriented person is one who seeks to accomplish a task in the shortest time with the least expenditure of human energy (Berry et al., 2002; Farquhar and Rowley, 2009).

In the marketing literature, convenience orientation is, for example, measured in terms of stage in a person's life cycle, family size, economic status, social status, and education (Sundström and Radon, 2015). Similar characteristics of convenience orientation might be developed for individuals in the elite regarding white-collar crime (Yasir et al., 2021).

Convenience orientation is introduced in this book as an explanation for white-collar crime among chief executives and other privileged individuals in politics, public administration, and private businesses. This book thus makes a case for a specific way of explaining elite member behavior.

Compliance and conformance to avoid crime convenience is not just a matter of individual and organizational wrongdoing that harms other individuals and organizations. It is also a matter of global sustainability as described by the

DOI: 10.4324/9781003379249-3

United Nations (UN). The UN Sustainable Development Goal 16 concerns 12 targets for promoting peace, justice, and strong institutions (Windsor, 2022).

Compliance in Corporate Governance

Corporate governance refers to mechanisms to protect and enforce stakeholders' rights by monitoring executives by transparency and holding them accountable. Corporate governance mediates between the various interests of internal and external stakeholders. Fotaki et al. (2020: 19) argued by their research results that compliance complements corporate governance:

> Compliance, although not sufficient in itself, serves as a complementary mechanism strengthening the effects of ethical values and creating the conditions by which instrumental values can act in favor of corporate governance. The results highlight that governance benefits can emanate from maintaining high ethical standards as well as from synergies between compliance and a focus on organizational values.

Kourula et al. (2019: 1104) defined governance as those private actors that direct behaviors in business conduct by rulemaking, enforcement, and sanctioning:

> By "governance" we refer not to corporate governance, but to the wider concept of societal governance, that of the collective means to give "direction to society" which we take to include direction to society's politics and markets.

This wide definition of governance is supported by Davies and Malik (2022), who emphasized regulatory regimes and criminal justice interventions in support of political priorities that give direction to corporate governance. Similarly, Johnson (2022: 23) reviewed a hybrid regulatory approach toward the enforcement of corporate financial crime in the United Kingdom and the United States, where an element of the approach is deferred prosecution agreements that "impose a financial penalty and behavioral commitments on a corporate entity for a defined period of time in exchange for the deferral of a criminal prosecution".

When there is suspicion of corporate white-collar crime, the governance branch typically involved should be the compliance function, potentially cooperating with internal and external auditors as well as various controllers (Maher et al., 2019; Schneider and Scherer, 2019). Internal or external fraud examiners have the task of investigating suspicions by reconstructing past events and sequences of events. If fraud examiners find sufficient evidence of law violation, then the case stops, moves internally, or moves externally to the national criminal justice system. If secrecy to protect corporate reputation is the main concern, then the case typically stops and remains internal.

However, organizations with inefficient or non-existing compliance functions or governance branch generally contribute to disorganized institutional deterioration. Schneider and Scherer (2019: 1147) argued that "the extent to which state authorities can regulate the externalities and the behavior of multinational corporations is limited", and that "aps in governance abound in today's globalized world". There is an erosion of state power and a shift toward private regulation (Aguilera et al., 2018). Critics claim that national governments collectively are taking limited initiatives through the OECD, European Union, UN, and other multinational organizations (Eberlein, 2019; Ken and León, 2021; Witt et al., 2021; Zysman-Quirós, 2020).

In contrast to the traditional agency perspective of a board's inability to control management, the multiple agency perspective includes various stakeholders as principals in their use of mechanisms to control management (Fotaki et al., 2020: 20):

> It considers a host of monitoring and incentives alignment mechanisms, as potential remedies for the multiple agency problems arising within a listed firm due to information asymmetries and conflicts of interest among various principals and agents.

The perspective of principal and agent suggests that when a principal delegates some tasks to an agent, the principal is often unable to control what the agent is doing (Bosse and Phillips, 2016). Agency problems occur when principal and agent have different risk willingness and different preferences, and knowledge asymmetry regarding tasks exists (Eisenhardt, 1989). The principal–agent perspective (or simply agency perspective) can illuminate fraud and corruption in an organizational context. The traditional principal may be a board of a company that leaves the corporate management to the chief executive officer (CEO). The CEO is then the agent in the relationship. The CEO in turn may entrust tasks to other executives, where the CEO becomes the principal, while people in positions such as chief financial officer (CFO), chief operating officer (COO), and chief technology officer (CTO) are agents (Stiffler, 2022). Agents perform tasks on behalf of principals (Pillay and Kluvers, 2014). The multiple agency perspective suggests that various stakeholders in combination might enable reduction or avoidance in principal–agent problems from opportunistic behavior by corporate executives.

Fotaki et al. (2020: 23) argued that "compliance with a given set of structural corporate governance regulatory requirements guarantees that the firm adopts the relevant practices to avoid legal liabilities":

> This means that compliance is primarily a quantitative issue, i.e., it denotes the number of corporate governance practices the firm reports that it adopts out of the set of best practices that it adheres to. We argue that compliance can affect the influence of enacted ethical and instrumental values on corporate governance for the following reasons. On one side, compliance with codes of best practices can also provide a compass to principals and agents, educating and guiding them on governance best practice.

> It defines roles and increases actors' participation in the governance-related issues, activating a process of learning and fostering a culture of corporate governance. On the other hand, compliance safeguards the firm against legal liabilities resulting also in some levels of accountability over the long term. In this context, principals, being usually assigned the monitoring role, have the confidence that agents at least adhere to rules and regulations regarding corporate governance.

Allocation of control rights to strategic resources might vary with governance structures (Rashid et al., 2022). In addition, residual rights of control occur because of incomplete organizing of exchanges. Alvarez and Parker (2009) argued that incomplete contract theory suggests that the relevant party to an exchange should receive these residual rights in order to maximize its overall value for the organization. That is the party that expects to create the most value from the exchange.

Mehrpouya and Salles-Djelic (2019: 13) argued that the discourse and rituals of transparency, account-giving, and verification are central to corporate governance:

> Transparency has been a normative shell through which financial accounting and audit standards have been pushed around the world. Under the contemporary governance paradigm, financial disclosure regimes are an important dimension of what it means to make organizations, states and individuals transparent and accountable. Champions of transparency, such as the former head of the IMF, Michel Camdessus, describe transparency as the "golden rule" of the new international financial system, "absolutely central to the task of civilizing globalization". Transparency implies unhindered access to information for the public. However, the definition of the public, targets and beneficiaries of transparency, along with associated programs and technologies, has been contested and has evolved through time.

Fotaki et al. (2020) studied 234 companies listed on the Athens Stock Exchange in Greece. The companies had issued their balance sheets and therefore also their corporate governance statements. The study findings suggest that interactions with compliance by corporate governance enhance the positive effects of ethical values, whereas compliance can also alter the role of instrumental values in favor of corporate governance. Study results suggested that compliance over a period of several years might increase the engagement of principals and agents with and learning of corporate governance issues.

Regarding environmental management and regulation compliance, Ballesteros et al. (2021) argued that introducing the social dimensions of environmental problems into governance has a positive impact. They studied shellfish poaching as an act of noncompliance with the laws that regulate fisheries governance outside Galicia in Spain.

Remaking Capitalism for Social Acceptance

Lucas et al. (2022: 958) argued that "a growing chorus off activists, academics, entrepreneurs, investors, and policymakers has expressed interest in remaking capitalism into a more just, sustainable, and inclusive economic system":

> Rather than serving shareholders only, companies have been admonished to generate value for all stakeholders, including employees, customers, suppliers, and communities.

Certification might be an avenue for the social license to operate as discussed by Lucas et al. (2022). Certification can be a device for authenticating values amid efforts to remake capitalism. Certification is an attempt to reconfigure organizational fields and reshape their collective values. Certification of social license moves far beyond traditional quality standard certificates such as ISO 9000. It is a matter of long-term vision of value-laden certification where various stakeholders rather than shareholders exclusively determine business direction. Values are here understood as abstract conceptions of desirable ends and goals that address specific circumstances and around which means and actions are oriented. Values can also be understood in the cultural perspective where they are manifested in various artifacts, rituals, and symbols.

The research by Lucas et al. (2022) exemplified certification by the B Lab that is a nonprofit network attempting to transform the global economy to benefit all people, communities, and the planet. The B Lab can issue a B Corp certification to corporations that contribute to an inclusive, equitable, and regenerative economy. Certification is based on standards defining social, environmental, and governance best practices for businesses. Sample questions from the B Lab assessment of companies include (www.bcorporation.net):

- Governance: What portion of your management is evaluated in writing on their performance with regard to corporate, social, and environmental targets?
- Workers: What % of the company is owned by full-time workers (excluding founders/executives)?
- Community: What % of management is from underrepresented populations? (This includes women, minority/previously excluded populations, people with disabilities, and/or people living in low-income communities.)
- Environment: Does your company monitor and record its universal waste production?
- Customers: How do you verify that your product improves the impact of your client organizations?

Lucas et al. (2022) studied legislation versus certification. They found that weak sustainability legislation in a jurisdiction tends to increase pressures toward value-driven business by adopting and maintaining a more rigorous and voluntary form of governance, for example in the form of third-party certification. Weak sustainability legislation might increase the need for value authentication that is social verification of a firm's values-based commitments by way of a more rigorous governance standard.

Lucas et al. (2022) reflected on the relationship between the legal license to operate and the social license to operate, where the latter was exemplified by certification. They argued that the traditional view tells us that new legislative rules positively reshape organizational impacts on society and the natural environment. The new legislative rules are then typically a result of social movements. However, since the strength of legislation may differ in terms of restrictiveness and enforcement, some legislation can be ambiguous as to both performance requirements and the related means for compliance. Legislation tends to take into account all imaginable circumstances and therefore remain full of weaknesses despite the social movements that triggered it. Legislative reform is therefore not at all the culmination of successful institutional change where alternative forms of governance like certifications for the social license to operate could become redundant.

Responses to Normative Pressures

Normative pressures refer to socially derived expectations. Often, normative pressures are a multiplicity of different expectations from a plurality of institutional demands (Durand et al., 2019: 301):

> Normative pressures are the evaluative and obligatory dimensions of an institutional order that weigh on an organization to gain, maintain, and defend its legitimacy.

Durand et al. (2019) made a distinction between willingness and ability of organizations to respond to normative pressures. The willingness derives from issue salience that refers to the extent to which a stakeholder issue resonates with and is prioritized by management. Issue salience is a perceptual outcome of a cognition process among decision makers. The ability derives from available resources and capabilities that lead to an assessment of taking or not taking action on the issue from a cost-benefit point of view. Therefore, even when an issue is highly salient, the enterprise that is subject to pressure may not respond.

On the basis of the willingness and ability of organizations to respond to normative pressures, compliance and conformity can be either symbolic or substantive (Durand et al., 2019: 300):

> Symbolic responses, on the one hand, describe managers' promises to engage in practice changes they have not yet implemented or may not implement, as well as nominal actions to produce impressions of more material change. Substantive responses, on the other hand, refer to managers' implementation of significant changes that involve material costs and

are not easily reversible, such as revamping deep-seated practices and inefficient distribution processes, or buying and selling divisions. While such distinction in responses is well observed in practice and well established in the literature, bridging symbolic and substantive responses with conformity and compliance is a distinctive contribution of the model we propose.

An example of symbolism in many business organizations is the ceremonial adoption of a code of ethics potentially copied from other business organizations or implemented in the organizations by external consultants. An example of substance is managerial training after organizational change caused by normative pressures.

In their model of organizational responses to normative pressures, Durand et al. (2019) proposed that a corporation may choose to respond to some issues but not to other issues based on varying assessment of issue salience as well as of resource mobilization. Some issues might be met with complete inaction; some might be met with symbolic action, while other issues might be met with substantive action. In the model, assessment of an issue as salient is a necessary but not sufficient condition for initiating a response. The model assesses possible organizational responses along two main dimensions. The first dimension ranges from inaction via symbolic to substantive responses, while the second dimension ranges from non-compliance via compliance to conformity. Four main categories of responses then emerge: (1) symbolic compliance, (2) substantive compliance, (3) symbolic conformity, and (4) substantive conformity. The model assumes that substantive actions are more costly and less reversible than symbolic actions. Substantive actions require a greater extent of resource mobilization that can close for other resorts in response to normative pressures.

The main premise of Durand et al.'s (2019) model is that boards with management decide the relevant response to any issue of normative pressure after considering issue salience and cost–benefit ratio, where the latter should be less than one for taking action and more than one for not taking action. This premise leads some businesses to respond symbolically, while others respond substantively, since various businesses even in the same industry might have different salience perceptions and different cost–benefit calculations. For example, the normative pressure not only for financial performance but also for socioenvironmental performance might cause different salience perceptions and different advantages and disadvantages if addressed by various enterprises.

The perspective of Durand et al. (2019) can be extended into a dynamic view of responses to normative pressures by comparison with companies hit by scandals. Gottschalk and Benson (2020) identified various paths of evolution of corporate accounts of scandals from exposure to investigation. Their analysis showed that denial of wrongdoing in several cases is replaced by admission of wrongdoing and scapegoating, while obfuscation of wrongdoing is replaced by denial or acceptance off responsibility and scapegoating.

Similarly, responses to normative pressures might initially take the form of inaction followed by symbolism. If the normative pressure continues and the issue is perceived as salient, while the cost–benefit ratio is considered less than one, then the next decision might be to implement a substantive action. Issue salience is perceptual as the same issue may not only be differentially evaluated as salient across decision makers and organizations but also be differentially evaluated as salient by the same decision maker and organization over time.

The purpose of Durand et al.'s (2019: 314) article was to present a "theoretical model describing the organizational decision-making process through which organizations choose whether and how to respond to normative pressures":

> By arguing that decision makers independently perceive the salience of an issue and concurrently evaluate the costs and benefits of mobilizing resources to address it, we highlight the sources of response heterogeneity across firms and across issues. These two factors account for both the willingness and ability of organizations to respond to normative pressures. In addition, they help to predict the different responses (inaction, symbolic and substantive conformity and compliance) that advance the neoinstitutional literature by streamlining and enriching the more traditional list of strategic responses to institutional pressures.

In the research by Durand (2019), corporate compliance and conformity are both a matter of issue salience and profitability in terms of benefits exceeding cost. This might seem strange since lack of compliance represents violations of laws and regulations, while lack of conformity represents violations of norms and expectations. It seems more serious to violate laws than norms for corporations. However, if issue salience reflects the seriousness of non-compliance versus non-conformity, then the difference between the two is implicitly covered in the suggested model.

Research Perspectives on Compliance

The word compliance can be defined as the act of adhering to or conforming to a law, rule, guideline, code, demand, or request. In a business environment, conforming is referred to as corporate compliance. Corporate compliance involves keeping a watchful eye on an ever-changing legal, regulatory, and moral climate, and making the changes necessary for the business to continue operating in good standing within its industry, community, and customer base to the satisfaction of all stakeholders. Compliance can be defined as "the internal programs that organizations adopt in order to educate employees, improve ethical norms, and detect and prevent violations of law" (Baer, 2009: 949).

Corporate compliance is a matter of organizational ability to carry out business activities without violating formal laws, the spirit of the laws, regulations and rules, ethics within and outside the organization, corporate culture in terms of norms and values, and other forms of guiding principles for the business. Corporate compliance is the ability to lead large groups of people toward achieving certain standards of conduct when performing their activities.

Compliance refers to obeying the formal rules and regulations as well as the informal norms and attitudes in force in a given situation (Desai, 2016; Durand et al., 2019).

Corporate compliance extends beyond mere legal and regulatory conformity into the realm of promoting organizational ethics and corporate integrity (Dion, 2008, 2009, 2019, 2020). Corporate compliance programs require monitoring, auditing, corrective actions, and system modifications or redesign to prevent future problem behavior (Andreisova, 2016; Majluf and Navarrete, 2011; Peterson, 2013; Remisova et al., 2019). A company's intolerance for wrongdoing is evidenced by corporate action taken consistent with its corporate compliance effort. Corporate compliance functions need internal and external intelligence to collect information on a continuous basis to prevent and detect deviant behaviors. If a corporate compliance function never prevents or detects actual incidents of wrongdoing, then it is likely that incidents escape under the radar (Desai, 2016; Williams et al., 2019), rather than it is a situation characterized by the absence of wrongdoing.

A distinction can be made between external and internal compliance (Kawasaki, 2020). External compliance is concerned with the laws, rules, and other regulations from a government that spell out how an organization should conduct itself. External compliance is also concerned with the local norms and values in the organizational environment. Internal compliance is concerned with internal policies and procedures that are implemented in the organizational structure as well as the organizational culture, where structure refers to the division of labor to complete tasks, while culture refers to the norms and values among organizational members when completing tasks. It is a matter of external and internal restraints from social control that influences organizational members toward conformance (Abadinsky, 2007).

When reviewing the corruption scandal at Siemens in Germany, Eberl et al. (2015) emphasized organizational rule adjustments such as strengthening of internal guidelines in order to close potential gaps, extension and specification of compliance rules for all employees and suppliers, general interdiction of consultancy contracts in sales and distribution, and guidelines on presents and invitations.

Ahrne and Brunsson (2011) described characteristics of an organization as membership, hierarchy, monitor, and sanctions. Organizations decide about membership and thus who will be allowed to join the organization as employees. Membership brings a certain identity with it, where the identity differs from that of non-members. Organizations include a hierarchy where there is a duty to oblige others to comply with decisions. Hierarchy entails a form of organized power. Organizations can issue commands, and they can decide upon rules that its members are expected to follow in their actions. An organization has the right to monitor compliance with its commands and rules (Kawasaki, 2020; Rooij and Fine, 2020). Organizations have the right to decide about sanctions, both positive and negative. They can decide to change a member's status by using promotions, grading systems, awards, diplomas, and medals.

In this hierarchical perspective, compliance at the top is far more difficult to monitor than compliance further down in the organization.

Compliance is linked to corporate social responsibility (CSR). To take on CSR means to pay back to society. Pay-back is the opposite of causing costs to society. CSR is supposed to be a self-regulatory mechanism whereby a business monitors and ensures its active compliance with the spirit of the law, ethical standards, and national and international norms (Zhang, 2021). CSR is a concept whereby companies integrate social and environmental concern in their business operations and in the interaction with their stakeholders on a voluntary basis (Ditlev-Simonsen, 2014).

While research perspectives on compliance are still very limited, CSR is receiving increased attention, sometimes linked to the concept of governance. CSR, governance, and compliance with laws and regulations are three approaches often suggested to combat fraud and corruption in organizations. CSR is defined as discretionary corporate initiatives and activities intended to further social welfare (Carnahan et al., 2017). Today, companies are expected to take on responsibilities beyond regulatory compliance and posting profits (Ditlev-Simonsen, 2014: 117):

> How companies engage the environment, human rights, ethics, corruption, employee rights, donations, volunteer work, contributions to the community and relationships with suppliers are typically viewed as components of CSR.

Scherer and Palazzo (2011: 906) claimed that globalization is a given and not something we can opt out from and that this makes a new perspective on CSR necessary and unavoidable:

> In order to respond to the globalization phenomenon and the emerging post-national constellation, it is necessary to acknowledge a new political role of business that goes beyond mere compliance with legal standards and conformity with moral rules.

CSR is described as a leadership task. Board members and chief executives in an organization have a particular responsibility to make sure that the organization is in compliance with laws and regulations, and that the organization makes contributions to society wherever relevant. Chief executives should make the organization accountable, compensate for negative impacts, contribute to societal welfare, operate business ethically, take responsibility for society, and manage in relation with society.

Engdahl (2013: 332) found that duality in terms of segregation of duties might ensure regulatory compliance in banking and finance:

> Today the segregation of duties is commonly used to ensure regulatory compliance in various industries. . . . The argument is made that an

> effective duality-based segregation-of-duties type control system presupposes social relations characterized by relative autonomy and third-party dependence, along with work task interdependence.

The CEO is the only executive at level 1 in the hierarchy of an organization (Davidson et al., 2019). All other executives are at lower levels. Above the CEO, a number of board members who have major positions elsewhere show up from time to time. Hambrick et al. (2015) found that boards often fail in their monitoring responsibilities. One reason is that many board members are missing some of the following attributes: independence, expertise in the domain, bandwidth, and motivation. Hambrick et al. (2015: 324) expressed surprise that investigative journalists succeed while board members fail:

> On the face of it, this study applauds the role of the press as governance watchdog, but it also raises deeper questions: If journalists could spot these frauds using public sources, why couldn't the companies' boards have detected them? For that matter, why couldn't the boards have spotted the frauds when they were first being perpetrated? And what kind of tone did these boards set that would prompt their companies' CEOs and other executives to engage in such acts and think they could get away with it?

CEOs typically enjoy substantial individual freedom in their professions with little or no control (Khanna et al., 2015). Fraud examiners recommend more control of CEOs because of failing compliance (e.g., Bruun Hjejle, 2018; Clifford Chance, 2020; KPMG, 2020a, 2020b; Plesner, 2020; Sands, 2019). It starts already with travel expenses by CEOs that typically find approval by a subordinate – the chief CFO. Control of the CEO is less likely to succeed by a group of people – the board. Rather, the chairperson of the board should control and approve all financial activities of the CEO. Furthermore, the CEO should never be able to act alone in major business activities. The chief compliance officer in the organization should have a special assignment of monitoring CEO activities and reporting findings to the chairperson. Cowen et al. (2016: 152) suggested that employment contracts for CEOs should have a clause related to misconduct and crime:

> For example, a claw back could be triggered by a financial restatement that happens after an executive's dismissal or by new evidence that surfaces indicating he or she engaged in misconduct while serving as CEO. Claw backs can also force terminated executives to repay benefits if there is evidence their actions have violated restrictive covenants.

As suggested in agency theory, CEOs have a tendency to become opportunistic agents (Shen, 2003). On the basis of their charisma, external stakeholders and board members lose control over CEO activities (Fanelli and Misangyi, 2006).

Therefore, Cowen's (2016) proposal of employment contracts with repayment option may cause a decline in white-collar crime by CEOs.

In the perspective of preventing and prosecuting corporate crime, Haines and Macdonald (2021: 299) argued that addressing corporate crime and harm is not simply an issue of enforcement and compliance:

> Neither is it one of digging deeper to find the ultimate root of the problem – the reproduction of power relations is nothing new to criminology. Understanding the direction of prevailing winds that shape business activity is important though in understanding where change is possible. Grappling with injustice is just that – looking for sources of influence ultimately requires going beyond blanket classifications of law – in all its forms – as either helpful or unhelpful, and understanding which law, from which place and used in which way within a field of struggle is important.

Lehman et al. (2020) introduced rule complexity as a research perspective on compliance. The perspective claims that it sometimes is impossible to understand what is right and what is wrong. Some laws, rules, and regulations are so complex that compliance becomes random. Some rules are more complex to the extent that they have more connections to or functional dependencies upon other rules in the same system.

Legalistic and Formalistic Approaches

The popular choice of strengthening the formalistic compliance function in organizations is no substantive action (Eberl et al., 2015: 1207):

> Internal rule adjustments have the potential to signal a voluntary willingness to change the moral standards of an organization, whereas simple compliance with external legal requirements may prove less effective.

Legalistic remedies do generally have little effect on integrity when they are inconsistent with individual and cultural values. Trust cannot be re-established by formal, legalistic measures. Instead, the value inconsistencies have to be addressed directly. However, in a short-term perspective, the approach of window dressing by a strengthened compliance function might temporarily contribute to trust repair. Window dressing is the act or the instance of making something appear better than it actually is. Formal control mechanisms are a window dressing approach that might reduce trust (Eberl et al., 2015: 1207):

> For some scholars formal control replaces or even diminishes trust. It is argued that extensive monitoring undermines trust. Formal control may create stress and therefore negatively affect trust. Others, who claim that trust and formal control complement each other, at least implicitly, emphasize the importance of formal organizational rules in ensuring consistent behavior. It is argued that organizational rules define normative

> expectations, thereby providing a feeling of certainty and guidance for interactions between organizational members. Following this thought, commonly accepted rules are fundamental for trustworthiness since they make behavior more predictable.

Actors in auditing and compliance functions in business and public enterprises seem to have a preference toward formal rules and guidelines in the form of window dressing rather than detection of potential offenders (Desai, 2016). Alon et al. (2019) argued that accounting and auditing functions have undergone a legitimacy crisis in recent years because of formal rather than substantial financial reviews.

Compliance emerged as an important management topic following a stream of corporate scandals in the United States and many other nations. Companies and industries adopted internal policies and procedures for reporting and trying to prevent misconduct (Chen and Soltes, 2018: 119):

> Those efforts helped assuage legislators who had sought to more heavily regulate and penalize firms for dishonest practices. Self-policing appealed to business leaders as a way to avoid the cost and disruption of additional regulation. It also eased the investigative burden on regulators, and many people believed it would successfully deter wrongdoing.

But it did not. Compliance programs did not deter wrongdoing. Compliance programs served mainly as window dressing to indicate a clean and professional front end of the organization with all its problems hidden inside. Chen and Soltes (2018) argued that the solution to this problem is to link compliance initiatives to business objectives.

Antitrust is yet another approach to compliance. Antitrust refers to laws, regulations, guidelines, and other measures that encourage competition by limiting the power of any particular firm and by preventing deviant executives from pursuing the route of crime networks such as cartels with other businesses in the same industry. An example mentioned by Edelman (2021) is the airline industry in the United States where there is an oligopoly of four major airlines. Antitrust is a matter of compliance not only at the organizational level but also at the national and global levels as "a global consensus has emerged recognizing the central role that competition law plays in promoting a nation's prosperity" (Yoo et al., 2021: 843).

Compliance Audits and Risk Assessment

Compliance audits gauge how well organizations ensure adherence to various applicable laws and other regulatory compliances (Thottoli, 2021: 137):

> It helps avoid risk of fines, penalties and closure of business. Compliance audit gives specific attention to assessing compliance by criteria derived from responsible authorities.

Compliance risk assessment is about introduction of a systematic approach to "the entity's identification of relevant risks to achievement of its objectives, forming a basis for determining how risks should be managed" (Marchetti, 2012: 74). Risk assessment is a process that has to include potential deviant behaviors among board members and corporate executives to make more informed business decisions. As Koller (2005: 28) noted, "fostering a risk assessment process upon an organization will not only change how opportunities or liabilities are assessed but will significantly alter the way an organization makes critical decisions".

Some organizations are characterized by rotten apples, while others are characterized by rotten barrels (Boateng et al., 2021; Gottschalk, 2012). While it might be comforting to assume that there is only one bad apple when a corporate crisis occurs, compliance functions have to look for rotten barrels involving larger parts of the business. While occupational crime is associated with bad apples, corporate crime is associated with systems failure. Bad apples theory represents an individualistic approach in criminology, while systems failure theory represents a business approach in criminology (Heath, 2008: 601):

> If the individualistic approach were correct, then one would expect to find a fairly random distribution of white collar crime throughout various sectors of the economy, depending upon where individuals suffering from poor character or excess greed wound up working. Yet, what one finds instead are very high concentrations of criminal activity in particular sectors of the economy. Furthermore, these pockets of crime often persist quite stubbornly over time, despite a complete changeover in the personnel involved.

It is certainly an interesting issue whether to view white-collar misconduct and crime as acts of individuals perceived as "rotten apples" or as an indication of systems failure in the company, the industry, or the society as a whole. The perspective of occupational crime is favoring the individualistic model of deviance, which is a human failure model of misconduct and crime. This rotten apple view of white-collar crime is a comfortable perspective to adopt for business organizations as it allows them to look no further than suspect individuals. It is only when other forms of group and/or systemic corruption and other kinds of crime erupt upon a business enterprise that a more critical look is taken of white-collar criminality. Furthermore, when serious misconduct occurs and is repeated, there seems to be a tendency to consider crime as a result of bad practice, lack of resources, or mismanagement, rather than acts of criminals.

Fraud Examinations of Compliance Failures

At Wells Fargo in the United States, corporate control functions were constrained by the decentralized organizational structure (Shearman Sterling, 2017; Shichor and Heeren, 2021). Fraud examiners excused corporate control functions since they suffered from harm by the decentralized organizational structure and a culture of substantial independence for business units. "That's how they taught us to do it". This is a phrase illustrating learned deviance and inadequate deterrence. Leasure and Zhang (2018) studied reports of Wells Fargo and Morgan Stanley being engaged in widespread fraudulent sales practices in the retail banking industry. They found that the underlying deviance had been taught by senior management, and that new employees were taught these fraudulent practices. Furthermore, they found that ethics and compliance practices and policies were largely ineffective in curtailing such conduct. Wells Fargo was fined US$185 million for fraudulently opening accounts at its Community Bank. Community Bank opened as many as two million fake accounts in an effort to meet wildly unrealistic sales goals. The CEO at Community Bank resigned before the fraud examination report by Shearman Sterling (2017) was published. The Community Bank at Wells Fargo was held responsible based on two laws, the Sarbanes-Oxley Act and the Dodd-Frank Act (Shichor and Heeren, 2021: 105):

> Both laws have provisions for claw backs of compensation, which is a notable feature of the penalties imposed on Wells. In addition, both laws require corporations to be concerned about internal governance, including the operation of the Board, corporate risk and compliance, and improved shareholder input. Sarbanes-Oxley reinforces these concerns by criminally penalizing any interference by a corporation which obstructs a governmental investigation of the corporation. This kind of provision seems to have played an important role in the ongoing revelations about the misdeeds of Wells Fargo.

At Samherji in Iceland, it was detected by investigative journalists that the fishing company was involved in corruption in Africa to obtain fishing rights along the coast of Namibia (Kleinfeld, 2019, 2020). Samherji (2020) then published the following press release on July 29, 2020, using the company website (www.samherji.is/en/moya/news/samherjis-namibia-investigation-finalized) to emphasize corporate commitment to compliance after a fraud examination by law firm Wikborg Rein:

> Long before Wikborg Rein's conclusions emerged, Samherji put in place a number of measures to safeguard against further exposure to wrongdoing committed by individuals. All operations in Namibia were stopped already in 2019. On 17 January 2020 Samherji announced that it was in process of launching a modern state-of-the art compliance program which is being implemented throughout our global organization this year: www.samherji.is/en/moya/news/samherji-to-implement-corporate-governance-and-compliance-system.
>
> That work is already well underway. Samherji's ambition is to be a pioneer in compliance, governance and internal control within the global fisheries industries.

> Samherji will also proactively keep reaching out to relevant authorities that show dedication to mutual cooperation, offering assistance and cooperation during ongoing investigations into the Namibia-related allegations. An agreement is now made for Wikborg Rein to meet with the Icelandic District Prosecutor in the fall. Several meetings have further been held with Namibian authorities in an effort to explore the basis for similar cooperation there.

At General Motors in the United States, sufficient resources for executives comprehensively to address safety and compliance issues were not ensured. The internal investigation report by Valukas (2014) was concerned with the safety defects in the Cobalt at GM. The fraud examiners found that departments, divisions, and groups did not have substantial responsibilities concerning the identification, investigation, or remediation of safety issues. No regular communication with employees about safety took place at GM. There was no awareness of safety issues. Employees were not encouraged to raise any concerns they had about safety or compliance. There was a culture of fear of retaliation when employees reported concerns regarding actual or potential safety-related defects or potential non-compliance with the federal standards. Owners of safety and compliance issues could not be identified at GM. Therefore, accountability could not be addressed. Internal roles did not define responsibilities and accountability for those involved in processes related to the evaluation and resolution of safety issues, including responsibilities for feeding items into the relevant work process. Roles of committees were not clarified. A person on each such committee was not designated as a safety liaison with responsibility for elevating safety issues. Appropriate identification, elevation, and resolution of safety and compliance issues were not included as a factor in employee performance evaluations. Employees were not required to certify that they had reported any safety issues, which they were aware of, and to identify, as part of that certification, any safety issues they were aware of that had not been resolved. Coordination between groups was never formalized, and no coordination occurred between engineering teams with accountability for safety and compliance issues. The CEO, who had hired Valukas (2014), was blamed in the fraud examination report. Others further down the GM hierarchy were attributed blame and had to leave the corporation as organizational scapegoats.

At Wirecard in Germany, fraud examiners from KPMG (2020a, 2020b) did not provide a clean bill of health since they in their report criticize Wirecard's internal controls and compliance functions. In their final report, examiners detailed shortcomings in Wirecard's internal controls and compliance functions and outlined severe doubts about the company's accounting practices. However, fraud examiners did neither confirm nor reject accounting manipulation and other kinds of financial wrongdoing. Therefore, Wirecard management quickly stated that "no evidence was found for the publicly raised allegations of balance sheet manipulation" (Storbeck, 2020). Nevertheless, the financial enterprise collapsed half a year later. While some ignored violations of laws in achieving goals, others wanted to watch compliance, which created an ethical climate conflict. The CEO was arrested in June 2020. The second-in-command who oversaw operations in Asia escaped arrest and was on the run. A key Wirecard business partner suddenly died. Consultants had helped Wirecard prepare a plan of Project Panther to take over Deutsche Bank. To do so, the value of Wirecard needed to exceed the value of Deutsche Bank. The scheme was detected by investigative journalists at *Financial Times* (Storbeck, 2020).

At the Office of the Sheriff in Philadelphia in the United States, contracts did not find compliance with the terms of the home rule charter, but they were not readily accessible for public review, and were not internally circulated and made known within the Office of the Sheriff (Deloitte, 2011: 14):

> The deficiencies in the contracting process weakened the Sheriff's Office ability to determine the accuracy and legitimacy of vendor invoices, particularly those of the Office's largest vendor.

The sheriff and his office did not exercise oversight of the invoices and did not minimize advertising costs and other expenses. Under the sheriff's tenure, there were few internal controls relating to vendor invoices and their fees. The director of compliance in the office did not notice any deviance.

At the International Biathlon Union in Austria, there were no restrictions on being the union president and how many periods he could be in such a central position without being replaced. The IBU president had been a central figure in shaping the business, culture, ethics, structure, and compliance of right and wrong at IBU as an organization. The suspected fraud was concerned with the president receiving favors and bribes from Russian biathlon union officials in terms of expensive adventure trips and access to Russian prostitutes. When the report by the Commission (2021) was published, the president resigned and became subject to criminal investigation.

At British Petroleum in the United States, Freeh (2013) had a mandate of examining and evaluating the internal compliance program in their claims office. In the aftermath of the Deepwater Horizon oil spill on April 20, 2010, and in an effort to begin to fulfill its obligations under the Oil Pollution Act, British Petroleum established a facility to receive and to process claims. They paid compensation to individuals and businesses affected by the spill. The BP facility paid claims for losses resulting from lost earnings or lost profits, removal and cleanup costs, damage to real or personal property, loss of subsistence use of natural resources, and physical injury or death. The total compensation was US$11 billion. Freeh (2013) concluded that attorneys in the claims office might have violated the federal criminal statutes regarding fraud, money laundering, conspiracy, or perjury. The investigator recommended that law enforcement should take over the case and conduct a criminal investigation in this matter. Attorneys had been presenting claims on behalf of victims as well as approving claims on behalf of petroleum company BP. It was a profitable assignment for attorneys, and some attorneys made it allegedly even more profitable for themselves by kickbacks and by both applying for and approving compensations.

At Oceanteam in the Netherlands, a consequence of the fraud examination by Sands (2019) was that both the chairman and the chief executive had to leave their positions at the corporation. Another consequence was the complete restructuring of compliance functions. However, the new management did not appreciate the investigation report by Sands (2019). They distanced themselves from the whole investigation affair, and they expressed dissatisfaction with the costs that the company had to carry for the examination that was initiated by a shareholder.

At the social security agency in Norway, they were reluctant to comply with European EEA rules. The reluctance of an agency to comply with EEA rules becomes stronger when the rules are both complicated and in conflict with political priorities. Over the course of many years, the Norwegian Labor and Welfare Administration (NAV) has applied the requirement of stay in Norway under the Norwegian National Insurance Act for recipients of social security benefits such as sickness compensation, attendance allowance, and work assessment allowance in a manner contrary to and in conflict with European commitments. However, within Europe, Norwegians are allowed to move freely independent of their status. Employees at NAV as well as ministry officials, police investigators, state prosecutors, defense lawyers, judges at criminal courts, officers at correctional institutions, academic researchers, and law professors have all ignored or misunderstood European social security regulations. While not a member of the European Union, Norway has signed a number of treaties requiring the country to align with most EU regulations. Many innocent Norwegian welfare recipients have been incarcerated wrongfully because NAV claimed it was illegal for them to stay in other European countries while receiving the generous social benefits from their home country Norway (NOU, 2020).

Maturity Model for Corporate Compliance

Stages of growth models for maturity levels help to assess and evaluate a variety of phenomena (e.g., Chen et al., 2021; Masood, 2020; Mondani and Rostami, 2021; Röglinger et al., 2012; Solli-Sæther and Gottschalk, 2015). Stage models predict the development or evolution of investigative maturity from basic performance to superior results (Iannacci et al., 2019: 310):

> They also suggest that this development is progressive (i.e., each successive stage is better than the previous one), stepwise (i.e., each step is a necessary prerequisite for the following step in the sequence), and prescriptive (i.e., each step must occur in a prescribed order in accordance with a pre-existing plan or vision), thus emphasizing the chain of successful events rather than the mechanisms by which subsequent stages come about.

Antonsen and Madsen (2021) suggested a maturity model for the compliance function of investment firms. Their assessment model for compliance maturity suggests a path of evolution wherein the compliance function matures from being reactive and inconsistent to becoming a proactive and integrated part of an investment firm's business practice. They defined a number of key enablers of a compliance function in the areas of technology, coordination, policies and processes, resources, and business integrity. Technology is applied to increase effectiveness, efficiency, and transparency. Coordination is a matter of improved cooperation and communication. Policies and processes work better when they are clearly defined and implemented. Appropriate resources must be allocated to the compliance function. Business integrity is the quality of acting in accordance with the moral values, norms, and rules that are considered valid and relevant within the context in which the actor operates (Loyens et al., 2021). Integrity refers to taking responsibility for the representation of the self and one's commitments (Gardiner et al., 2017).

The maturity model suggested by Antonsen and Madsen (2021) has four levels:

- Level 1: Reactive and inconsistent. All processes are manual, no systems in place; no functional access and communication with other business lines; policies and processes not documented, ad hoc response to incidents; insufficient resources allocated; and compliancy viewed as a necessary evil.
- Level 2: Organized but reactive. Some processes are automated while others are manual; defined lines of communication with other business lines and mutual functional access; defined and documented compliance function but not integrated into the workflow; appropriate resources necessary to achieve compliance; and business ethics and values are defined centrally.
- Level 3: Actively managed and understood. All processes are supported by automated systems; all business lines work toward shared goals and initiatives; compliance function understood by employees and integrated into the workflow; scalable risk-adjusted resource deployment assessment of resources done periodically; and time is spent consulting and involving employees in business ethics and values.
- Level 4: Proactive and implemented. All processes are supported by and integrated in one and the same automated system; alignment of strategy, processes, and technology to shared goals to improve effectiveness; compliance function integrated into the workflow, continuously measured and improved; resources continuously monitored and effectively adapted to changes in compliance requirements; a healthy compliance culture is fostered, and employees naturally promote it.

Antonsen and Madsen (2021) tested their compliance model based on an interview with the head of compliance and risk at a Norwegian investment firm. The interviewee was concerned with an effective compliance function described as working among management and employees preventively by explaining why the regulations are formed as they are. The interviewee emphasized that compliance principles serve as a sales argument to the firm's clients. In terms of the compliance model, the researchers found that the firm was at level 4 regarding business integrity since the board and management focused on building a compliance culture. When and where in doubt, control systems were in place to ensure that optimal priorities applied. Policies and processes as well as resources were also assessed at level 4. Coordination was assessed at level 3 since communication gaps could still be found. Technology was assessed at level 2 since some processes were automated while others were performed manually.

References

Abadinsky, H. (2007). *Organized Crime*, Eighth Edition, Thomson Wadsworth, Belmont, CA.

Aguilera, R.V., Judge, W.Q. and Terjesen, S.A. (2018). Corporate governance deviance, *Academy of Management Review*, 43 (1), 87–109.

Ahrne, G. and Brunsson, N. (2011). Organization outside organizations: The significance of partial organization, *Organization*, 18 (1), 83–104.

Alon, A., Mennicken, A. and Samsonova-Taddei, A. (2019). Dynamics and limits of regulatory privatization: Reorganizing audit oversight in Russia, *Organization Studies*, 40 (8), 1217–1240.

Alvarez, S.A. and Parker, S.C. (2009). Emerging firms and the allocation of control rights: A Bayesian approach, *Academy of Management Review*, 34 (2), 209–227.

Andreisova, L. (2016). Building and maintaining an effective compliance program, *International Journal of Organizational Leadership*, 5 (1), 24–39.

Antonsen, H.H. and Madsen, Ø. (2021). Developing a maturity model for the compliance function of investment firms: A preliminary case study from Norway, *Administrative Sciences*, 11, 109, published online doi.org/10.3390/admsci11040109.

Baer, M.H. (2009). Governing corporate compliance, *Boston College Law Review*, 50 (4), 949–1019.

Ballesteros, H.M., Rodriguez-Rodriguez, G., Ferreiro-Seoane, F.J. and Martinez-Cabrera, H. (2021). The fewer insider poachers, the more normative compliance: Clues for managing poaching in the shellfish sector, *Deviant Behavior*, 42 (6), 747–761.

Berry, L.L., Seiders, K. and Grewal, D. (2002). Understanding service convenience, *Journal of Marketing*, 66, 1–17.

Boateng, F.D., Hsieh, M.L. and Pryce, D.K. (2021). Police criminality: Nature and extent of crimes committed by female police officers, *Police Quarterly*, published online doi: 10.1177/10986111211044070.

Bosse, D.A. and Phillips, R.A. (2016). Agency theory and bounded self-interest, *Academy of Management Review*, 41 (2), 276–297.

Bruun Hjejle. (2018). *Report on the Non-Resident Portfolio at Danske Bank's Estonian branch*, law firm Bruun Hjejle, Copenhagen, Denmark, 87 pages.

Carnahan, S., Kryscynski, D. and Olson, D. (2017). When does corporate social responsibility reduce employee turnover? Evidence from attorneys before and after 9/11, *Academy of Management Journal*, 60 (5), 1932–1962.

Chen, H. and Soltes, E. (2018). Why your compliance programs fail – and how to fix them, *Harvard Business Review*, March–April, 116–123.

Chen, W., Liu, C., Xing, F., Peng, G. and Yang, X. (2021). Establishment of a maturity model to assess the development of industrial AI in smart manufacturing, *Journal of Enterprise Information Management*, published online doi: 10.1108/JEIM-10–2020–0387.

Clifford Chance. (2020). *Report of Investigation on Swedbank*, law firm Clifford Chance, Washington, DC, 218 pages.

Commission. (2021). *Final Report of the IBU External Review Commission*, IBU External Review Commission: Jonathan Taylor, Vincent Defrasne, Christian Dorda, Tanja Haug, Anja Martin, and Lauren Pagé, January 28, 220 pages.

Cowen, A.P., King, A.W. and Marcel, J.J. (2016). CEO severance agreements: A theoretical examination and research agenda, *Academy of Management Review*, 41 (1), 151–169.

Davidson, R.H., Dey, A. and Smith, A.J. (2019). CEO materialism and corporate social responsibility, *The Accounting Review*, 94 (1), 101–126.

Davies, J. and Malik, H. (2022). Challenging existing regulatory approaches for white-collar and corporate crimes, *Journal of White Collar and Corporate Crime*, 3 (1), 3–6.

Deloitte. (2011). *Forensic Investigation Report: Office of the Philadelphia Sheriff*, Deloitte Financial Advisory Services LLP, Philadelphia, PA, https://controller.phila.gov/wp-content/uploads/2018/06/CityController_ForensicReport_October2011(full).pdf, retrieved September 23, 2018.

Desai, V.M. (2016). Under the radar: Regulatory collaborations and their selective use to facilitate organizational compliance, *Academy of Management Journal*, 59 (2), 636–657.

Dion, M. (2008). Ethical leadership and crime prevention in the organizational setting, *Journal of Financial Crime*, 15 (3), 308–319.

Dion, M. (2009). Corporate crime and the dysfunction of value networks, *Journal of Financial Crime*, 16 (4), 436–445.

Dion, M. (2019). A Gadamerian perspective on financial crimes, *Journal of Financial Crime*, 26 (3), 836–860.

Dion, M. (2020). Bribery, extortion and "morally ambiguous" leadership in organizations, *Journal of Financial Crime*, 27 (4), 1027–1046.

Ditlev-Simonsen, C.D. (2014). Are non-financial CSR reports trustworthy? A study of the extent to which non-financial reports reflect the media perception of the company's behaviour, *Issues in Social and Environmental Accounting*, 8 (2), 116–133.

Durand, R., Hawn, O. and Ioannou, I. (2019). Willing and able: A general model of organizational responses to normative pressures, *Academy of Management Review*, 44 (2), 299–320.

Eberl, P., Geiger, D. and Assländer, M.S. (2015). Repairing trust in an organization after integrity violations. The ambivalence of organizational rule adjustments, *Organization Studies*, 36 (9), 1205–1235.

Eberlein, B. (2019). Who fills the global governance gap? Rethinking the roles of business and government in global governance, *Organization Studies*, 40 (8), 1125–1146.

Edelman, J. (2021). Reviving antitrust enforcement in the airline industry, *Michigan Law Review*, 120 (1), 125–155.

Eisenhardt, K.M. (1989). Agency theory: An assessment and review, *Academy of Management Review*, 14 (1), 57–74.

Engdahl, O. (2013). Ensuring regulatory compliance in banking and finance through effective controls: The principle of duality in the segregation of duties, *Regulation & Governance*, 8 (3), 332–349.

Fanelli, A. and Misangyi, V.F. (2006). Bringing out charisma: CEO charisma and external stakeholders, *Academy of Management Review*, 31 (4), 1049–1061.

Farquhar, J.D. and Rowley, J. (2009). Convenience: A services perspective, *Marketing Theory*, 9 (4), 425–438.

Fotaki, M., Lioukas, S. and Voudouris, I. (2020). Ethos in destiny: Organizational values and compliance in corporate governance, *Journal of Business Ethics*, 166, 19–37.

Freeh, L.J. (2013). *Independent External Investigation of the Deepwater Horizon Court Supervised Settlement Program, Report of Special Master Louis J. Freeh*, September 6, www.laed.uscourts.gov/sites/default/files/OilSpill/Orders/Report11287.pdf, retrieved September 14, 2018.

Gardiner, S., Parry, J. and Robinson, S. (2017). Integrity and the corruption debate in sport: Where is the integrity? *European Sport Management Quarterly*, 17 (1), 6–23.

Gottschalk, P. (2012). White-collar crime and police crime: Rotten apples or rotten barrels? *Critical Criminology*, 20 (2), 169.182.

Gottschalk, P. and Benson, M.L. (2020). The evolution of corporate accounts of scandals from exposure to investigation, *British Journal of Criminology*, 60, 949–969.

Haines, F. and Macdonald, K. (2021). Grappling with injustice: Corporate crime, multinational business and interrogation of law in context, *Theoretical Criminology*, 25 (2), 284–303.

Hambrick, D.C., Misangyi, V.F. and Park, C.A. (2015). The quad model for identifying a corporate director's potential for effective monitoring: Toward a new theory of board sufficiency, *Academy of Management Review*, 40 (3), 323–344.

Heath, J. (2008). Business ethics and moral motivation: A criminological perspective, *Journal of Business Ethics*, 83, 595–614.

Iannacci, F., Seepma, A.P., Blok, C. and Resca, A. (2019). Reappraising maturity models in e-government research: The trajectory-turning point theory, *Journal of Strategic Information Systems*, 28, 310–329.

Johnson, D. (2022). What are the merits of taking a hybrid regulatory approach toward the enforcement of corporate financial crime in the United Kingdom and United States of America? *Journal of White Collar and Corporate Crime*, 3 (1), 23–32.

Kawasaki, T. (2020). Review of comparative studies on white-collar and corporate crime, in: Rorie, M.L. (editor), *The Handbook of White-Collar Crime*, Wiley & Sons, Hoboken, NJ, chapter 27, pages 437–447.

Ken, I. and León, K.S. (2021). Necropolitical governance and state-corporate harms: Covid-19 and the U.S. pork packing industry, *Journal of White Collar and Corporate Crime*, published online doi: 10.1177/2631309X211011037.

Khanna, V., Kim, E.H. and Lu, Y. (2015). CEO connectedness and corporate fraud, *The Journal of Finance*, 70, 1203–1252.

Kleinfeld, J. (2019). Anatomy of a Bribe: A deep dive into an underworld of corruption, news organization *Al Jazeera*, www.aljazeera.com, retrieved December 1.

Kleinfeld, J. (2020). Corruption allegations in Namibian 5G deal with Huawei, *News Organization Al Jazeera*, www.aljazeera.com, retrieved July 15.

Koller, G. (2005). *Risk Assessment and Decision Making in Business and Industry: A Practical Guide*, Boca Raton, FL: Chapman & Hall/CRC Press.

Kourula, A., Moon, J., Salles-Djelic, M.L. and Wicker, C. (2019). New roles of government in the governance of business conduct: Implications for management and organizational research, *Organization Studies*, 40 (8), 1101–1123.

KPMG. (2020a). *Report Concerning the Independent Special Investigation at Wirecard AG*, April 27, audit firm KPMG, Munich, Germany, 74 pages.

KPMG. (2020b). *Bericht über die unabhängige Sonderuntersuchung*, Wirecard AG, München, 27. April, 74 pages.

Leasure, P. and Zhang, G. (2018). "That's how they taught us to do it": Learned deviance and inadequate deterrents in retail banking, *Deviant Behavior*, 39 (5), 603–616.

Lehman, D.W., Cooil, B. and Ramanujam, R. (2020). The effects of rule complexity on organizational noncompliance and remediation: Evidence from restaurant health inspections, *Journal of Management*, 46 (8), 1436–1468.

Loyens, K., Claringbould, I., Heres-van Rossem, L. and Eekeren, Frank van. (2021). The social construction of integrity: A qualitative case study in Dutch football, *Sports in Society*, published online doi: 10.1080/17430437.2021.1877661.

Lucas, D.S., Grimes, M.G. and Gehman, J. (2022). Remaking capitalism: The strength of weak legislation in mobilizing B corporation certification, *Academy of Management Journal*, 65 (3), 958–987.

Maher, R., Valenzuela, F. and Böhm, S. (2019). The enduring state: An analysis of governance-making in three mining conflicts, *Organization Studies*, 40 (8), 1169–1192.

Mai, H.T.X. and Olsen, S.O. (2016). Consumer participation in self-production: The role of control mechanisms, convenience orientation, and moral obligation, *Journal of Marketing Theory and Practice*, 24 (2), 209–223.

Majluf, N.S. and Navarrete, C.M. (2011). A two-component compliance and ethics program model: An empirical application to Chilean corporations, *Journal of Business Ethics*, 100 (4), 567–579.

Marchetti, A.M. (2012). *Enterprise Risk Management Best Practices: From Assessment to Ongoing Compliance*, John Wiley & Sons, Hoboken, NJ.

Masood, T. (2020). A machine learning approach for performance-oriented decision support in service-oriented architecture, *Journal of Intelligent Information Systems*, published online doi: 10.1007/s10844-020-00617-6.

Mehrpouya, A. and Salles-Djelic, M.L. (2019). Seeing like the market: Exploring the mutual rise of transparency and accounting in transnational economic and market governance, *Accounting, Organizations and Society*, 76, 12–31.

Mondani, H. and Rostami, A. (2021). Uncovering the degree of criminal organization: Swedish street gangs and the role of mobility and co-offending networks, *Social Science Research*, published online doi: 10.1016/j.ssresearch.2021.102657.

NOU. (2020). *Blindsonen: Gransking av feilpraktiseringen av folketrygdlovens oppholdskrav ved reiser i EØS-området (The Blind Spot: Investigation of the Incorrect Practice of the National Insurance Act's Residence Requirements When Traveling in the EEA Area)*, Norges offentlige utredninger (Norway's public inquiries) 2020:9, 328 pages, Oslo, Norway.

Peterson, E.A. (2013). Compliance and ethics programs: Competitive advantage through the law, *Journal of Management and Governance*, 17 (4), 1027–1045.

Pillay, S. and Kluvers, R. (2014). An institutional theory perspective on corruption: The case of a developing democracy, *Financial Accountability & Management*, 30 (1), 95–119.

Plesner. (2020). *Response to DFSA-letter: Anmodning om redegørelse om Danske Bank A/S' gældsinddrivelsessystem (Response to DFSA Letter: Request for Account Concerning Danske Bank Inc.'s Debt Collection System)*, investigation report by Danske Bank, law firm Plesner, Copenhagen, Denmark, 120 pages.

Rashid, A., Al-Mamun, A., Roudaki, H. and Yasser, Q.R. (2022). An overview of corporate fraud and its prevention approach, *Australasian Accounting, Business and Finance Journal*, 16 (1), Article 6, 101–118.

Remisova, A., Lasakova, A. and Kirchmayer, Z. (2019). Influence of formal ethics program components on managerial ethical behavior, *Journal of Business Ethics*, 160 (1), 151–166.

Röglinger, M., Pöppelbuss, J. and Becker, J. (2012). Maturity model in business process management, *Business Process Management Journal*, 18 (2), 328–346.

Rooij, B. and Fine, A. (2020). Preventing corporate crime from within: Compliance management, whistleblowing, and internal monitoring, in: Rorie, M.L. (editor), *The Handbook of White-Collar Crime*, Chapter 15, Wiley & Sons, Hoboken, NJ, pages 229–245.

Samherji. (2020). *Samherji's Namibia investigation finalized*, Samherji ice fresh seafood, website www.samherji.is/en/moya/news/samherjis-namibia-investigation-finalized, Akureyri, Iceland, published by margret@samherji.is.

Sands. (2019). *Factual report Oceanteam: Investigation of related party transactions*, report of investigation, 256 pages, law firm Sands, Oslo, Norway.

Scherer, A. and Palazzo, G. (2011). The new political role of business in a globalized world: A review of a new perspective on CSR and its implications for the firm, governance, and democracy, *Journal of Management Studies*, 48 (4), 899–931.

Schneider, A. and Scherer, A.G. (2019). State governance beyond the 'shadow of hierarchy': A social mechanisms perspective on governmental CSR policies, *Organization Studies*, 40 (8), 1147–1168.

Shearman Sterling. (2017). *Independent Directors of the Board of Wells Fargo & Company: Sales Practices Investigation Report*, law firm Shearman Sterling, New York, NY, 113 pages.

Shen, W. (2003). The dynamics of the CEO-board relationship: An evolutionary perspective, *Academy of Management Review*, 28 (3), 466–476.

Shichor, D. and Heeren, J.W. (2021). Reflecting on corporate crime and control: The Wells Fargo banking saga, *Journal of White Collar and Corporate Crime*, 2 (2), 97–108.

Solli-Sæther, H. and Gottschalk, P. (2015). Stages-of-growth in outsourcing, offshoring and backsourcing: Back to the future? *Journal of Computer Information Systems*, 55 (2), 88–94.

Stiffler, C.E. (2022). *Understanding the Role of Chief Financial Officers in the Strategic Planning and Decision-Making Process of Defense Contractors in the Washington, D.C. Region*, A dissertation submitted to the Nathan M. Bisk College of Business at Florida Institute of Technology in partial fulfillment of the requirements for the degree of Doctor of Business Administration, Melbourne, Florida, May, 172 pages.

Storbeck, O. (2020). Wirecard: The frantic final months of a fraudulent operation, *Financial Times*, www.ft.com, retrieved August 25.

Sundström, M. and Radon, A. (2015). Utilizing the concept of convenience as a business opportunity in emerging markets, *Organizations and Markets in Emerging Economies*, 6 (2), 7–21.

Thottoli, M.M. (2021). The relevance of compliance audit on companies' compliance with disclosure guidelines of financial statements, *Journal of Investment Compliance*, 22 (2), 137–150.

Valukas, A.R. (2014). *Report to board of directors of General Motors Company regarding ignition switch recalls*, law firm Jenner & Block, May 29, 325 pages, www.beasleyallen.com/webfiles/valukas-report-on-gm-redacted.pdf.

Williams, M.L., Levi, M., Burnap, P. and Gundur, R.V. (2019). Under the corporate radar: Examining insider business cybercrime victimization through an application of routine activities theory, *Deviant Behavior*, 40 (9), 1119–1131.

Windsor, D. (2022). Aligning MNEs with SDGs: Peace, justice and strong institutions, in: McIntyre, J.R., Ivanaj, S. and Ivanaj, V. (editors), *The Role of Multinational Enterprises in Supporting the United Nation's SDGs*, Edward Elgar Publishing, UK, Cheltenham.

Witt, M.A., Fainshmidt, S. and Aguilera, R.V. (2021). Our board, our rules: Nonconformity to global corporate governance norms, *Administrative Science Quarterly*, 1–36, published online doi: 10.1177/00018392211022726.

Yasir, A., Ahmed, A. and Anum, L. (2021). Corporate financial crimes in Pakistan – A review and analysis, *Journal of Financial Crime*, published online doi: 10.1108/JFC-2021-0233.

Yoo, C.S., Fetzer, T., Jiang, S. and Huang, Y. (2021). Due process in antitrust enforcement: Normative and comparative perspectives, *Southern California Law Review*, 94 (4), 843–926.

Zhang, J. (2021). The practice of CSR development and its performing mechanism – case study of P&G, *Journal of Sociology and Ethnology*, 3, 100–110.

Zysman-Quirós, D. (2020). White-collar crime in South and Central America: Corporate-state crime, governance, and the high impact of the Odebrecht corruption case, in: Rorie, M.L. (editor), *The Handbook of White-Collar Crime*, Wiley & Sons, Hoboken, NJ, chapter 23, pages 363–380.

2 Profiling White-Collar Offenders

The perspective of convenience theory emphasizes that white-collar offenders have financial motives from either possibilities or threats, and they have opportunity in their professions both to commit financial crime and to conceal it. Furthermore, their deviance willingness might derive from personal choice or perceived innocence. A total of 14 convenience themes are suggested in the structural convenience model, where only a few typically apply to a specific offender at an identified incident. By including some themes while disregarding others, an offender profile will emerge. Profiles thus vary among offenders. Some have an opportunity structure mainly of committing crime, while others have an opportunity structure of concealing crime. Some made crime a rational choice, while others deny wrongdoing. The structural model might be a useful tool in fraud investigations, defense strategies, as well as prosecution approaches.

As emphasized by Hoekstra and Verhoeven (2021), high-status fraud suspects tend to have certain characteristics such as a tendency of narcissistic traits. The suspects that they studied were white-collar criminals who Sutherland (1983) described as persons of considerable respectability and high social status belonging to elite groups in society and committing financial crime during their regular work in their privileged professional positions. White-collar offenders are relevant and interesting to study since they abuse trust and their open-resource access to commit and conceal wrongdoing in their occupations.

A theoretical perspective to study profiling of offenders is the convenience theory (Asting and Gottschalk, 2022; Braaten and Vaughn, 2019; Dearden and Gottschalk, 2020; Stadler and Gottschalk, 2022). The convenience theory suggests that a financial motivation, an organizational situation, and a deviant attitude can make financial crime attractive for white-collar offenders. Convenience is both an absolute and a relative concept. In this research, we apply the relative concept by comparing the convenience of legitimate versus illegitimate means to achieve objectives. The relative concept refers to the efficiency in time and effort to complete a task as well as the level of pain and strain in legal versus illegal acts (Engdahl, 2015). Generally, a convenient individual is neither bad nor lazy. In fact, the person can be considered smart and rational

DOI: 10.4324/9781003379249-4

since the person spends as little time and effort as possible on achieving objectives (Sundström and Radon, 2015). In this line of thinking, Agnew (2014: 2) suggested that "crime is often the most expedient way to get what you want", and that "fraud is often easier, simpler, faster, more exciting, and more certain than other means of securing one's ends".

The idea presented in this chapter suggests that a visual representation and a verbal explanation of offender profiles might enhance the understanding of white-collar offenders. By selecting the main theme(s) for motive, the main theme(s) for opportunity, and the main theme(s) for willingness, a profile of the offender will emerge. The profile serves to create a narrative of the offense and the offender, where pieces of information in each actual case are assigned to specified convenience themes in the structural model.

The convenience theory has similarities to the more famous fraud triangle (Cressey, 1972; Wells, 1997) that suggests three conditions for fraud by potential offenders. First, there are incentives or pressures. Next, there are crime opportunities. Finally, there is a positive attitude toward deviance and rationalization of deviance acts. While such conditions also apply also to the convenience triangle of motive-opportunity-willingness, there are three distinct differences. First, convenience is a relative concept, indicating that offenders have the option of alternative actions to reach their goals where their behavior does not involve illegitimate actions. While the fraud triangle suggests that increased opportunities will stimulate crime tendencies, the convenience triangle suggests that relative opportunities will stimulate such tendencies. In the convenience perspective, there is no reason to commit crime, even if there are ample and attractive opportunities, as long as alternative – and more convenient – decisions involving legitimate behavior may lead to the same result or even to a better result. The extent of relative convenience rather than the extent of absolute opportunity determines whether an offense seems attractive. Depending on the convenience orientation, that is the extent of emphasis on convenience, an extremely convenience oriented elite member may resort quicker to illegal activities when legal activities are slightly more stressful. On the other hand, a less conveniently oriented decision maker may try intensely to solve problems and explore opportunities without violating the law.

Second, while the fraud triangle refers to opportunity in general, the convenience triangle refers to opportunity in an occupational setting of status and access. Offenders have privileged access to resources to commit and conceal wrongdoing. There is often too much trust and lack of control that cause convenient opportunities for elite members.

Third, the extent of opportunity is not only a constant or a variable that is externally determined. Rather, a potential offender can create and expand the opportunity space over time. By reducing transparency, controlling information flows, threatening potential whistleblowers, collecting decision rights, controlling information flows, and by authoritarian leadership styles, a potential offender can develop an opportunity space that grows conveniently over time.

This chapter presents the structural model of convenience theory with 14 convenience themes. Offender profiling occurs when some of the 14 themes are identified as relevant for a suspected white-collar offender.

Structural Convenience Model

A combination of motive, opportunity, and willingness determines the extent of white-collar crime convenience as illustrated in the structural model in Figure 2.1 and as described by Gottschalk (2021: 14):

> In the financial motive dimension, profit might be a goal in itself or an enabler to exploit possibilities and to avoid threats. Possibilities and threats exist both for individual members of the organization as well as for the organization as a whole. It is convenient to exploit possibilities and to avoid threats by financial means.
>
> In the organizational opportunity dimension, convenience can exist both to commit white-collar crime and to conceal white-collar crime. Offenders have high social status in privileged positions, and they have legitimate access to crime resources. Disorganized institutional deterioration causes decay, lack of oversight and guardianship cause chaos, while criminal market structures cause collapse.
>
> The personal willingness for deviant behavior focuses on offender choice and perceived innocence. The choice of crime can be caused by deviant identity, rational consideration, or learning from others. Justification and neutralization cause the perceived innocence at crime. Identity, rationality, learning, justification, and neutralization all contribute to making white-collar crime action a convenient behavior for offenders.

As illustrated in the figure, there are 14 potential themes that might contribute to a profile of the white-collar offender. These themes are presented in the following.

Profiling Motive Convenience

At the individual level of possibilities, greed is the most frequently mentioned motive for financial crime by white-collar offenders. Goldstraw-White (2012) defined greed as socially constructed needs and desires that can never be completely covered or contended. Sajko et al. (2021: 961) studied CEO greed where they defined greed as self-interest by excessive materialistic desire and lack of concern for the well-being of others:

> Greed, which is most commonly defined as an excessive materialistic desire to acquire personal wealth, can be seen as the "dark" end of the self-interest continuum – that is, hyper-self-interest. . . . While self-interest

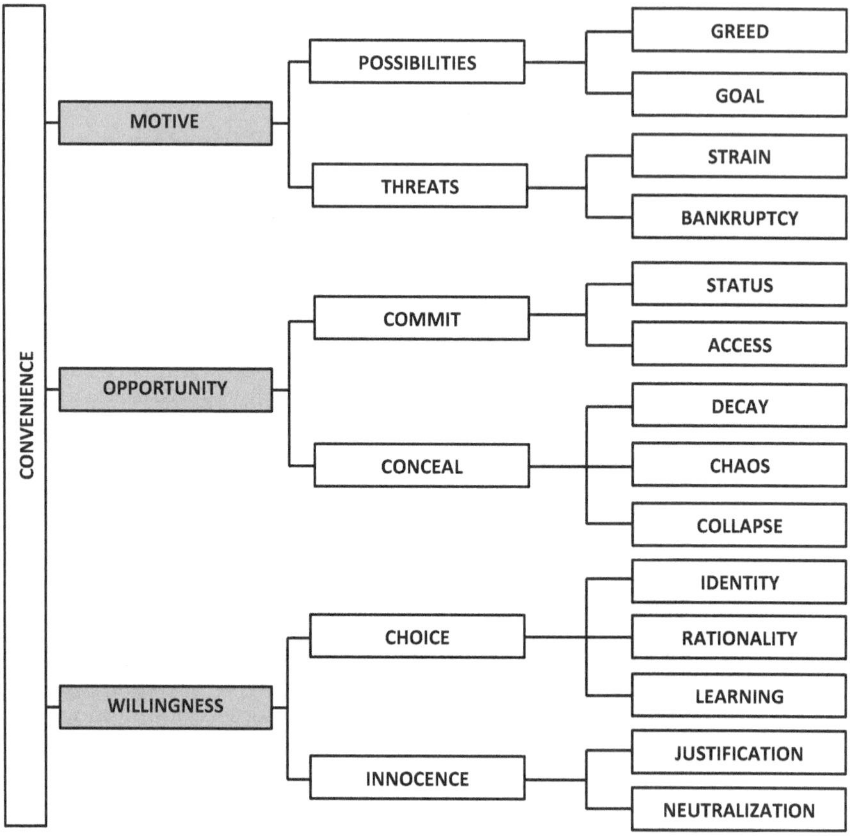

Figure 2.1 Structural model of convenience propositions

> is morally neutral, greed carries a moral charge. . . . Greed by definition implies a lack of concern for the well-being of others.

The pyramid of needs is another well-known motive for financial crime by white-collar offenders along the motive-possibilities-individual axis in the structural model in the figure. Higher up in the pyramid, privileged individuals strive for status, recognition, and admiration (Maslow, 1943). High up in the pyramid, combined with greed, we find the American dream of prosperity and success as the ultimate goal of life. It is an extremely one-sided emphasis on accumulated wealth and big spending. Other values, such as family well-being and personal health, are less important in many cultures.

Along the motive-threats-individual axis in the structural model, the strain perspective has become one of the leading theoretical explanations for crime.

The strain perspective argues that a range of factors influence whether individuals cope with strains through crime (Thaxton and Agnew, 2018: 888):

> Criminal coping is said to be most likely among those with poor coping skills and resources, little social support, low social control, beliefs favorable to crime, criminal associates, and opportunities for crime.

Escalation of commitment to ambitious business goals might cause an increase in the likelihood of wrongdoing (Sleesman et al., 2018) along the motive-possibilities-corporate axis in the structural model. For example, Welsh and Ordonez (2014) found that high performance goals cause unethical behavior. Escalation of commitment is defined as "decision-making in the face of negative feedback about prior resource allocations, uncertainty surrounding the likelihood of goal attainment, and choice about whether to continue" (Keil et al., 2000: 632). When executives perceive high performance goals as critical and invariable, individual desperation for achievement of the goals might be the result (Kuvaas et al., 2016: 401):

> Perceiving goals as invariable refers to the extent to which employees believe that the goals in a performance management system represent absolute standards that they must meet without exception, even if they think other factors are more important.

In many organizations, ends in terms of objectives justify means in terms of deviant actions. Welsh et al. (2020) argued that high performance goals are important not only because of rewards associated with goal attainment but also because of changing morale reasoning processes related to the goals (Gottschalk, 2021: 19):

> As such, high goal commitment facilitates unethical behavior by increasing not only the motivation to achieve the goal but also the motivation to justify doing so by any means necessary Locatelli et al., 2017). This is known as state morale disagreement, a process through which individuals justify unethical behavior (Moore, 2015). It is part of the dark side of ambitious goals.

The final convenience theme in the motive category is painful corporate economic threats (Gottschalk, 2022: 36):

> The threat of corporate collapse and bankruptcy might cause exploration and exploitation of illegal avenues to survive, where moral panic can occur (Kang and Thosuwanchot, 2017). The survival of the corporation can become so important that no means come across as unacceptable in the current situation. Sometimes, fraud and corruption are considered

> temporary measures to recover from a crisis (Geest et al., 2017), where the measures will be terminated when the crisis is over. A crisis is a fundamental threat to the organization, which is often characterized by ambiguity of cause, effect, and means of resolution (König et al., 2020).

Markets with crime forces can represent painful corporate economic threats for corporations that prefer to stay on the right side of the law. In many markets, there are cartels that regulate the supply side (Goncharov and Peter, 2019: 152):

> Cartel members seek to act collectively, as if they were a single monopolist, thereby maximizing the collective profit. By doing so, cartels violate competition policy and severely reduce consumer welfare through price-fixing activities that increase the price of goods far beyond the competitive level.

Chattopadhyay et al. (2001) studied organizational actions in response to threats and found that threats are associated with urgency, difficulty, and high stakes. Threats are often noticed very late, by both individuals and organizations. Handling threats thus becomes a matter of urgency. Individuals and firms "fail to detect threats and prevent calamities not because of an absence of signals or insufficient knowledge (or faulty awareness), but because attention bandwidth and information-processing fidelity are inherently limited" (Downing et al., 2019: 1890).

Profiling Opportunity Convenience

In the perspective of crime-as-a-choice, the status of the offender can make illegitimate actions relatively more convenient compared to legitimate actions (Kakkar et al., 2020: 532):

> Status is a property that rests in the eyes of others and is conferred to individuals who are deemed to have a higher rank or social standing in a pecking order based on a mutually valued set of social attributes. Higher social status or rank grants its holder a host of tangible benefits in both professional and personal domains. For instance, high-status actors are sought by groups for advice, are paid higher, receive unsolicited help, and are credited disproportionately in joint tasks. In innumerable ways, our social ecosystem consistently rewards those with high status.

In their criminological profile of white-collar crime, Eaton and Korach (2016) emphasized authority that is a result of status. Offenders have an appreciation of and confidence in their own authority. Authority is the power or right to give orders, make decisions, and enforce obedience.

The opportunity-commit-access line in the structural model suggests that white-collar offenders typically have legitimate access to resources to commit financial crime. A resource is an enabler applied and used to complete a task.

According to Petrocelli et al. (2003), access to resources equates access to power since resources are enablers to accomplish desired actions. Legitimate access to resources includes entrance to premises, passwords to systems, and leadership of employees (Benson and Simpson, 2018; Williams et al., 2019). Specialized access in routine activities enables offenders to hide deviant transactions in a flow of legitimate transactions (Cohen and Felson, 1979).

In the role of an entrepreneur, the trusted offender might have even easier access to crime resources for illegal entrepreneurship (Peixoto et al., 2021). Scheaf and Wood (2021: 2) found that entrepreneurial fraud has stimulated a wide array of research related to white-collar crime, where they provided the following definition of entrepreneurial fraud:

> Enterprising individuals (alone or in groups) deceiving stakeholders by sharing statements about their identity, individual capabilities, elements of new market offerings, and/or new venture activities that they know to be false in order to obtain something of value.

Opportunity is any "potential course of action, made possible by a particular set of social conditions, which has been symbolically incorporated into an actor's repertoire of behavioral possibilities" (Coleman, 1987: 409). A criminal opportunity is "the presence of a favorable combination of circumstances that renders a possible course of action relevant" (Aguilera and Vadera (2008: 434).

As suggested by Berghoff and Spiekermann (2018: 290), sophisticated concealment is an important factor in white-collar crime:

> The privileged position of white-collar criminals is the result of several factors. Their offences are especially difficult to prosecute because the perpetrators use sophisticated means to conceal them. They can also often afford the best lawyers and have the political clout to influence the legislative process to their advantage and, if need be, to bribe prosecutors and judges. Additionally, the class bias of the courts works to their benefit. The law is often seen as not binding, at least not for and by economic elites.

Crime concealment becomes more convenient when there is organizational decay in the form of institutional deterioration and moral collapse (Shadnam and Lawrence (2011: 379):

> Our theory of moral collapse has two main elements. First, we argue that morality in organizations is embedded in nested systems of individuals, organizations and moral communities in which ideology and regulation flow "down" from moral communities through organizations to individuals, and moral ideas and influence flow "upward" from individuals through organizations to moral communities. Second, we argue that moral collapse is associated with breakdowns in these flows and explore conditions under which such breakdowns are likely to occur.

Lack of oversight and guardianship can create a chaos that improves the convenient opportunity to conceal financial crime in the organizational setting for a white-collar offender. Managers can withhold bad news by accounting misrepresentation, since financial statements are a substantive component of a firm's communications with its stakeholders (Gupta et al., 2020). Internal and external auditors who depend on approval of their continued engagement can be reluctant to report deviance and wrongdoing. Mohliver (2019: 310) found that some auditors prioritize their clients' interests over their legal obligation by recommending client malfeasance, for example, in terms of illegal stock option backdating:

> The findings suggest that professional experts' involvement in the diffusion of liminal practices is highly responsive to the institutional environment.

Auditors are supposed to serve as gatekeepers to protect shareholders and report directly to shareholder representatives on the board of directors, but auditors become surprisingly often hired by corporate management to whom they are loyal. Reporting fraud to public authorities will also harm auditors (Mohliver, 2019: 316):

> As organizations, audit firms are often severely penalized for client malfeasance. Yet the individual auditors working for these firms are susceptible to "motivated blindness" stemming from conflicts of interest that bias their moral judgment toward choices that help their clients.

While disorganized institutional deterioration causes decay, and lack of oversight and guardianship causes chaos, criminal market structures cause external collapse. Collapse of legitimacy is the final convenience theme in the opportunity category. Collapse might be caused by rule complexity preventing compliance (Lehman et al., 2020), participation in crime networks such as cartels to survive in the industry (Nielsen, 2003), and financial crime as the usual way of doing business in markets with crime forces such as cartels (Chang et al., 2005).

Rule complexity can create a situation where nobody is able to tell whether an action represents a criminal offense (Lehman et al., 2020). Furthermore, Eberlein (2019) argued that globalization opens markets for corporations but outstrips the capacity of states to regulate and enforce laws on cross-border business conduct for the public good. Similarly, Schneider and Scherer (2019: 1147) argued that "the extent to which state authorities can regulate the externalities and the behavior of multinational corporations is limited", and that "gaps in governance abound in today's globalized world". Maher et al. (2019) found that governments not just in global business but also in local business are reluctant to intervene.

A cartel is a typical criminal network involving chief executives from competing firms who have chosen to have their businesses cooperate illegally on the market. A cartel is collective misconduct of firms (Bertrand and Lumineau,

2016: 983): "Instead of competing with one another, cartel members rely on each other's agreed course of action".

Profiling Willingness Convenience

A corporation can initially be blamed for a scandal, yet corporate accounts and the secrecy of offenders can make corporate crime seem less serious (Schoultz and Flyghed, 2021a, 2021b). Dewan and Jensen (2020: 1657) studied high social status individuals in times of scandals that can change the role of status from being an asset to being a liability:

> Because scandal diminishes the effectiveness of factors that make status an asset, status offers less protection during a scandal. At the same time that scandal decreases the protective benefits of status, the factors that make status a liability remain or are augmented.

As illustrated in the figure, the willingness for deviant behavior derives from choice and innocence. White-collar crime can be the result of a choice based on identity, rationality, and learning, and white-collar crime can be the result of innocence based on justification and neutralization. Typically, there is a lack of self-control where self-control reflects an individual's ability to override desires and urges (Liang et al., 2016):

> Effective human functioning requires the capacity to transcend primal desires and habitual behaviors in order to behave in a socially appropriate manner. When self-control fails, individuals disregard the long-term implications of their behaviors and succumb to their desires, such as eating fatty foods, cheating on a partner, or engaging in unethical behaviors. Ultimately, self-control failure contributes to poor physical and mental health, crime, and low-quality interpersonal relationships.

Identity is the first convenience theme in the willingness category. Crime as a choice can be based on an identity that makes it acceptable for elite members to violate laws, regulations, and guidelines (Petrocelli et al., 2003), on a professional deviant identity label by self (Obodaru, 2017), on an identity of a narcissist expecting preferential treatment from extraordinary capabilities (Zvi and Elaad, 2018), on deviant identity labeling by others (Mingus and Burchfield, 2012), on reputation adaption to individual labels (Bernburg et al., 2006), and on narcissistic identification with the organization where there is no difference between company money and personal money (Galvin et al., 2015). Identification with the organization is the process through which an individual's identity becomes entangled with, and imprinted by, the corporation. The person's unique sense of self comes to be understood in reference to that organization, where the organization defines individual self.

The economic model of rational self-interest is all about weighing up the pros and cons of alternative courses of action (Gottschalk, 2020: 66):

> When the desire increases, then the benefits in the rational benefit-cost comparison increase that in turn influences willingness. The rational choice perspective simply states that when benefits exceed costs, we would all do it. The perspective is explicitly a result of the self-regarding preference assumption, where rationality is restricted to self-interested materialism.
>
> (Paternoster et al., 2018)

Learning from others by differential association was introduced by Sutherland (1983), who coined the term white-collar crime several decades earlier. The differential association perspective suggests that offenders associate with those who agree with them, while they distance themselves from those who disagree with them. The choice of crime is thus caused by social learning from others with whom offenders associate.

In elite setting, interactions with deviant others promote criminal activity (Gottschalk, 2020: 67):

> The essence of differential association is that criminal behavior is learned, and the main part of learning comes from within important personal groups. Exposure to the attitudes of members of the organization that either favor or reject legal codes influences the attitudes of the individual. The individual will go on to commit crime, if the person exposes himself or herself more to attitudes that favor law violation than to attitudes that favor abiding the law (Wood and Alleyne, 2010). Learning from others is an active process. Differential association can occur in the organizational setting, but does not as such increase the organizational opportunity to commit crime. Rather, differential association belongs to the behavioral willingness category of convenience, as crime learning makes it more convenient to favor law violation. Differential association by individuals can occur outside the organizational setting, such as exposure to law-violation attitudes early in life, exposure to law-violation attitudes over a prolonged period in different situations, and exposure to law-violation attitudes from people they like and respect. Once the appropriate attitudes have developed, young people learn the skills of criminality in much the same way as they would learn any other skill, which is by example and training (Wood and Alleyne, 2010). Individuals embedded within structural units by differential association become vulnerable to attitudes in favor of or opposed to delinquent and criminal behavior. Differential reinforcement of crime convenience develops over time as individuals become vulnerable to various associations and definitions conducive to delinquency.
>
> (Hoffmann, 2002)

In their criminological profile of white-collar crime, Eaton and Korach (2016) emphasized cultural hedonism, narcissistic personality disorder, and low self-control as determinants of deviant behavior by white-collar offenders. Hedonism refers to a strong attention to pleasure, narcissism refers to excessive admiration of oneself, and self-control refers to the ability to regulate one's behavior.

Justification of crime might refer to an offender claiming that the deviant act was no wrongdoing or resulting from upper echelon biased information selection. Offenders may justify by negative life events that have occurred, by peer pressure, or by disappointing work context that causes entitlement (Schoen et al., 2021: 730):

> People use justification mechanisms to protect their sense of self. People who sincerely believe that they are a specific kind of person but routinely demonstrate behaviors that indicate otherwise may avoid cognitive dissonance and maintain their sense of self by using justification mechanisms that allow them to "explain away" their behavior.

When offenders apply neutralization techniques (Sykes and Matza, 1957), they deny responsibility for the incident, they deny injury from the incident, and they deny the existence of victims from the incident. Offenders claim action was a result of higher loyalties, the action was the outcome of a dilemma trade-off, and the action is quite normal. They justify the necessity of their own behaviors where it was necessary to carry out the action. They claim role in society where it is a natural maneuver among elite members. They gather support, where nobody thinks it was wrong. They claim rule complexity, where it is impossible to understand what is right and what is wrong.

Visual Offender Profile Representation

Ever since Sutherland (1983) introduced the term white-collar criminals to identify privileged individuals who abuse their professional positions for illegitimate financial gain, a number of scholars have applied various theoretical perspectives on the white-collar crime phenomenon. Most of these scholars belong to the criminal justice and criminology community, but some can also be found in sociology, psychology, management, and organizational behavior. Their accumulated work is impressive and immense, and it is indeed a challenging task to create an umbrella term to cover the various perspectives.

This chapter has taken on the challenging task of integrating all main perspectives under the umbrella term of convenience theory. Rather than being a completely new and revolutionary theory to explain and predict, as well as prevent and detect economic crime among members of the upper echelon in society, the theory instead combines perspectives into three main dimensions of motive, opportunity, and willingness.

The idea presented here in this chapter suggests that a visual representation and a verbal explanation of offender profiles might enhance the understanding of white-collar offenders. By selecting the main theme(s) for motive, the main theme(s) for opportunity, and the main theme(s) for willingness, a profile of the offender will emerge. This chapter claims to offer a useful tool and strategy in creating profiles for fraud investigation, defense strategies, and prosecution approaches by offering the theoretical perspective of the convenience model.

Specifically, an investigation can benefit from early convenience hypotheses to direct attention in suspect interrogations and witness interviews toward guilt versus innocence. For example, if status seems to be the main determinant, others will typically have noticed deviant behavior without telling. At the search of evidence later in an investigation, the opportunity convenience of committing versus concealing wrongdoing can direct the reconstruction of events and sequences of events. For example, lack of control and guardianship might direct attention toward the role of auditors (Mohliver, 2019).

The defense can benefit from convenience hypotheses concerned with possibilities or threats as motive, and the lack of investigation evidence in committing or concealing the suggested wrongdoing. Furthermore, the defense can identify characteristics of the defendant as a follower rather than a leader in crime, and as a victim rather than an offender in crime. Scapegoating is a form of denial of responsibility accompanied with placement of blame on an individual or group of individuals (Lee and Robinson, 2000; Resodihardjo et al., 2015; Xie and Keh, 2016; Schoultz and Flyghed, 2021a, 2021b).

The prosecution can benefit from convenience perspectives by presenting in court relevant negative motives of the offender. The opportunities for concealment and the extent of concealment can indicate the extent of planned wrongdoing. The deviant behavior might be classified as rational actions rather than justifiable mistakes. Defense accounts such as denials, promises, excuses, reparations, and other defense explanations to influence the extent of trust (Benson, 2019; Kim et al., 2009; Schoultz and Flyghed, 2020) might be overshadowed by attribution of responsibility to the defendant to cause a defense response of admissions (Gottschalk and Benson, 2020).

There are a number of avenues for future research to improve the convenience profiling model that is currently based on various – and potentially rival – theoretical explanations of crime, ranging from control to strain and learning theories. Concerns regarding irreconcilable assumptions about human nature might be addressed in future research by looking at works by Akers (2013), Gottschalk (2020, 2021, 2022), Hirschi (1979), and Thornberry (1987).

The theory of convenience is an emerging approach to understand certain offenders. Maybe it not only is suited for financial crime but might also be used to explain a broader typology of offenses, including state-corporate crime. However, typologies and empirical testing is far beyond the scope of this chapter.

References

Agnew, R. (2014). Social concern and crime: Moving beyond the assumption of simple self-interest, *Criminology*, 52 (1), 1–32.

Aguilera, R.V. and Vadera, A.K. (2008). The dark side of authority: Antecedents, mechanisms, and outcomes of organizational corruption, *Journal of Business Ethics*, 77, 431–449.

Akers, R.L. (2013). *Criminological Theories: Introduction and Evaluation*, Routledge, London, UK.

Asting, C. and Gottschalk, P. (2022). Attorney fraud in the law firm: A case study of crime convenience theory and crime signal detection theory, *Deviant Behavior*, published online doi: 10.1080/01639625.2022.2071657.

Benson, M.L. (2019). The neutralization of corporate crime: Organizational and state-facilitated denials of corporate harm and wrongdoing, *Journal of White Collar and Corporate Crime*, https://ascdwcc.org/journal-of-white-collar-and-corporate-crime/, retrieved April 2.

Benson, M.L. and Simpson, S.S. (2018). *White-Collar Crime: An Opportunity Perspective*, Third Edition, Routledge, New York, NY.

Berghoff, H. and Spiekermann, U. (2018). Shady business: On the history of white-collar crime, *Business History*, 60 (3), 289–304.

Bernburg, J.G., Krohn, M.D. and Rivera, C. (2006). Official labeling, criminal embeddedness, and subsequent delinquency, *Journal of Research in Crime and Delinquency*, 43 (1), 67–88.

Bertrand, O. and Lumineau, F. (2016). Partners in crime: The effects of diversity on the longevity of cartels, *Academy of Management Journal*, 59 (3), 983–1008.

Braaten, C.N. and Vaughn, M.S. (2019). Convenience theory of cryptocurrency crime: A content analysis of U.S. federal court decisions, *Deviant Behavior*, published online https://doi.org/10.1080/01639625.2019.1706706.

Chang, J.J., Lu, H.C. and Chen, M. (2005). Organized crime or individual crime? Endogenous size of a criminal organization and the optimal law enforcement, *Economic Inquiry*, 43 (3), 661–675.

Chattopadhyay, P., Glick, W.H. and Huber, G.P. (2001). Organizational actions in response to threats and opportunities, *Academy of Management Journal*, 44 (5), 937–955.

Cohen, L.E. and Felson, M. (1979). Social change and crime rate trends: A routine activity approach, *American Sociological Review*, 44, 588–608.

Coleman, J. (1987). Toward an integrated theory of white-collar crime, *American Journal of Sociology*, 93 (2), 406–439.

Cressey, D. (1972). *Criminal Organization: Its Elementary Forms*, Harper and Row, New York, NY.

Dearden, T.E. and Gottschalk, P. (2020). Gender and white-collar crime: Convenience in target selection, *Deviant Behavior*, published online doi: 10.1080/01639625.2020.1756428.

Dewan, Y. and Jensen, M. (2020). Catching the big fish: The role of scandals in making status a liability, *Academy of Management Journal*, 63 (5), 1652–1678.

Downing, S.T., Kang, J.S. and Markman, G.D. (2019). What you don't see can hurt you: Awareness cues to profile indirect competitors, *Academy of Management Journal*, 62 (6), 1872–1900.

Eaton, T.V. and Korach, S. (2016). A criminological profile of white-collar crime, *Journal of Applied Business Research*, 32 (1), 129–142.

Eberlein, B. (2019). Who fills the global governance gap? Rethinking the roles of business and government in global governance, *Organization Studies*, 40 (8), 1125–1146.

Engdahl, O. (2015). White-collar crime and first-time adult-onset offending: Explorations in the concept of negative life events as turning points, *International Journal of Law, Crime and Justice*, 43 (1), 1–16.

Galvin, B.M., Lange, D. and Ashforth, B.E. (2015). Narcissistic organizational identification: Seeing oneself as central to the organization's identity, *Academy of Management Review*, 40 (2), 163–181.

Geest, V.R., Weisburd, D. and Blokland, A.A.J. (2017). Developmental trajectories of offenders convicted of fraud: A follow-up to age 50 in a Dutch conviction cohort, *European Journal of Criminology*, 14 (5), 543–565.
Goldstraw-White, J. (2012). *White-Collar Crime: Accounts of Offending Behavior*, Palgrave Macmillan, London, UK.
Goncharov, I. and Peter, C.D. (2019). Does reporting transparency affect industry coordination? Evidence from the duration of international cartels, *The Accounting Review*, 94 (3), 149–175.
Gottschalk, P. (2020). *The Convenience of White-Collar Crime in Business*, Springer Nature, Switzerland, Cham.
Gottschalk, P. (2021). *Trusted White-Collar Offenders: Global Cases Studies of Crime Convenience*, Palgrave Macmillan, Springer Nature, Switzerland, Cham.
Gottschalk, P. (2022). *The Convenience of Corporate Crime: Financial Motive – Organizational Opportunity – Executive Willingness*, De Gruyter, Germany, Berlin.
Gottschalk, P. and Benson, M.L. (2020). The evolution of corporate accounts of scandals from exposure to investigation, *British Journal of Criminology*, 60, 949–969.
Gupta, V.K., Mortal, S., Chakrabarty, B., Guo, X. and Turban, D.B. (2020). CFO gender and financial statement irregularities, *Academy of Management Journal*, 63 (3), 802–831.
Hirschi, T. (1979). Separate and unequal is better, *Journal of Research in Crime and Delinquency*, 16 (1), 34–38.
Hoekstra, M.R. and Verhoeven, W.J. (2021). Investigative interviewing of high-status fraud suspects, *Journal of Investigative Psychology and Offender Profiling*, 18 (3), 185–200.
Hoffmann, J.P. (2002). A contextual analysis of differential association, social control, and strain theories of delinquency, *Social Forces*, 81 (3), 753–785.
Kakkar, H., Sivanathan, N. and Gobel, M.S. (2020). Fall from grace: The role of dominance and prestige in the punishment of high-status actors, *Academy of Management Journal*, 63 (2), 530–553.
Kang, E. and Thosuwanchot, N. (2017). An application of Durkheim's four categories of suicide to organizational crimes, *Deviant Behavior*, 38 (5), 493–513.
Keil, M., Mann, J. and Rai, A. (2000). Why software projects escalate: An empirical analysis and test of four theoretical models, *MIS Quarterly*, 24 (4), 631–664.
Kim, P.H., Dirks, K.T. and Cooper, C.D. (2009). The repair of trust: A dynamic bilateral perspective and multilevel conceptualization, *Academy of Management Review*, 34 (3), 401–422.
König, A., Graf-Vlachy, L., Bundy, J. and Little, L.M. (2020). A blessing and a curse: How CEOs' trait empathy affects their management of organizational crisis, *Academy of Management Review*, 45 (1), 130–153.
Kuvaas, B., Buch, R. and Dysvik, A. (2016). Performance management: Perceiving goals as invariable and implications for perceived job autonomy and work performance, *Human Resource Management*, 55 (3), 401–412.
Lee, F. and Robinson, R.J. (2000). An attributional analysis of social accounts: Implications of playing the blame game, *Journal of Applied Social Psychology*, 30 (9), 1853–1879.
Lehman, D.W., Cooil, B. and Ramanujam, R. (2020). The effects of rule complexity on organizational noncompliance and remediation: Evidence from restaurant health inspections, *Journal of Management*, 46 (8), 1436–1468.
Liang, L.H., Lian, H., Brown, D.J., Ferris, D.J., Hanig, S. and Keeping, L.M. (2016). Why are abusive supervisors abusive? A dual-system self-control model, *Academy of Management Journal*, 59 (4), 1385–1406.

Locatelli, G., Mariani, G., Sainati, T. and Greco, M. (2017). Corruption in public projects and megaprojects: There is an elephant in the room! *International Journal of Project Management*, 35 (3), 252–268.

Maher, R., Valenzuela, F. and Böhm, S. (2019). The enduring state: An analysis of governance-making in three mining conflicts, *Organization Studies*, 40 (8), 1169–1192.

Maslow, A.H. (1943). A theory of human motivation, *Psychological Review*, 50 (4), 370–396.

Mingus, W. and Burchfield, K.B. (2012). From prison to integration: Applying modified labeling theory to sex offenders, *Criminal Justice Studies*, 25 (1), 97–109.

Mohliver, A. (2019). How misconduct spreads: Auditors' role in the diffusion of stock-option backdating, *Administrative Science Quarterly*, 64 (2), 310–336.

Moore, C. (2015). Moral disengagement, *Current Opinion in Psychology*, 6, 199–2014.

Nielsen, R.P. (2003). Corruption networks and implications for ethical corruption reform, *Journal of Business Ethics*, 42 (2), 125–149.

Obodaru, O. (2017). Forgone, but not forgotten: Toward a theory of forgone professional identities, *Academy of Management Journal*, 60 (2), 523–553.

Paternoster, R., Jaynes, C.M. and Wilson, T. (2018). Rational choice theory and interest in the "fortune of others", *Journal of Research in Crime and Delinquency*, 54 (6), 847–868.

Peixoto, A., Gouveia, T., Sousa, P., Faria, R. and Almeida, P.R. (2021). Dark personality traits and tolerance towards unethical behaviors on entrepreneurship: A comparison between entrepreneurs and non-entrepreneurs, *Journal of White Collar and Corporate Crime*, published online doi: 10.1177/2631309X211029877.

Petrocelli, M., Piquero, A.R. and Smith, M.R. (2003). Conflict theory and racial profiling: An empirical analysis of police traffic stop data, *Journal of Criminal Justice*, 31 (1), 1–11.

Resodihardjo, S.L., Carroll, B.J., Eijk, C.J.A. and Maris, S. (2015). Why traditional responses to blame games fail: The importance of context, rituals, and sub-blame games in the face of raves gone wrong, *Public Administration*, 94 (2), 350–363.

Sajko, M., Boone, C. and Buyl, T. (2021). CEO greed, corporate social responsibility, and organizational resilience to systemic shocks, *Journal of Management*, 47 (4), 957–992.

Scheaf, D.J. and Wood, M.S. (2021). Entrepreneurial fraud: A multidisciplinary review and synthesized framework, *Entrepreneurship: Theory and Practice*, 1–36, published online doi: 10.1177/0422587211001818.

Schneider, A. and Scherer, A.G. (2019). State governance beyond the 'shadow of hierarchy': A social mechanisms perspective on governmental CSR policies, *Organization Studies*, 40 (8), 1147–1168.

Schoen, J.L., DeSimone, J.A., Meyer, R.D., Schnure, K.A. and LeBreton, J.M. (2021). Identifying, defining, and measuring justification mechanisms: The implicit biases underlying individual differences, *Journal of Management*, 47 (3), 716–744.

Schoultz, I. and Flyghed, J. (2020). Denials and confessions: An analysis of the temporalization of neutralizations of corporate crime, *International Journal of Law, Crime and Justice*, published online doi.org/10.1016/j.ijlcj.2020.100389.

Schoultz, I. and Flyghed, J. (2021a). "We have been thrown under the bus": Corporate versus individual defense mechanisms against transnational corporate bribery charges, *Journal of White Collar and Corporate Crime*, 2 (1), 24–35.

Schoultz, I. and Flyghed, J. (2021b). Performing unbelonging in court: Observations from a transnational corporate bribery trial – A dramaturgical approach, *Crime, Law and Social Change*, published online doi: 10.1007/s10611-021-09990-x.

Shadnam, M. and Lawrence, T.B. (2011). Understanding widespread misconduct in organizations: An institutional theory of moral collapse, *Business Ethics Quarterly*, 21 (3), 379–407.

Sleesman, D.J., Lennard, A.C., McNamara, G. and Conlon, D.E. (2018). Putting escalation of commitment in context: A multilevel review and analysis, *Academy of Management Annals*, 12 (1), 178–207.

Stadler, W.A. and Gottschalk, P. (2022). Testing convenience theory for white-collar crime: Perceptions of potential offenders and non-offenders, *Deviant Behavior*, 43 (7), 804–820.

Sundström, M. and Radon, A. (2015). Utilizing the concept of convenience as a business opportunity in emerging markets, *Organizations and Markets in Emerging Economies*, 6 (2), 7–21.

Sutherland, E.H. (1983). *White Collar Crime – The Uncut Version*, Yale University Press, New Haven, CT.

Sykes, G. and Matza, D. (1957). Techniques of neutralization: A theory of delinquency, *American Sociological Review*, 22 (6), 664–670.

Thaxton, S. and Agnew, R. (2018). When criminal coping is likely: An examination of conditioning effects in general strain theory, *Journal of Quantitative Criminology*, 34, 887–920.

Thornberry, T.P. (1987). Toward an interactional theory of delinquency, *Criminology*, 25 (4), 863–892.

Wells, J.T. (1997). *Occupational Fraud and Abuse*, Obsidian Publishing Company, Austin, TX.

Welsh, D.T., Baer, M.D., Session, H. and Garud, N. (2020). Motivated to disengage: The ethical consequences of goal commitment and moral disengagement in goal setting, *Journal of Organizational Behavior*, 1–15, published online doi: 10.1002/job.2467.

Welsh, D.T. and Ordonez, L.D. (2014). The dark side of consecutive high performance goals: Linking goal setting, depletion, and unethical behavior, *Organizational Behavior and Human Decision Processes*, 123, 79–89.

Williams, M.L., Levi, M., Burnap, P. and Gundur, R.V. (2019). Under the corporate radar: Examining insider business cybercrime victimization through an application of routine activities theory, *Deviant Behavior*, 40 (9), 1119–1131.

Wood, J. and Alleyne, E. (2010). Street gang theory and research: Where are we now and where do we go from here? *Aggression and Violent Behavior*, 15, 100–111.

Xie, Y. and Keh, H.T. (2016). Taming the blame game: Using promotion programs to counter product-harm crises, *Journal of Advertising*, 45 (2), 211–226.

Zvi, L. and Elaad, E. (2018). Correlates of narcissism, self-reported lies, and self-assessed abilities to tell and detect lies, tell truths, and believe others, *Journal of Investigative Psychology and Offender Profiling*, 15, 271–286.

3 Convenient Corruption in Sports

As the flow of money into the sport industry increases, and the prestige of sport events increases, the attractiveness of wrongdoing also increases. The theory of convenience suggests that there is a financial motive, an organizational opportunity, and a personal willingness for deviant behavior that cause corruption. This chapter demonstrates the potential of applying the theory of convenience to three case studies of corruption in sport: FIFA World Cup, Berkley coaches, and IBU president. There are several benefits from this application of theory. The structural model of convenience theory helps identify relevant as well as irrelevant convenience themes that can direct attention in detection and prevention of corruption. Furthermore, cases of corruption in sport have different convenience structures that invite contingent approaches to law enforcement. Also, the extent of convenience can be identified by underlying factors in each theme. For example, the convenience of corruption is very different when it is mainly found in committing versus concealing wrongdoing. This chapter thus provides a template for future studies of corruption in sport.

A fraud investigation report by Garcia (2014) found evidence of corruption when the football association FIFA in Switzerland allocated world cups to Russia in 2018 and to Qatar in 2022. A fraud investigation report by Howle (2020) found evidence of corruption in the athletes' department at the University of California, Berkley, in the United States, where wealthy parents bribed coaches to have their children accepted at the university. A fraud investigation report by Taylor (2021) found evidence of corruption at the International Biathlon Union (IBU) in Austria, where the Russian biathlon union bribed the IBU president to avoid attention to doping scandals.

These are just three examples of numerous corruption scandals in sport (Gardiner et al., 2017; Kihl et al., 2017; Kulczycki and Koenigstorfer, 2016; Rossi et al., 2019), where corruption in sport is defined as "any illegal, immoral or unethical activity that attempts at deliberately distorting the outcome of a contest for the personal material gain of one or more parties involved in that activity" (Gorse and Chadwick, 2011: 5). Examples of corrupt sport include manipulation of top-level sport events worldwide, match-fixing, doping, and intimidation of referees (Stathopoulou et al., 2021).

DOI: 10.4324/9781003379249-5

This chapter aims at identifying convenience themes in sport corruption based on fraud investigation reports. Convenience is savings in time and effort as well as avoidance of strain and pain to get what the offenders want. As Agnew (2014: 2) formulates it: "crime is often the most expedient way to get what you want" and "fraud is often easier, simpler, faster, more exciting, and more certain than other means of securing one's ends".

This chapter starts with a brief review of the literature regarding corruption in sport and its consequences. Next, the chapter introduces the theory of convenience that suggests financial gain or financial threat as the motive for corruption, organizational opportunity to commit and conceal corruption, and personal willingness for deviant behavior. Then this chapter returns to the three examples of fraud investigation reports mentioned earlier (e.g., Garcia, 2014; Howle, 2020; Taylor, 2021) to discuss corruption convenience in sport by identifying relevant convenience themes in each case.

Characteristics of Sport Corruption

Stathopoulou et al. (2021: 1) found that sport "has ripened into a global industry that captivates the crowds worldwide, mobilizes billions of people, and creates millions of jobs". The global sport market is now reaching US$400 billion. With the magnitude and growth of money involved in the sport industry, there are also criminal forces that explore and exploit the industry (Scalia, 2022). An important criminal force is corruption that generally refers to the giving, requesting, or accepting of an improper advantage related to a position, office, or assignment (Ashforth et al., 2008). The improper advantage does not have to be connected to a specific action or to not doing this action (Artello and Albanese, 2021). It will be sufficient if the advantage can be linked to a person's position, office, or assignment. An individual or group is guilty of corruption if they accept money or money's worth for doing something that he or she is under a duty to do anyway, that he is under a duty not to do, or to exercise a legitimate discretion for improper reason. Corruption is to destroy or pervert the integrity or fidelity of a person in his or her discharge of duty, it is to induce to act dishonestly or unfaithfully, and it is to bribe or to be bribed. Corruption involves behavior on the part of officials in the public or private sector, in which they improperly and unlawfully enrich themselves or others important to them by abusing the privileged positions that they occupy. Corruption entails "mistreatment of suppliers, customers, or competitors" (Kolthoff, 2020: 434).

Stathopoulou et al. (2021) studied the blinding effects of team identification on sport corruption. Their research perspective was particularistic versus universalistic moral norms. Strong particularistic moral norms lead to a strong loyalty to the favored sport team, sport arena, or sport such as football or biathlon. It does not matter to a stakeholder whether the favored entity is involved in corruption because of the stakeholder's strong in-group loyalty. Strong universalistic moral norms, on the other hand, lead to favoring fairness and social justice generally. It does then matter to the stakeholder whether the favored entity is involved in corruption because the universalistic rejection of deviance such as corrupt behavior is stronger than the in-group loyalty.

Specifically, Stathopoulou et al. (2021) examined how identification with a football team influences perceptions of corruption. Other variables in their research included satisfaction, trust, and intention to attend football matches. Research results indicated that the relationships between perceived sport corruption, satisfaction, and attendance were conditional, where the condition was the moderating effect of team identification as well as the indirect effects of attendance in highly corrupt countries. While the domination of universalistic moral norms will harm sport in cases of corruption, the domination of particularistic moral norms will have little or no negative effect on the industry in cases of corruption.

Harm from detection of corruption might be the result of the stigma effect or the competition effect. A stigma is a social attribute that discredits the individual, organization, or industry as possessing a fundamental flaw (Naumovska and Lavie, 2021). The stigma effect implies that the sport industry or parts of it suffers harm collectively. The competition effect implies that non-accused clubs or sport enjoy a spillover effect from accused clubs or sport. Traditionally, as argued by Naumovska and Lavie (2021: 1130), "research on misconduct suggests that accusations against industry peers generate negative consequences for non-accused firms". Researchers have thus suggested a stigma effect that generates a negative spillover, whereby other sporting units and sport events in the accused entity's industry suffer market loss following the accusation.

However, Naumovska and Lavie (2021: 1131) introduced a counterargument, "predicting a positive spillover to non-accused firms following an accusation against their industry peer". Alleged wrongdoing ascribed to a competitor can improve the competitive position of competing units and events in the same industry. Non-accused entities can benefit from the revelation of financial misconduct by an industry peer. Major customers such as sponsors and television networks might not only consider, but actually carry out a switch of their business to other units and entities in the same industry. Then one sport organizer's loss is its competitor's gain.

An important stakeholder group in the sport industry is sponsors (Kulczycki and Koenigstorfer, 2016), since "sport provides corporations with a platform to enhance corporate image and reputation, build brand equity, develop relationships with key stakeholders, and enjoy the benefits of positive image spillover" (Roberts et al., 2018: 20). Business enterprises enter into agreements with rights-holders in the sport industry to benefit from that association. When possibility of positive image spillover is harmed by corruption, the issue of sponsor reaction is of interest. An example is the German sportswear company Puma that ended its contract with a foreign football association after compelling evidence that four of the football teams in the association had fixed their games. Other examples of sponsors that have pulled out of sport are Adidas, Audi, Deutsche Telekom, and Rabobank.

When an incident of corruption causes a scandal, the initial reaction by the accused is often an attempt to protect the sport business in initial accounts. An account is a statement made by the alleged corrupt entity to explain negative behavior that has become subject to inquiry by stakeholders and outsiders (Gottschalk and Benson, 2020). A scandal is "an unexpected, publicly known, and harmful event that has high levels of initial uncertainty, interferes with the normal operation of an organization, and generates widespread, intuitive, and negative perceptions" externally (Bundy and Pfarrer, 2015: 350). As a scandal evolves, the club or another accused has to make statements to explain unanticipated negative conduct in the form of accounts of incidents. Scapegoating is an attempt of diverting attention from the organization and transferring responsibility for corruption to a few symbolic figures (Schoultz and Flyghed, 2021). Depending on the extent of success in accounts giving and scapegoating, the club or industry may suffer more or less harm and loss from the corruption scandal.

Corruption itself causes harm to the sport industry in terms of "competitive damage generated by any kind of undertaking viewed as prohibited by law, unjust and dishonest established on shared global rules and restrictions" (Ionescu, 2015: 109). Corruption is "distorting the outcome of a contest" (Stathopoulou et al. 2021: 1), and "corruption in sport equates the deviation from public expectations that sport will be played and administered in an honest manner" (Masters, 2015: 113).

While Olympic games seem to be the most prestigious and attractive arena for top athletes, the International Olympic Committee (IOC) as such is not well regarded because of suspected financial misconduct (Mason et al., 2006: 57):

> As allegations of corruption among IOC members grew and the media focused more attention on this story, Olympic sponsors became concerned about how the issue might affect the image of the IOC and, by association, their own organizations.

The high status of the games and the low status of the organizer of the games might be explained by the blinding effect of sport events. Also, particularistic rather than universalistic moral norms seem to apply to the situation. However, the aforementioned quote suggests potential stigma effect harming sponsors of events from the bad reputation of the organizer.

It has been suggested that corruption in sport is quite common, while the consequences of corruption are not necessarily very harmful to sport. Therefore, corruption might be an attractive and convenient approach for individuals and enterprises that want to enrich themselves and who are willing to do it in illegitimate ways.

Convenience in Sport Corruption

The theory of convenience suggests that corruption and other forms of financial crime can be triggered by a motive of possibilities or threats and can be conveniently committed and concealed in a professional setting by individuals who demonstrate willingness for deviant behavior. The theory was introduced a few years ago (Gottschalk, 2017) and has since been given favorable reviews (e.g., Hansen, 2020; Oka, 2021; Vasiu and Podgor, 2019) and has been applied by a number of scholars (e.g., Asting and Gottschalk, 2022; Braaten and Vaughn, 2019; Dearden and Gottschalk, 2020; Desmond et al., 2022; Stadler and Gottschalk, 2022; Qu, 2021).

The convenience triangle of motive, opportunity, and willingness has some similarities with the traditional fraud triangle (Murphy and Free, 2015). At the core of the theory is the human desire for convenience in terms of little time and effort, combined with avoidance of strain and pain, to complete a task and reach an objective. The theory is illustrated in Figure 3.1 by its structural model in terms of three convenience dimensions and 14 convenience themes.

Along the motive dimension, there are possibilities or threats for the individual or the enterprise that make corruption attractive. The opportunity for

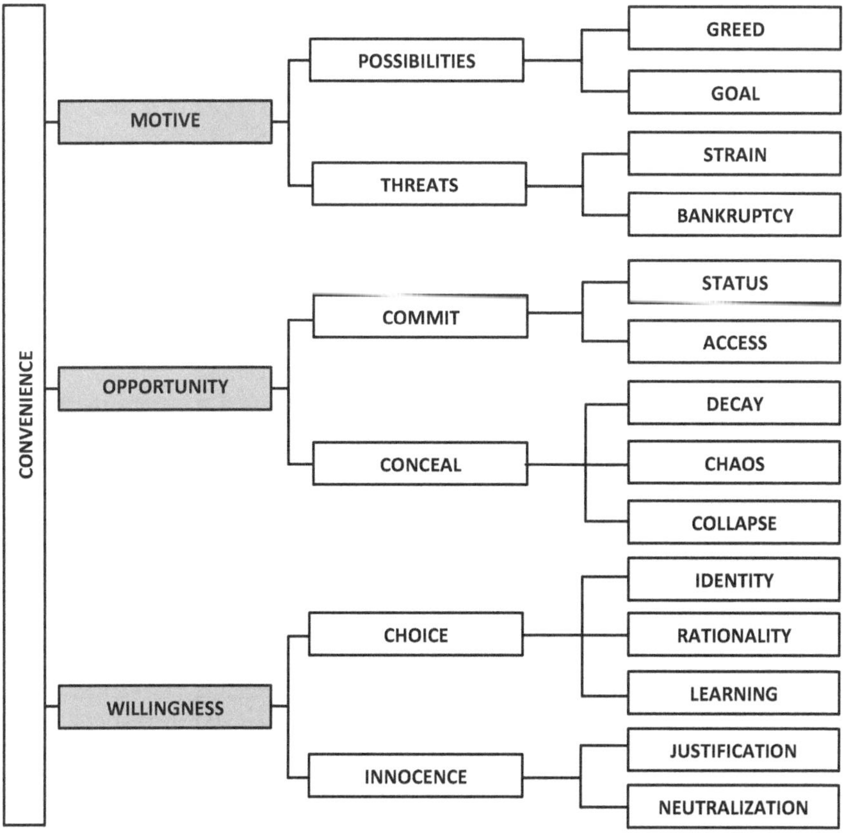

Figure 3.1 Structural model of convenience propositions for corruption in sports

corruption, both for the briber and for the bribed, is to commit and conceal wrongdoing in a professional setting. The offender may have a high status and legitimate access to resources. The professional setting can be characterized by institutional deterioration causing decay, lack of oversight and guardianship causing chaos, and criminal market forces causing collapse. The offender demonstrates willingness for deviant behavior based on choice or innocence, where rational choice, learning from others, and deviant identity are three convenience themes for choice, while justification and neutralization are two convenience themes for innocence.

Corrupt Sport Nations

Media reports suggested that the reason why the international football association FIFA's world cups ended up in Russia in 2018 and in Qatar in 2022 was corruption (Blitz, 2013; Kerr, 2014). Members of the executive committee at FIFA did allegedly receive bribes not only from the winning nations Russia and Qatar but also from losing competitors such as Australia (Smyth, 2015). On December 2, 2010, the executive committee of FIFA, using an anonymous voting procedure, determined the hosts for the 2018 and 2022 FIFA World Cup tournaments. Allegations of corruption related to the voting process had surfaced even before the final vote that December day in Zürich in Switzerland. Ever since, there have been persistent allegations of misconduct with respect to the selection process (Ahmed and Agini, 2021). In 2017, British newspaper The Guardian reported that a FIFA official allegedly took bribes to back Qatar's 2022 world cup bid (Laughland, 2017):

> Julio Grondona, a senior vice-president at Fifa and head of the Argentinian football association until his death in 2014, allegedly told the witness, Alejandro Burzaco, an Argentinian sports marketing executive, that he was owed the money in exchange for his vote, which helped Qatar secure the lucrative tournament.

Three years earlier, in 2014, the Garcia report was completed. The Garcia (2014) report was an investigation produced by Michael Garcia and Cornel Borbély into allegations of corruption in world football's governing body triggered by the early rumors after the anonym vote in 2010. FIFA appointed Garcia and Borbély in 2012 to investigate ethical breaches at FIFA. The two examiners quickly focused on persistent public accusations of bribery in the 2018 and 2022 world cup bids. FIFA kept the Garcia (2014) report secret for several years before it leaked to a German newspaper, which caused FIFA subsequently to release the report to the public in 2017.

Both briber and bribed in a corruption relationship have their financial motives, organizational opportunities, as well as willingness for deviant behaviors. In Figure 3.2, illustrations for the bribers – the applicant nations – are with texture, while illustrations for the bribed – the FIFA officials – are with dark

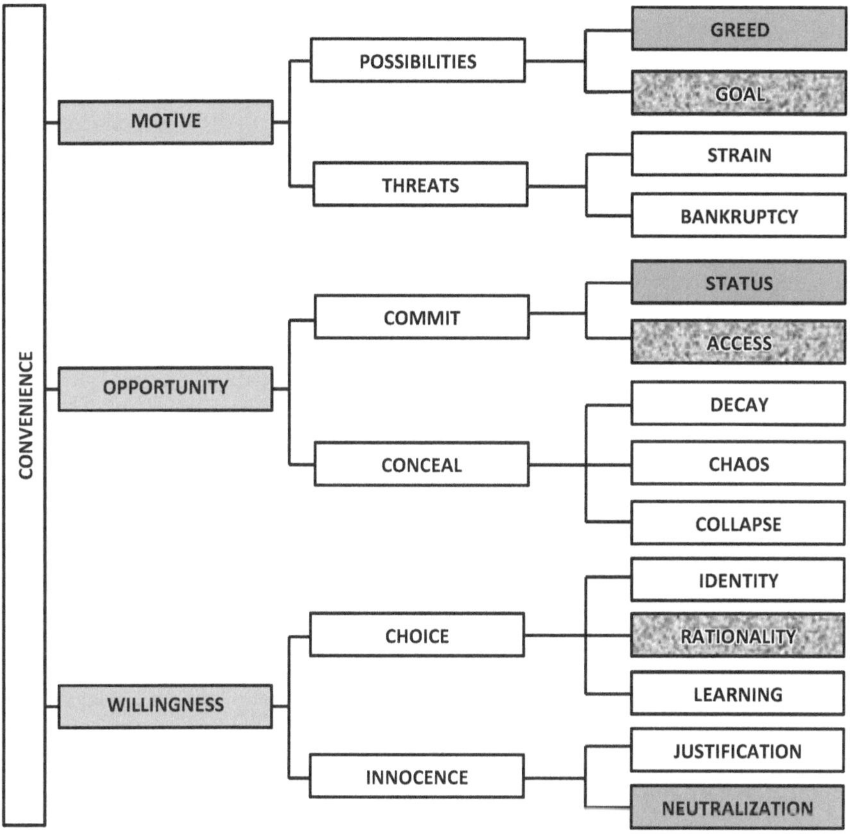

Figure 3.2 Convenience themes in the case of FIFA World Cup

gray. The bribers have a motive of winning the bid for the world cup, which leads to prestige for the country. It is a situation where business objectives justify means (Jonnergård et al., 2010).

The bribed committee members, on the other hand, can make an extraordinary profit, which is possible because of the position at FIFA (Pontell et al., 2014). The bribers have access to resources to bribe members (Benson and Simpson, 2018). It is a rational choice for the bribers to get involved in corruption to improve the nations' chances of winning the bid (Pratt and Cullen, 2005). The bribed can neutralize potential feelings of guilt by arguing that their vote did not change from corruption (Sykes and Matza, 1957).

The relevant convenience themes for the briber are thus corporate possibilities, access to resources, and rational choice, while relevant convenience themes for the bribed are individual possibilities, status, and neutralization, as illustrated in Figure 3.2.

Corrupt Sport Coaches

The University of California was investigated by the auditor of the state of California. The California state auditor found that qualified students faced an inconsistent and unfair admissions system that had been improperly influence by relationships and monetary donations (Howle, 2020). Several rich and mighty people were involved in the corruption scandal (Chaffin, 2020; Levenson, 2020).

On May 22, 2020, Hollywood actress Lori Anne Loughlin pleaded guilty to federal program corruption as she had bribed sport coaches at the University of California to enable her children's admissions to Berkley (Levenson, 2020). The bribed coaches admitted the children as athletic recruits despite the children having low athletic abilities in the relevant sport (Chaffin, 2020). The corrupt university officials wrongfully and deliberately classified the two Loughlin daughters as qualified and promising for the women's rowing team although none of them had any experience from the sport of rowing, and none of them had any plans of entering into the sport. Loughlin and her husband Mossimo Giannulli paid half a million dollars in bribes to the Berkley coaches for the corrupt university service of admittance (Madani, 2021). On August 21, 2020, the wealthy and influential actress Loughlin was sentenced to two months in prison while her husband, an American fashion designer, was sentenced to five months (Puente, 2020; Taylor, 2020).

While pleading guilty, Loughlin said in court that she acted out of love and care for her daughters. This statement is in line with the financial crime motive of social concern. Agnew (2014) introduced the motive of social concern by crime, where the offender has a desire to help others and thus is moving beyond the simple self-interest often assumed in white-collar offenses. However, as argued by Paternoster et al. (2018), helping others can be a self-interested, rational action that claims social concern, where offenders such as Loughlin and Giannulli could satisfy their need in Maslow's (1943) hierarchy for being perceived as caring, loving, and helping parents. Social concern belongs to the convenience theme of motive-possibilities-individual as illustrated in Figure 3.3.

Agnew (2014) argued that social concern consists of four elements, namely, (1) individuals, such as parents, care about the welfare of others, such as their children; (2) parents want close ties with their children; (3) the parents may think of following moral guidelines such as innocent people should not suffer harm, although qualified students were not admitted as a consequence; and (4) the parents tend to seek confirmation through other people's actions and norms such as confirmation bias from a similar situation at Yale university.

In the opportunity dimension of convenience theory, actress Loughlin had high social status as indicated in Figure 3.3. Movie stars such as Loughlin become popular and often idol to their fans. Movie stars tend to be icons with high, sometimes heroic, status in society. Loughlin fell from grace as she lost position of honor and admiration in the privileged roles of actress and producer

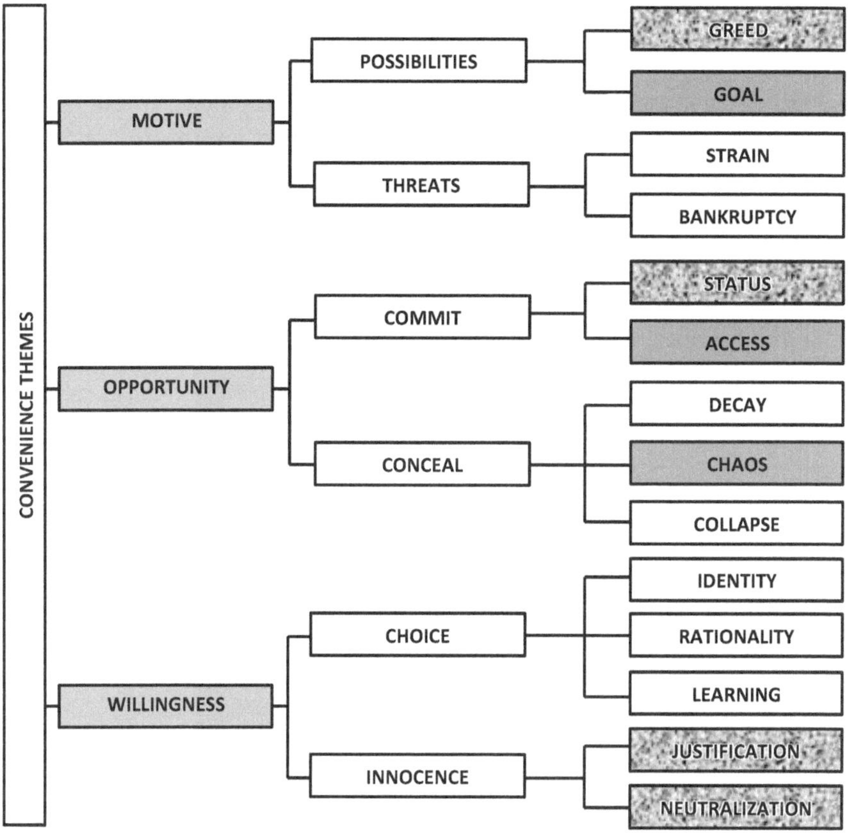

Figure 3.3 Convenience themes in the case of university admittance

(Starr, 2021). Status is an individual's social rank within a formal or informal hierarchy, or the person's relative standing along a valued social dimension such as fame. Status is the extent to which an individual is respected and admired by others, and status is the outcome of a subjective assessment process (McClean et al., 2018). High-status individuals enjoy greater respect and deference from, as well as power and influence over, those who are positioned lower in the social hierarchy (Kakkar et al., 2020: 532):

> Status is a property that rests in the eyes of others and is conferred to individuals who are deemed to have a higher rank or social standing in a pecking order based on a mutually valued set of social attributes.

Especially individuals with high status based on prestige such as Loughlin, rather than dominance, tend to be excused for whatever wrongdoing they commit (Kakkar et al., 2020). This was evidenced by her return to television after prison time for the college admission scandal (Madani, 2021).

The willingness of actress Loughlin to bribe university officials might derive from an innocence perspective of both justification and neutralization (Sykes and Matza, 1957). She found the act of wrongdoing morally justifiable (Schnatterly et al., 2018), probably based on upper echelon information selection (Gamache and McNamara, 2019). The actress felt an obligation to help her daughters into a respectable educational institution. The relevant convenience themes are illustrated by texture color in Figure 3.3.

In our main perspective of convenient corruption in sport, campus staff took advantage of weaknesses in admissions processes inappropriately to admit students by returning favors to donors, family, and friends. As coaches at universities have a responsibility to secure funding to their sport teams, where they rely on donations as a revenue source, it was corporate rather than individual possibilities as illustrated by gray color in Figure 3.3 (Howle, 2020: 19):

> Generally, coaches at the campuses are contractually responsible for fundraising for their teams and use that funding to pay for expenses such as team travel, athletic scholarships, and salaries for coaches and support staff. Their reliance on donations to support the continued existence of their teams can put pressure on coaches to use their significant influence over the admissions process to falsely designate applicants as qualified athletes to cultivate a positive relationship with prospective or existing donors.

Athletic coaches do not necessarily have high status, but they have access to resources to admit non-qualified individuals to their teams and thus to the university. Their willingness might rest on a loyalty to the university in terms of financing own teams to succeed in future sport events. The convenience theme of neutralization thus applies to both briber and bribed in this case.

Howle (2020: 19) emphasized the lack of control and guardianship indicated as chaos in Figure 3.3:

> The campuses' athletics admissions processes are open to abuse because they allow for a large percentage of applicants to gain admission on the basis of much different considerations than the general applicant pool, and there is inadequate oversight of these admissions processes.

Despite the vulnerability to abuse the athletics admissions process, Howle (2020: 19) found that none of the four campuses of the University of California that was reviewed had "implemented effective safeguards against inappropriate admissions activity in the years leading up to the national admissions scandal".

Corrupt Biathlon President

Russian doping whistleblower Grigory Rodchenkov told the media about organized doping of Russian athletes at the Sochi Winter Olympics. Rodchenkov had been the head of Russia's national anti-doping laboratory. Rodchenkov's allegations were confirmed by the independent McLaren (2016) report, leading to Russia's partial bans from the 2016 Summer Olympics as well as the 2018 and 2022 Winter Olympics. Rodchenkov's allegations and the McLaren (2016) findings led to an investigation particularly targeted at the management at the IBU. When the IBU report was released (Taylor, 2021), the *New York Times* wrote about it under the heading "Hunting trips, sex, and cash: How grooming biathlon's leader paid off for Russia: An investigation accuses biathlon's long-time president of accepting gifts from Russians and then doing the country's bidding as a doping scandal swirled" (Panja, 2021):

> The president of the International Biathlon Union told the police that the young woman who had come to his hotel in Moscow was a prostitute, but he was hazy on the details. He did not remember the date or even who had paid for her services, he said, but it had assuredly not been him. The president, Anders Besseberg, had led biathlon's governing body for more than two decades by then, and he was accustomed to receiving gifts from his Russian hosts. Like a chocolate on his pillow or a gift bag placed on a chair in his hotel room, the company of a young woman during a trip to a World Cup biathlon event was not uncommon.
>
> And for decades, according to a report commissioned by biathlon's new leadership, Besseberg repaid the Russian favors by doing the country's bidding – defending its athletes, assailing its critics and even blocking efforts to root out doping by its teams. The yearlong effort to groom Besseberg, and later his top deputy, was so effective that at the height of Russia's state-run doping scandal one Russian official boasted to a colleague that the country had little to fear in biathlon – a grueling endurance sport that combines precision shooting with cross-country ski racing – because he had Besseberg "under his control".

The IBU is headquartered in Salzburg in Austria. Biathlon is a winter sport that combines cross-country skiing and rifle shooting. It is treated as a race, with contestants skiing through a cross-country trail where distance is divided into shooting rounds. Major biathlon nations include France, Russia, Sweden, and Norway. Biathlon is a very popular sport among spectators, both present at shooting stadiums and in front of television screens all over the world. The business of biathlon events has grown significantly in recent decades, and rumors of both corruption and doping have flourished for several years in the media.

The potential offender in this case study is Anders Besseberg who appeared in the view of the fraud examiners to have had no regard for ethical values and no real interest in protecting the sport from cheating. Taylor (2021) claimed that Besseberg was enabled by a complete lack of basic governance safeguards that left integrity decisions in the sole hands of himself and his allies on the IBU executive board, with no checks and balances, no transparency, and no accountability. The use of the term integrity "has in recent years become common currency in the sports world" (Gardiner et al., 2017: 7), where integrity refers to the quality of acting in accordance with the moral values, norms, and rules that are considered valid and relevant within the context in which the actor operates (Loyens et al., 2021). The external fraud examiners alleged that Besseberg had been bribed by Russian officials by more than €300,000.

In the financial motive dimension of convenience theory, he was allegedly interested in hunting trips and sex paid for by others, in addition to cash (Taylor, 2021: 63):

> The police also seized thirteen watches at Mr Besseberg's home. Four of them were from specific sporting events, the other nine watches being luxury brands like RAM (2), Omega Broad Arrow, Ulysse Nardin (2), Hublot Geneve, Poljot, and two unknown brands (both probably Russian). Mr Besseberg confirmed that he had received the Omega watch (worth about Euro 20,000) as a personal present in March 2011 in Khanty-Mansiysk, to mark the occasion of the 100th IBU Executive Board meeting and his 65th birthday. He said a blue watch (brand unknown, probably *Naprer') was given to him by Alexander Tikhonov, but he could not provide the occasion or the date of the gift, just that it was at an IBU World Cup event at Holmenkollen. That leaves seven watches of unclear provenance. Mr Besseberg himself did not state that he had bought them or indicate how he had obtained them.

Besseberg climbed the hierarchy of needs for status and success (Maslow, 1943). He had contributed to the success of biathlon sport and probably wanted to satisfy the need for acclaim as a narcissist (Chatterjee and Pollock, 2017). He was allegedly greedy as well (Goldstraw-White, 2012). The motive for alleged wrongdoing was thus individual possibilities as indicated in Figure 3.4.

In the opportunity dimension of convenience theory, Taylor (2021:1) argued that Besseberg's allegedly corrupt behavior was

> enabled by a complete lack of basic governance safeguards that left integrity decisions in the sole hands of the President and his allies on the IBU Executive Board, with no checks and balances, no transparency, and no accountability whatsoever to keep them honest.

which made that "Mr. Besseberg's proclaimed commitment to clean sport was, in the Commission's view, a charade". As indicated in Figure 3.4, there was a combination of status and decay that made alleged wrongdoing convenient. While status enabled commitment of wrongdoing (Patel and Cooper, 2014; Pontell et al., 2014), decay enabled concealment of wrongdoing (Crosina and Pratt, 2019; Eberl et al., 2015; Rooij and Fine, 2020). The president of the biathlon union in the United States, Max Cobb, claimed that Besseberg behaved like and had the status of a king (Christiansen et al., 2021).

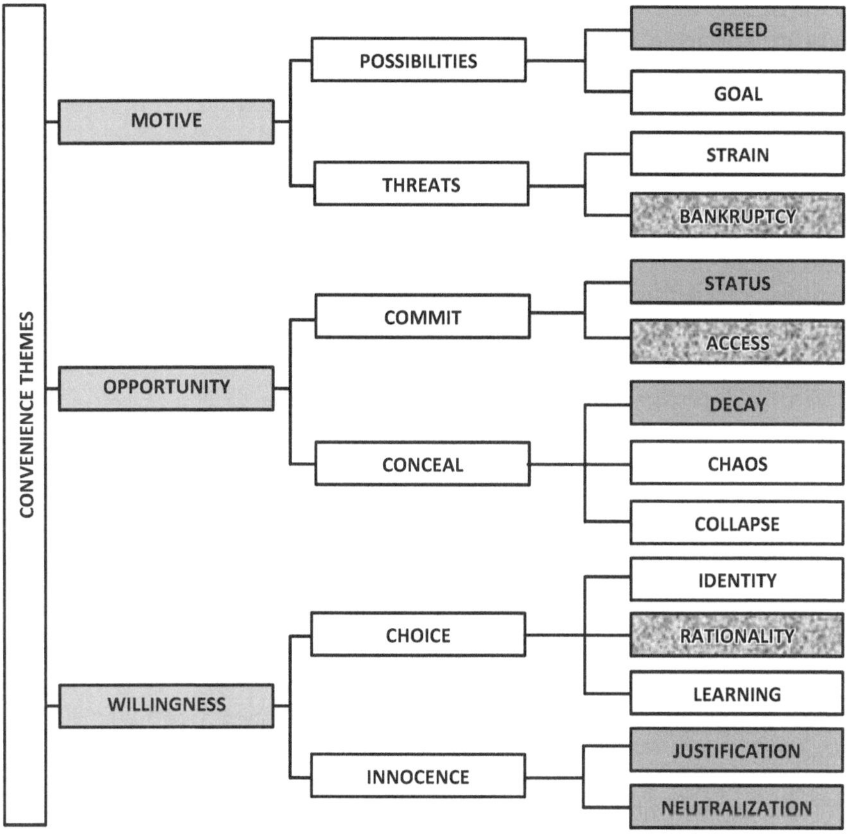

Figure 3.4 Convenience themes in the case of doping

In the willingness dimension of convenience theory, Taylor (2021: 1) claimed that Besseberg could justify and neutralize his deviant behavior:

> This final report of the independent IBU External Review Commission (the Commission) identifies what the Commission considers to be evidence of systematic corrupt and unethical conduct at the very top of the IBU for a decade (2008 to 2018) and more, by a president (Anders Besseberg, IBU President 1993 to 2018) who appears, in the view of the Commission, to have had no regard for ethical values and no real interest in protecting the sport from cheating.

Besseberg's alleged deviant behavior seems to be in accordance with the differential association perspective, where an offender associates with those who agree with him, and distances him from those who are critical to his activities (Sutherland, 1983). It is a matter of learning from others, who in this case are Russian officials. It was then a rational choice, where perception of benefits exceeded perceptions of costs (Pratt and Cullen, 2005). Probably did behavioral reinforcement of deviance occur over time (Benartzi et al., 2017). Besseberg may have been sliding on the slippery slope (Welsh et al., 2014) with a lack of self-control (Gottfredson and Hirschi, 1990).

While IBU president Besseberg was the assumed bribed with convenience themes as indicated in gray color in Figure 3.4, Russian biathlon officials were the assumed bribers with convenience themes as indicated in texture color. Russian officials faced a threat of having their top athletes banned from international competitions that involve both prestige and money (Chattopadhyay et al., 2001). They had access to resources to bribe the IBU president in various ways (Wheelock et al., 2011). It was a rational choice (Pratt and Cullen, 2005).

Bribers and Bribed Officials

The structural model of convenience theory is a template to identify relevant convenience themes in a potential corruption case. As illustrated in the three cases above from Switzerland involving Russia and Qatar, from the United States involving several elite universities, and from Austria involving Russia, convenience themes vary according to the situation and whether the offender is a bribing organization or a bribed individual. In addition to identify convenience themes in a specific case, the structural model might also help in identifying the extent of convenience for each theme. For example, the status of IBU president Besseberg, who was accused of being bribed by Russian biathlon officials, was extremely solid based on his position in the biathlon sport for decades as well as the Russian vulnerability from exposure of the doping scandal depending on Besseberg's handling of the scandal.

The bribed FIFA officials in Switzerland, the bribed university sport coaches in the United States, as well as the alleged bribed IBU president in Austria had a motive of individual possibilities, a trustworthy status in the opportunity dimension, and willingness based on neutralization. In addition, the opportunity structure for the biathlon president included lack of oversight and guardianship causing decay, and the willingness structure included justification by socializing with key biathlon nations that was important to the president.

The bribers in Switzerland had a goal of corporate possibilities by making FIFA officials assign the world cup to their nations. Both winning countries, such as Russia and Qatar, as well as losing countries, such as Australia, were allegedly on the bribing side. The bribers had access to resources to get involved in corruption, which was a rational choice in the willingness dimension. Rational here means that the expected benefits exceeded the expected costs of corruption.

The Russian bribers had similar motives, opportunities, and willingness themes as the FIFA bribers. The bribers in the United States had a goal of individual possibilities by making coaches admit their children to high-ranking universities. The offenders had status, and they justified the wrongdoing by concern for others – that is their own children.

In conclusion, this chapter has explored the potential of applying the theory of convenience to case studies of corruption in sport. There are three benefits from this application of theory. First, the structural model of convenience theory helps identify relevant as well as irrelevant convenience themes that can direct attention in detection and prevention of corruption. Second, cases of corruption in sport have different convenience structures that invite contingent approaches to law enforcement. Third, the extent of convenience can be identified by underlying factors in each theme. For example, the convenience of corruption is very different when it is mainly found in committing versus concealing wrongdoing. This chapter has thus provided a template for future studies of sport corruption.

Furthermore, this chapter has demonstrated the use of investigation reports by fraud examiners as an empirical basis to study alleged wrongdoing. A fraud examiner is a financial detective in the private or public policing business undertaking internal investigations in client or associated organizations. The fraud examiner conducts inquiries by undertaking factual reviews of documents, interviews with whistleblowers and suspects, and other investigative steps. The expectation is that fraud examiners such as Garcia (2014), Howle (2020), and Taylor (2021) will uncover and verify the facts of the case, reconstruct past events and sequences of events, and thereby allowing harmed organizations to make informed decisions to either litigate or resolve matters (King, 2021; Meerts, 2020).

References

Agnew, R. (2014). Social concern and crime: Moving beyond the assumption of simple self-interest, *Criminology*, 52 (1), 1–32.

Ahmed, M. and Agini, S. (2021). Blatter and Platini face fraud charges in FIFA corruption bribe, *Financial Times*, www.ft.com, retrieved November 2.

Artello, K. and Albanese, J.S. (2021). Culture of corruption: Prosecutions, persistence, and desistence, *Public Integrity*, pages 1–21, published online doi: 10.1080/10999922.2021.1881300.

Ashforth, B.E., Gioia, D.A., Robinson, S.L. and Trevino, L.K. (2008). Re-reviewing organizational corruption, *Academy of Management Review*, 33 (3), 670–684.

Asting, C. and Gottschalk, P. (2022). Attorney fraud in the law firm: A case study of crime convenience theory and crime signal detection theory, *Deviant Behavior*, published online doi: 10.1080/01639625.2022.2071657.

Benartzi, S., Beshears, J., Milkman, K.L., Sunstein, C.R., Thaler, R.H., Shankar, M., Tucker-Ray, W., Congdon, W.J. and Galing, S. (2017). Should governments invest more in nudging? *Psychological Science*, 28 (8), 1041–1055.

Benson, M.L. and Simpson, S.S. (2018). *White-Collar Crime: An Opportunity Perspective*, Third Edition, Routledge, New York, NY.

Blitz, R. (2013). Fifa feels the heat over Qatar World Cup choice, *Financial Times*, www.ft.com, retrieved October 3.

Braaten, C.N. and Vaughn, M.S. (2019). Convenience theory of cryptocurrency crime: A content analysis of U.S. federal court decisions, *Deviant Behavior*, published online https://doi.org/10.1080/01639625.2019.1706706.

Bundy, J. and Pfarrer, M.D. (2015). A burden of responsibility: The role of social approval at the onset of a crisis, *Academy of Management Review*, 40 (3), 345–369.

Chaffin, J. (2020). Ex-Pimco chief sentenced to 9 months for college bribes, *Financial Times*, www.ft.com, retrieved February 7.

Chatterjee, A. and Pollock, T.G. (2017). Master of puppets: How narcissistic CEOs construct their professional worlds, *Academy of Management Review*, 42 (4), 703–725.

Chattopadhyay, P., Glick, W.H. and Huber, G.P. (2001). Organizational actions in response to threats and opportunities, *Academy of Management Journal*, 44 (5), 937–955.

Christiansen, A.K., Friberg, J. and Asbjørnsen, M. (2021). IBU-topp om Besseberg: -Han var som en valgt konge (IBU Top About Besseberg: He Was Like an Elected King), Daily Norwegian Newspaper *VG*, www.vg.no, retrieved January 29.

Crosina, E. and Pratt, M.G. (2019). Toward a model of organizational mourning: The case of former Lehman Brothers bankers, *Academy of Management Journal*, 62 (1), 66–98.

Dearden, T.E. and Gottschalk, P. (2020). Gender and white-collar crime: Convenience in target selection, *Deviant Behavior*, published online doi: 10.1080/01639625.2020.1756428.

Desmond, S.A., Rorie, M. and Sohoni, T. (2022). Working for God: Religion and occupational crime and deviance, *Deviant Behavior*, published online doi: 10.1080/01639625.2021.2022968.

Eberl, P., Geiger, D. and Assländer, M.S. (2015). Repairing trust in an organization after integrity violations. The ambivalence of organizational rule adjustments, *Organization Studies*, 36 (9), 1205–1235.

Gamache, D.L. and McNamara, G. (2019). Responding to bad press: How CEO temporal focus influences the sensitivity to negative media coverage of acquisitions, *Academy of Management Journal*, 62 (3), 918–943.

Garcia. (2014). *Report on the Inquiry Into the 2018/2022 Fifa World Cup Bidding Process*, investigatory chamber chairman Michael J. Garcia, Zürich, Switzerland, 359 pages.

Gardiner, S., Parry, J. and Robinson, S. (2017). Integrity and the corruption debate in sport: Where is the integrity? *European Sport Management Quarterly*, 17 (1), 6–23.

Goldstraw-White, J. (2012). *White-Collar Crime: Accounts of Offending Behavior*, Palgrave Macmillan, London, UK.

Gorse, S. and Chadwick, S. (2011). *The Prevalence of Corruption in International Sport – A Statistical Analysis*, Report prepared for the Remote Gambling Association and their partners, the European Gaming and Betting Association, and the European Sports Security Association, Centre for the International Business of Sports, UK, Coventry, 41 pages.

Gottfredson, M.R. and Hirschi, T. (1990). *A general theory of crime*, Stanford University Press, Stanford, CA.

Gottschalk, P. (2017). Convenience in white-collar crime: Introducing a core concept, *Deviant Behavior*, 38 (5), 605–619.

Gottschalk, P. and Benson, M.L. (2020). The evolution of corporate accounts of scandals from exposure to investigation, *British Journal of Criminology*, 60, 949–969.

Hansen, L.L. (2020). Review of the book "convenience triangle in white-collar crime: Case studies of fraud examinations", *Choice Connect*, vol. 57, no. 5, Association of College and Research Libraries, Middletown, CT.

Howle, E.M. (2020). *The University of California: Qualified Students Face an Inconsistent and Unfair Admissions System That Has Been Improperly Influenced by Relationships and Monetary Donations*, Report of Investigation, California State Auditor, 82 pages.

Ionescu, L. (2015). The economics of corruption in professional sport, *Economics, Management, and Financial Markets*, 10 (2), 109–114.

Jonnergård, K., Stafsudd, A. and Elg, U. (2010). Performance evaluations as gender barriers in professional organizations: A study of auditing firms, *Gender, Work and Organization*, 17 (6), 721–747.

Kakkar, H., Sivanathan, N. and Globel, M.S. (2020). Fall from grace: The role of dominance and prestige in punishment of high-status actors, *Academy of Management Journal*, 63 (2), 530–553.

Kerr, S. (2014). World Cup allegations crown bad year for Qatar, *Financial Times*, www.ft.com, retrieved June 6.

Kihl, L.A., Skinner, J. and Engelberg, T. (2017). Corruption in sport: Understanding the complexity of corruption, *European Sport Management Quarterly*, 17 (1), 1–5.

King, M. (2021). Profiting from a tainted trade: Private investigators' views on the popular culture glamorization of their trade, *Journal of Criminological Research Policy and Practice*, 7 (2), 112–125.

Kolthoff, E. (2020). Criminological responses to corruption, in: Graycar, A. (editor), *Handbook on Corruption, Ethics and Integrity in Public Administration*, Edward Elgar Publishing, Cheltenham, UK, chapter 30, 434–448.

Kulczycki, W. and Koenigstorfer, J. (2016). Why sponsors should worry about corruption as a mega sport event syndrome, *European Sport Management Quarterly*, 16 (5), 545–574.

Laughland, O. (2017). Fifa official took bribes to back Qatar's 2022 world cup bid, court hears, *The Guardian*, www.theguardian.com, retrieved November 15.

Levenson, M. (2020). Lori Loughlin begins 2-month sentence for role in admissions scandal, *The New York Times*, www.nytimes.com, retrieved October 30.

Loyens, K., Claringbould, I., Heres-van Rossem, L. and Eekeren, Frank van. (2021). The social construction of integrity: A qualitative case study in Dutch football, *Sports in Society*, published online doi: 10.1080/17430437.2021.1877661.

Madani, D. (2021). Lori Loughlin returns to television after prison time for college admissions scandal, *NBC News*, www.nbcnews.com, retrieved September 29.

Maslow, A.H. (1943). A theory of human motivation, *Psychological Review*, 50 (4), 370–396.

Mason, D.S., Thibault, L. and Misener, L. (2006). An agency theory perspective on corruption in sport: The case of the international Olympic committee, *Journal of Sport Management*, 20, 52–73.

Masters, A. (2015). Corruption in sports: From the playing field to the field of policy, *Policy and Society*, 34 (2), 111–123.

McClean, E.J., Martin, S.R., Emich, K.J. and Woodruff, T. (2018). The social consequences of voice: An examination of voice type and gender on status and subsequent leader emergence, *Academy of Management Journal*, 61 (5), 1869–1891.

McLaren, R.H. (2016). *The Independent Person Report: Wada Investigation of Sochi Allegations*, World Anti-Doping Agency Wada, www.wada-ama.org, retrieved July 16.

Meerts, C. (2020). Corporate investigations: Beyond notions of public-private relations, *Journal of Contemporary Criminal Justice*, 36 (1), 86–100.

Murphy, P.R. and Free, C. (2015). Broadening the fraud triangle: Instrumental climate and fraud, *Behavioral Research in Accounting*, 28 (1), 41–56.

Naumovska, I. and Lavie, D. (2021). When an industry peer is accused of financial misconduct: Stigma versus competition effects on non-accused firms, *Administrative Science Quarterly*, 66 (4), 1130–1172.

Oka, R. (2021). Introducing an anthropology of convenience, *Economic Anthropology*, 8 (2), 188–207.

Panja, T. (2021). Hunting trips, sex and cash: How grooming biathlon's leader paid off for Russia – An investigation accuses biathlon's longtime president of accepting gifts from Russians and then doing the country's bidding as a doping scandal swirled, *The New York Times*, www.nytimes.com, retrieved January 28.

Patel, P.C. and Cooper, D. (2014). Structural power equality between family and nonfamily TMT members and the performance of family firms, *Academy of Management Journal*, 57 (6), 1624–1649.

Paternoster, R., Jaynes, C.M. and Wilson, T. (2018). Rational choice theory and interest in the "fortune of others", *Journal of Research in Crime and Delinquency*, 54 (6), 847–868.

Pontell, H.N., Black, W.K. and Geis, G. (2014). Too big to fail, too powerful to jail? On the absence of criminal prosecutions after the 2008 financial meltdown, *Crime, Law and Social Change*, 61 (1), 1–13.

Pratt, T.C. and Cullen, F.T. (2005). Assessing macro-level predictors and theories of crime: A meta-analysis, *Crime and Justice*, 32, 373–450.

Puente, M. (2020). Lori Loughlin released from prison after serving 2-month sentence in college bribery scheme, *USA Today*, www.eu.usatoday.com, retrieved December 28.

Qu, J. (2021). The challenge against economic regulation ethics under the Covid-19 epidemic: An analysis of unethical behavior of convenience, *Converter Magazine*, 2021 (5), 74–79.

Roberts, S., Chadwick, S. and Anagnostopoulos, C. (2018). Sponsorship programmes and corruption in sports: Management responses to a growing threat, *Journal of Strategic Marketing*, 26 (1), 19–36.

Rooij, B. and Fine, A. (2020). Preventing corporate crime from within: Compliance management, whistleblowing, and internal monitoring, in: Rorie, M.L. (editor), *The Handbook of White-Collar Crime*, Wiley & Sons, Hoboken, NJ, chapter 15, pages 229–245.

Rossi, G., Goossens, D., Tanna, G.L.D. and Addesa, F. (2019. Football team performance efficiency and effectiveness in corruptive context: The Calciopoli case, *European Sport Management Quarterly*, 19 (5), 583–604.

Scalia, V. (2022). There are too many Christians involved: Cosa Nostra and professional football in Palermo, *Journal of White Collar and Corporate Crime*, pages 1–9, published online doi: 10.1177/2631309X221101048.

Schnatterly, K., Gangloff, K.A. and Tuschke, A. (2018). CEO wrongdoing: A review of pressure, opportunity, and rationalization, *Journal of Management*, 44 (6), 2405–2432.

Schoultz, I. and Flyghed, J. (2021). Performing unbelonging in court: Observations from a transnational corporate bribery trial – A dramaturgical approach, *Crime, Law and Social Change*, published online doi: 10.1007/s10611-021-09990-x.

Smyth, J. (2015). Australian police probe payments in failed bid to host World Cup, *Financial Times*, www.ft.com, retrieved June 4.

Stadler, W.A. and Gottschalk, P. (2022). Testing convenience theory for white-collar crime: Perceptions of potential offenders and non-offenders, *Deviant Behavior*, 43 (7), 804–820.

Starr, M. (2021). Disgraced Lori Loughlin shows no shame with 'family' TV comeback, *New York Post*, www.nypost.com, retrieved September 28.

Stathopoulou, A., Quansah, T.K. and Balabanis, G. (2021). The blinding effects of team identification on sports corruption: Cross-cultural evidence from Sub-Saharan African countries, *Journal of Business Ethics*, published online doi: 10.1007/s10551-021-04822-3.

Sutherland, E.H. (1983). *White Collar Crime – The Uncut Version*, Yale University Press, New Haven, CT.

Sykes, G.M. and Matza, D. (1957). Techniques of neutralization: A theory of delinquency, *American Sociological Review*, 22 (6), 664–670.

Taylor, J. (2021). *Final Report of the IBU External Review Commission*, International Biathlon Union, Austria, January 28, 220 pages.

Taylor, K. (2020). Lori Loughlin released from federal prison, *New York Times*, www.nytimes.com, retrieved December 28.

Vasiu, V.I. and Podgor, E.S. (2019). Organizational opportunity and deviant behavior: Convenience in white-collar crime, *Criminal Law and Criminal Justice Books*, Rutgers, the State University of New Jersey, July, www.clcjbooks.rutgers.edu.

Welsh, D.T., Ordonez, L.D., Snyder, D.G. and Christian, M.S. (2014). The slippery slope: How small ethical transgressions pave the way for larger future transgressions, *Journal of Applied Psychology*, 100 (1), 114–127.

Wheelock, D., Semukhina, O. and Demidov, N.N. (2011). Perceived group threat and punitive attitudes in Russia and the United States, *British Journal of Criminology*, 51, 937–959.

4 Economic Crime in the Fishing Industry

The fishing industry is suffering from lack of compliance causing the ocean to be emptied by sea creatures. Both possibilities and threats are motives for economic crime in the fishing industry, where greed and goal are linked to possibilities, while strain and bankruptcy are linked to threats. Legitimate access to vessels combined with institutional deterioration, lack of oversight and guardianship, and criminal market forces are important convenience issues when committing and concealing crime. On the basis of the theory of convenience, this chapter suggests that targeting such convenience issues in the implementation of regulation might disturb and reduce crime convenience for potential offenders. The structural model of convenience covers 14 potential issues where ten issues apply to economic crime in the fishing industry based on the reviewed research literature. This chapter claims to offer a useful tool and strategy in creating profiles of IUU fishing offenders for regulatory purposes, fraud investigations, and prosecution approaches by offering the theoretical perspective of the convenience model.

The fishing industry is suffering from lack of compliance causing the ocean to be emptied by sea creatures as exemplified by fishing outside Indonesia (Rønneberg, 2022: 12): "Every time they go out, there are more boats struggling to catch from an ever smaller fish stock". Indonesia is the second largest fishing nation after China. "The ocean might be empty in 2048" (Rønneberg, 2022: 12). Similarly, outside Galicia in Spain, "shellfish poaching is a far-reaching, endemic activity which is regarded as the main threat to the shell-fishing industry" (Ballesteros et al., 2021: 747):

> Galician shellfish poachers are many in number and type, acting for a variety of motives, poaching by using different degrees of investment, frequency, organization and technology. In Galicia, one of the most predatory poaching activities is carried out by licensed shellfish-gatherers, who combine legal shell-fishing with illegal extraction. These non-compliers are known as insider poachers.

Norway is the tenth largest fishery nation. In the threat assessment from the Norwegian National Authority for Investigation and Prosecution of Economic

DOI: 10.4324/9781003379249-6

and Environmental Crime (Økokrim, 2022: 28), economic crime in the fishing industry is emphasized:

> Fisheries crime deprives the community of great values. Marine resources are very important for value creation along the coast and for the Norwegian economy. Norwegian seafood is Norway's second largest export product after oil and gas, and the profit opportunity is great for several of the players in the industry. It is very likely that some fishermen and companies that receive fish are involved in systematic under and incorrect reporting of fish and shellfish. Fisheries crime undermines the conditions of competition in the industry, the community's gain form the values at sea and the authorities' management of fishery resources.
>
> Norwegian fishery resources and their great economic value attract actors who profit from systematic under and misreporting of catches at fish receptions. This takes place either in collaboration with the fishermen or by the receptions embezzling catch or catch value from the fishermen. In cooperation, the receptions compensate for under and error reporting by paying a higher price for the catch. The reception thus gets more raw materials and the vessel can catch more fish that it has on the quota.
>
> The use of pallet scales enables the rewriting of end notes. Furthermore, production where the fish is processed in several stages can facilitate the depreciation of a larger proportion of fish than is actually the case.
>
> Rewriting of species also provides financial benefits for both the fisherman and the reception. The fisherman receives a price that is above the minimum price for the reported species, while the reception pays less than half the price for an item that can be traded for full price in the market. Enterprises that own several reception centers or control several activities in the value chain attempt to camouflage under and incorrect reporting by moving seafood between the enterprises. Fish is also traded illegally through seemingly legitimate companies. Some companies that systematically commit and misreport fish also use vulnerable foreign labor, who have poor living conditions and who are exposed to unjustified deductions in wages. In some cases, companies that commit extensive fishing and work-related crime outcompetes the other law-abiding businesses and take over market shares and expand their vertical integration in the market. Actors who control companies in several parts of the value chain use their position to make a profit by putting the sale of illegally caught fish and shellfish into a system. The sale of illegally caught fish often takes place in the dark by the sale not being reported to the customs and tax authorities.

An example is the Norwegian fisherman Mikal Solhaug who was convicted to ten months in prison for misreporting catch. He did also have to pay a fine of NOK 300,000 (about US$30,000). Some years later, Solvang was again the defendant in court where a financial claim was secured by arrest in Solvang's fishing vessel (Horn, 2016).

> Illegal fishing is conducted by vessels of countries that are party to a fisheries organization but which operate in violation of its rules, or operate in a country's waters without permission, or on the high seas without showing a flag or other markings.
>
> (Sumaila et al., 2006: 696)

"Illegal fishing is a widespread, global phenomenon that is affecting already heavily depleted wild fish stocks, threatening marine habitats and contributing to marine pollution through discarded fishing gear" (Vince et al., 2021: 518). IUU fishing – Illegal, Unreported and Unregulated fishing – is often referred to in research on economic crime in the fishing industry (Petrossian and Pezzella, 2019: 122):

> IUU fishing refers to any fishing activity that is carried out in contravention of national, regional, and international fisheries regulations. Illegal fishing refers to operating a vessel in violation of the laws of a country, such as fishing without a license, fishing in violation of the terms of the license, fishing with illegal gear, fishing in closed or protected areas, or fishing during closed seasons. Unreported fishing pertains to misreporting catches to relevant national authorities or regional fisheries management organizations, in violation of the national and international regulations. Unregulated fishing refers to fishing in international waters without a nationality (i.e., carrying a flag), or fishing while flying the flag of a country not party to the regional fisheries management organization that manages the particular fishing region or specific species. . . .
>
> IUU fishers may also engage in seafood fraud, which involves mislabeling or using other deceptive marketing strategies along the seafood supply chain with respect to the quality, origin, quantity, or species. . . .
>
> Seafood fraud can occur anywhere along the seafood chain. The seafood chain is complex, involving a web of harvesters, importers and exporters, distributors (brokers, traders, middlemen, wholesalers), restaurants, supermarkets, and retail fish markets.

The convenience theory approach to economic crime in the fishing industry is concerned with identification of convenience themes with propositions. Convenience exists in the financial motive, the organizational opportunity, and the personal willingness for deviant behavior. These three themes can result in 14 convenience propositions (Gottschalk, 2022). For the phenomenon of IUU fishing, the offense can be examined by identifying relevant convenience issues in the structural model of crime convenience. Not all of the 14 issues will be relevant to create a narrative in one specific business such as the fishing industry. On the basis of the following review of research on IUU fishing, some of the 14 issues emerge as relevant along the motive, opportunity, as well as willingness dimensions. The approach to identification of relevant convenience propositions is a textual comparison of descriptions of convenience issues with descriptions of IUU fishing issues in the literature.

This research is important to ocean development and international law since identified convenience issues for offenders can stimulate jurisdictions to implement regulation that disturb and reduce the convenience of IUU fishing. By targeting identified convenience issues regarding motive, opportunity, as well as willingness for deviant behavior, regulation implementation might become more effective in the future.

Structural Model of Convenience

As documented by Gottschalk (2022), a combination of motive, opportunity, and willingness determine the extent of white-collar crime convenience as illustrated in the structural model in Figure 4.1. Convenience is a concept that

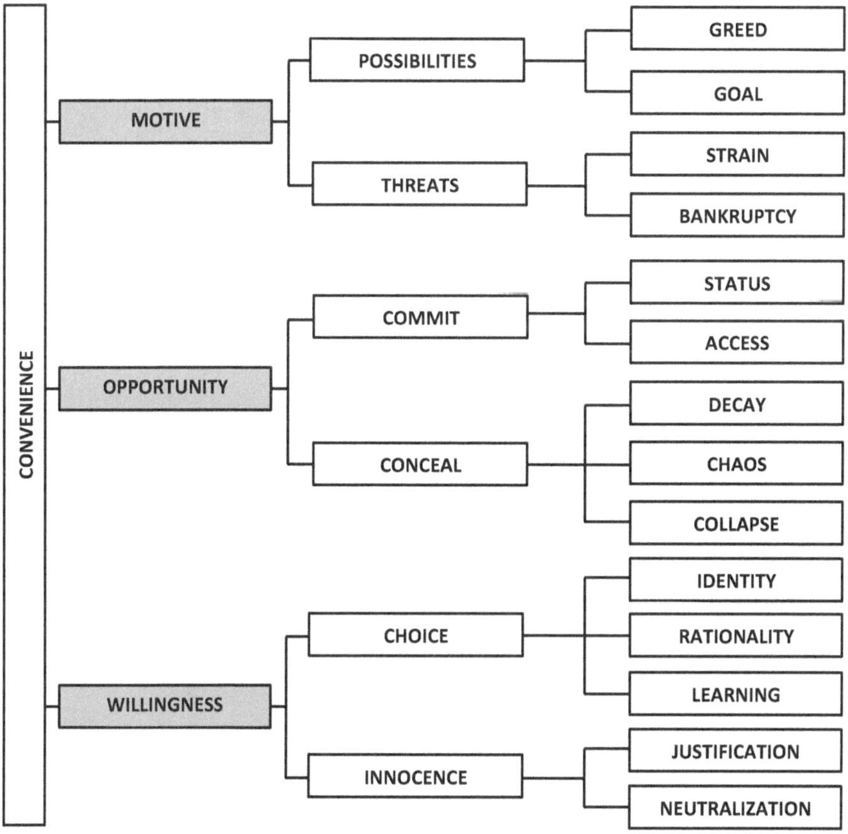

Figure 4.1 Structural model of convenience propositions

was theoretically mainly associated with efficiency in time savings. Today, convenience is associated with a number of other characteristics, such as reduced effort and reduced pain. Convenience is linked to terms such as fast, easy, and safe. Convenience says something about attractiveness and accessibility. A convenient individual is not necessarily neither bad nor lazy. On the contrary, the person can be seen as smart and rational (Sundström and Radon, 2015).

In the financial motive dimension, profit might be a goal in itself or an enabler to exploit possibilities and to avoid threats. Possibilities and threats exist both for individual fishers and for fishing enterprises. The possibility at the individual level is labeled greed (Sajko et al., 2021), and the possibility at the enterprise level is labeled goal (Schweitzer et al., 2004). The threat at the individual level is labeled strain (Thaxton and Agnew, 2018), and the threat at the enterprise level is labeled bankruptcy (Kang and Thosuwanchot, 2017).

In the organizational opportunity dimension, convenience can exist both to commit white-collar crime and to conceal white-collar crime. To commit crime, offenders might have high social status in privileged positions (Kakkar et al., 2020), and they typically have legitimate access to crime resources (Williams et al., 2019). To conceal crime, disorganized institutional deterioration causes decay (Rodriguez et al., 2005), lack of oversight and guardianship causes chaos (Berghoff, 2018; Chan and Gibbs, 2022), while criminal market structures cause collapse (Eberlein, 2019). Aguilera and Vadera (2008: 434) described a criminal opportunity as "the presence of a favorable combination of circumstances that renders a possible course of action relevant".

The personal willingness for deviant behavior focuses on offender choice and perceived innocence. The choice of crime can be caused by deviant identity (Obodaru, 2017), rational consideration (Welsh et al., 2014), or learning from others (Wood and Alleyne, 2010). Justification and neutralization cause the perceived innocence at crime. In a justification, the actor admits responsibility for the act in question but denies its pejorative and negative content (Schoen et al., 2021). By neutralizing guilt feelings, offenders do not feel accountable, ashamed, or responsible (Chen and Moosmayer, 2020). Identity, rationality, learning, justification, and neutralization all contribute to making white-collar crime action a convenient behavior for offenders.

Economic Motive Convenience

Gallic and Cox (2006: 690) emphasized that IUU fishing is economically motivated:

> IUU fishing is primarily an economic activity. Recognizing that incentives to engage in IUU fishing activities are also economic in nature, the general economics of crime and punishment can be used to model this phenomenon.

The possibilities open up for greed and goal as there is a growing and profitable demand for fish products (Petrossian and Pezzella, 2019: 122)

> IUU fishing is carried out primarily due to the rising global demand and the increasing value of fish and fish products. Fish serve as a valuable source of nutrition in many countries, and trade in fish contributes to the income and foreign exchange of these countries.

Overcapacity is a stimulating motive for illegal fishing (Gallic, 2008: 860):

> The prevalence of overcapacity in the worldwide fishing fleet, which incites operators to find the most profitable (although not permitted in their country of origin) way of using their capacities to the full and reducing fishing vessels and crew costs.

The possibilities are "creating higher revenues or lower costs" (Gallic, 2008: 861), and therefore it is more advantages for IUU fishing by vessels carrying flags of convenience (FOC) and others (Gallic, 2008: 860):

> In a nutshell, by circumventing national and international conservation measures, the advantage of IUU/FOC vessels is that they can produce more than when complying with rules and face reduced operating and risk costs.

Several economic and social drivers make IUU fishing attractive (Gallic, 2008: 861):

> Some are of economic nature, such as the prevalence of tax distortion systems (e.g. tax havens, which may provide IUU operators with low tax and reduce the cost of risk), inappropriate management regimes, the prevalence of some forms of subsidies (e.g. subsidies that reduce the cost of IUU fishing capacity), and some investment or fiscal rules (which may reduce the cost of IUU fishing capacity). Others are of social nature, such as the prevalence of poor economic and social conditions and outlooks in some countries, which may reduce the cost of fraud, crew costs, the cost of risk and the costs associated with maintaining appropriate safety and working standards, and, last but not least, the lack of knowledge on the seriousness of the problem, which may reduce the moral/reputation cost IUU operators might face.

Serdy (2017: 345) argued that IUU fishing can be an illegitimate short cut to a legitimate goal since "international fisheries regulations as treaty-based obligations bind only the parties to the treaty concerned and not third states without their consent". Achievement of goals is a strong motive in all kinds of businesses including the fishing industry (Gottschalk, 2022).

Along the motive propositions of threats, Sumaila et al. (2006: 697) emphasized that if the fisher is losing money in legal fishery, and there is the potential to derive benefits from illegal fishing then the probability of cheating increases: "There is also the factor of greed, i.e., the fisher may be making a profit but still engages in IUU fishing because of the desire to increase profits". Sumaila et al. (2006: 697) found that the "following factors are important in determining the potential benefit to the fisher if they cheat: catches, catch per unit, price, cost of fishing".

In the threat perspective, Gallic (2008: 860) argued that "crews originating from low income countries" might be particularly motivated for IUU. Similarly, Gallic and Cox (2006: 691) found that "the prevalence of poor economic conditions and prospects in some developing countries create a ready and cheap labor pool for IUU/FOC vessels".

Overcapacity can represent a possibility as well as a threat for the business (Gallic and Cox, 2006: 690):

> Overcapacity, ineffective management and subsidies are identified as three of the major economic causes of IUU fishing. At the level of the vessel, overcapacity can be caused by a situation of general imbalance between fishing capacities and fishing possibilities in the domestic fleet or inappropriate allocation off fishing rights, both of which result from inappropriate management regimes. The analysis shows that incentives to engage in IUU fishing exist as long as the expected return from using the excess capacity is greater than the regular best alternative, which is zero profit.

In many countries, fishing and the fish industry is subsidized by the state. Such state subsidies can motivate excessive activities to obtain larger sums of government funding. "The provision of subsidies that contribute to the maintenance, the development or the transfer of fishing capacities are likely to artificially reduce the cost of IUU fishing capacities both locally and internationally" (Gallic and Cox, 2006: 690). "One of the challenges for the Indonesian authorities is that the country's fishing industry is heavily subsidized. It helps to create jobs, which in turn makes it cramped at fishing spots" (Rønneberg, 2022: 12).

The aforementioned quotes from the research literature regarding motives for crime illustrate that all four propositions find support. There is both greed at the individual level and goal achievement at the business level, and there is both strain at the individual level and the possibility of bankruptcy at the business level that represent motives for IUU fishing as economic crime. This is illustrated in Figure 4.2.

Business Opportunity Convenience

Offender status might make IUU fishing convenient. High-status individuals enjoy greater respect and deference from, as well as power and influence

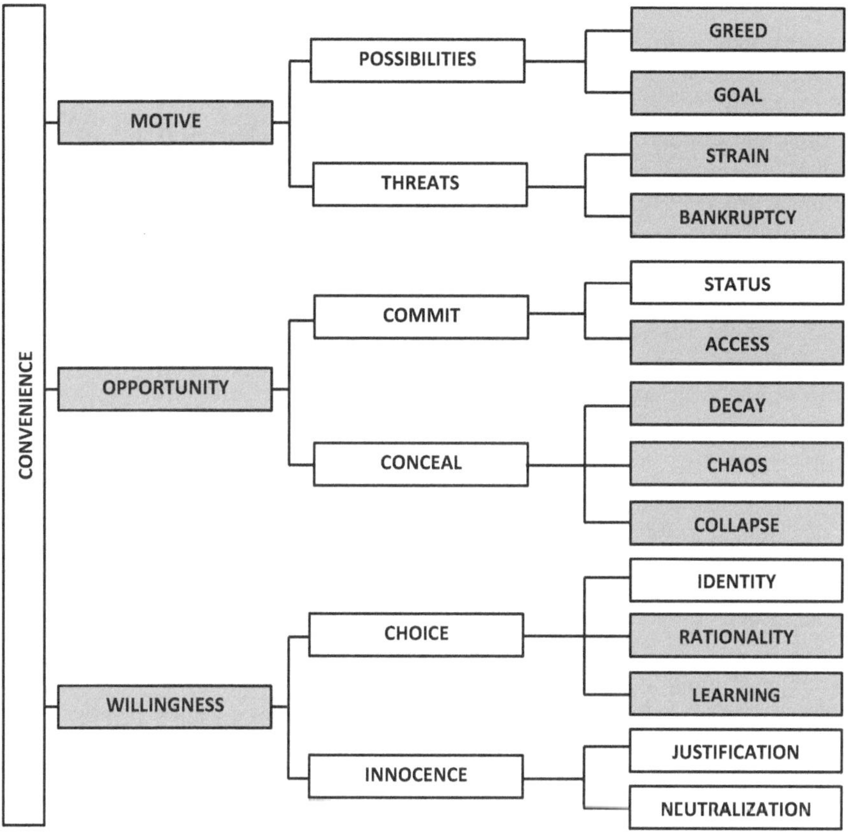

Figure 4.2 Convenience propositions for IUU fishing

over, those who are positioned lower in the social hierarchy (Kakkar et al., 2020: 532):

> Status is a property that rests in the eyes of others and is conferred to individuals who are deemed to have a higher rank or social standing in a pecking order based on a mutually valued set of social attributes. Higher social status or rank grants its holder a host of tangible benefits in both professional and personal domains. For instance, high-status actors are sought by groups for advice, are paid higher, receive unsolicited help, and are credited disproportionately in joint tasks. In innumerable ways, our social ecosystem consistently rewards those with high status.

Especially individuals with high status based on prestige rather than dominance tend to be excused for whatever wrongdoing they commit. Individuals who attain and maintain high rank by behaving in ways that are assertive, controlling, and intimidating are characterized as dominant. Individuals who attain and maintain high rank by their set of skills, knowledge, expertise, and their willingness to share these with others are characterized as prestigious (Kakkar et al., 2020).

The question here is whether high social status is typical for IUU offenders. It might be argued that some fishing companies are powerful and can influence political processes to obtain fishing licenses. An example is the Icelandic fishing company Samherji that succeeded in achieving fishing rights outside the coast of Namibia. Samherji was accused of paying bribes to trawl the African country's waters (Kleinfeld, 2019, 2021). The newspaper *Financial Times* reported in November 2019 that two ministers in Namibia had resigned and that Samherji's chief executive had temporarily stepped down over allegations that the company paid bribes for fishing quotas in the southern African nation's maritime waters (Cotterill, 2019; Kibar, 2020; Samherji, 2019; Seljan et al., 2019). Three years later, Namibia requested Interpol's aid in extraditing former Samherji executives (Ciric, 2022). The Al Jazeera news investigation by Kleinfeld (2019, 2021) as well as the Kveikur news investigation by Seljan et al. (2019) was reviewed by Bjarnadóttir (2020). She identified four issues of concern reported in the media: corruption within, exploitation of Namibian resources, reputation of Iceland internationally, and mistrust and disputes in government.

Another example might be countries where there is a form of state-corporate crime in fishing where the state is involved in illegal activities (Bernat and Whyte, 2020; Rothe and Medley, 2020). However, based on the reviewed literature, the typical IUU fisher does not seem to match the requirement of high status that makes crime convenient. Therefore, the status box in Figure 4.2 is not indicated in any way.

The access box in Figure 4.2 is indicated as a reflection of legitimate access to crime resources to commit IUU fishing. A resource is an enabler applied and used to satisfy human and organizational needs. A resource has utility and limited availability. The main resource for a fisher is legitimate access to a fishing boat. The resource-based perspective postulates that differences in individuals' opportunities find explanation in the extent of resource access and the ability to combine and exploit those resources (Aguilera and Vadera, 2008).

The convenient opportunity to conceal IUU fishing is dependent on institutional deterioration labeled decay, lack of control and guardianship labeled chaos, and criminal market forces labeled collapse. As indicated in Figure 4.2, all three convenience propositions might apply to IUU fishing.

In line with the decay perspective, some fishing companies are "mixing IUU catch along with regularly obtained catch" (Gallic and Cox, 2006: 691):

> The emergence of organized IUU fishing operations has facilitated and accelerated the development of IUU by reducing the monetary and transaction costs of engaging in IUU fishing (mainly the cost of risk and avoidance, fraud, registration operations).

> The development of highly complex company ownership structures has several effects which alter the economic balance sheet for these vessels.

In line with the chaos perspective, "using flags of convenience is one of the most common means for IUU fishing vessels to avoid penalties", as "these vessels deliberately register under flags of states that are reluctant to prosecute them" (Petrossian and Pezzella, 2019: 135). It has been suggested that the "root cause of IUU fishing is a lack of effective flag State control", and

> [T]his is because some States, after authorizing vessels to fly their flags, fail to meet their obligations under international law with respect to the supervision and control of these vessels, or do not provide proper authorizations for their vessels to fish once they assume the State's flag.
>
> (Kao, 2015: 5)

Similarly, Gallic (2008: 859) argued:

> Among IUU fishing activities, a particularly worsening situation consists in those IUU operations conducted by a citizen of a given State who registers and flags its vessel in a foreign State with the explicit objective to circumvent domestic and international regulations. While there is no universally agreed definition to describe such a situation, those States that are willing to have a vessel on their national registers without fully undertaking their obligations to exert Flag State jurisdiction and control are often referred to as Flag of Convenience (FOC) or Flag of Non Compliance (FONC) States.

The chaos perspective is supported by the lack of implementation of various regulatory measures. "Several regulatory mechanisms have been put in place at international, regional, and country levels to address the problem, but the implementation of these regulations remains a challenge" (Petrossian and Pezzella, 2019: 121). Lack of implementation causes lack of compliance with international law (Kim, 2019: 632), where compliance "denotes a state of conformity or identity between an actor's behavior and a specified rule", and implementation "refers to the process by which subjects of international law apply the law and take necessary measures to comply with it".

Lack of implementation causes "the incomprehensiveness and weakness of the current international framework for the sea, which allows the prevalence of Flag of Convenience (FOC) vessels as well as for some fishing practices to be beyond the reach of national and international regulations" (Gallic, 2008: 860). "As a result of this complicated web, tracing seafood back to its legal origin is nearly impossible" (Petrossian and Pezzella, 2019: 123). There is "insufficient level of monitoring, control and surveillance operations (leading to a low probability to be caught) and the insufficient level of sanctions (fines and non-monetary sanctions), which both reduce the cost of risk faced by IUU operators" (Gallic, 2008: 861).

The use of tax havens adds to the chaotic situation: "Vessel operators have the possibility of using the confidentiality or secrecy of banking institutions established in such places to hide their true identity, and thus avoid paying fines when their vessel is caught" (Gallic and Cox, 2006: 861).

Elvestad and Kvalvik (2015: 243) emphasized the lack of capacity and concern for control and guardianship:

> Coastal states have the right and responsibility to manage the fisheries resources under their jurisdiction, usually within their 200-nautical-mile exclusive economic zones, and to cooperate with flag states on monitoring, control, and surveillance of third-party state vessels. But lack of capacity or sufficient concern on the part of many countries has resulted in a mixed performance of coastal states in combating IUU fishing.

The norms of deviant behavior (Sumaila et al., 2006) might derive from challenging the legitimacy of regulations and the extent of rule complexity (Lehman et al., 2020). Rule complexity can create a situation where nobody is able to tell whether an action represented a criminal offense. It is impossible to understand what is right and what is wrong. Some laws, rules, and regulations are so complex that compliance becomes random depending on the local jurisdictions. The regulatory legal environment is supposed to define the boundaries of appropriate fishing conduct. However, legal complexity is often so extreme that even specialist compliance officers struggle to understand what to recommend to business executives in the organizations. This is especially so when operating internationally and globally where states do not agree on what should be legal and illegal activities (Boghossian and Marques, 2019; Pontell et al., 2020).

The collapse perspective seems supported by a local fisher Warhidin in Indonesia who said (Rønneberg, 2022: 12): "I do not understand why the authorities issue so many licenses" and "They should regulate the catch much more strictly" (Rønneberg, 2022: 12). Adapting to criminal market structures such as monopolies, cartels, crime networks, and state-corporate wrongdoing might seem necessary to stay in business (Bernat and Whyte, 2020; Goncharov and Peter, 2019).

Personal Willingness Convenience

Similar to offender status regarding opportunity, offender identity does not seem to be a relevant proposition for IUU fishing willingness. The powerful and wealthy in the upper class of society define their own identity in terms of what is right and what is wrong for them, sometimes in a state-corporate alignment (Bernat and Whyte, 2020; Rothe and Medley, 2020). If they themselves break their own laws, then there is a need to change the laws rather than punish law violators (Petrocelli et al., 2003). The question here is whether such deviant identity is typical for IUU offenders. On the basis of the reviewed literature, the typical IUU fisher does not seem to match the requirement of deviant identity that makes crime convenient. Therefore, the identity box in Figure 4.2 is not indicated in any way.

The rationality box in Figure 4.2 is indicated as a reflection of benefits exceeding costs and thus advantages exceeding disadvantages when committing IUU fishing. Sumaila et al. (2006: 696) argued that the expected benefits from illegal, unreported, and unregulated fishing far exceed the expected cost of being apprehended:

> For an assumed 1 in 5 chance of being apprehended, our calculations show that reported fines for the vessels apprehended will have to be increased by 24 times for the expected cost to be at least as much as the expected benefits.

Given that an assumed detection risk of 1 in 5 is far from reality, since the detection risk for similar crime is 1 to 10 or even 1 to 20 (Gottschalk and Gunnesdal, 2018), then a more appropriate argument would be to increase fines by 50 to 100 times for the expected cost to be at least as much as expected benefits.

In criminology, it is considered rational to commit crime if benefits exceed costs. An important cost element is the probability and severity of sanctions. Potential penalties include the amount of the fine, confiscation of the boat, confiscation of the catch, exclusion from the fishery, imprisonment, and history of prosecutions/application of the penalty. This is according to the deterrence perspective on crime (Rorie and West, 2022).

> The IUU fisher will choose the level of IUU activity such that the marginal revenue from the activity is greater or equal to the marginal cost of engaging in the activity, which in this study equates to the sum of the marginal cost of fishing and the marginal moral and social cost of engaging in IUU fishing.
>
> (Sumaila et al., 2006: 698)

The moral and social cost depends on the extent of law-abiding fishing versus legitimate fishing in the local community that is the extent of deviance perceived by the offender.

Lack of detection causes willingness among IUU fishers to engage in seafood fraud: "This is understandable given the significant monetary benefit of seafood fraud and the relatively low risk detection" and "The United States imports more than 90 percent of seafood to meet consumer demand; however, only 2 percent of the imported seafood is subject to inspection" (Petrossian and Pezzella, 2019: 122).

The learning box in Figure 4.2 is indicated as a reflection of socialization processes into crime. "In some fisheries (especially those associated with small-scale, traditional fisheries), individual behaviors are strongly influenced by the community" (Gallic, 2008: 860).

Sumaila et al., (2006: 698) classified a given population of fishers where they suggest that moderate violators are largest group:

> It has been observed that a given population of fishers, for example, can be classified into (i) chronic violators, (ii) moderate violators, and (iii) non-violators.
>
> Chronic and non-violators generally make up a small portion of a given population.
>
> The former have a tendency to undertake IUU activities no matter what, while non-violators will not engage in IUU fishing under any condition. Moderate violators, on the other hand, will only bypass regulations if the potential economic gain is high enough to cover the potential penalty they may face given the size of the penalty when caught, and the probability of being caught.

Linked to learning is social acceptance of noncompliance that might depend on a number of factors (Ballesteros et al. (2021: 748):

> The social acceptance of noncompliance varies significantly depending on certain contextual factors, such as the existence of alternative ways of life, social inequality, poverty, the perception of the validity of the rules, or the relationship between those who enforce the rules and those who follow them.

There is no evidence of perceived innocence in the reviewed literature so the final two boxes in Figure 4.2 are not indicated. Maybe some fishers admit responsibility but deny harm (Schoen et al., 2021), but this is not evident. Similarly, some IUU fishers might avoid guilt feelings (Chen and Moosmayer, 2020), but this is not evident.

IUU Fishing Convenience Propositions

Convenience theory is an emerging theoretical perspective to explain the phenomenon of economic crime where convenience was first introduced as a core concept by Gottschalk (2017). Recently, the theory has been reviewed (e.g., Chan and Gibbs, 2020; Hansen, 2020; Oka, 2021; Vasiu, 2021; Vasiu and Podgor, 2019) and applied by several scholars such as Asting and Gottschalk (2022), Braaten and Vaughn (2019), Dearden and Gottschalk (2020), Desmond et al. (2022), Qu (2021), Stadler and Gottschalk (2022), and Sterri and Borge (2022).

The idea presented in this chapter suggested that a visual representation and a verbal explanation of the typical offender profile might enhance the understanding of IUU fishing offenders. By selecting the main propositions for motive, opportunity, and willingness based on the reviewed literature, a profile of typical offenders emerged. The profile serves to create a narrative of economic crime in the fishing industry, where pieces of information in each case of an IUU offender are assigned specified convenience issues in the structural model. This chapter claims to offer a useful tool and strategy in creating profiles of IUU fishing offenders for regulatory purposes, fraud investigations, and prosecution approaches by offering the theoretical perspective of the convenience model.

On the basis of review of research literature on IUU fishing, ten out of 14 convenience propositions emerged as relevant in the fishing industry. Convenience of economic crime relates to both possibilities and threats for both individuals and groups. Legitimate access to vessels and other resources, decay, chaos, and collapse contribute to the convenience of IUU fishing that is a choice not made convenient by perceived innocence.

In conclusion, profiling IUU fishing in the perspective of convenience theory enabled identification of relevant issues regarding economic motive, professional opportunity, and willingness for deviant behavior. The relevant issues might be addressed in future regulatory reforms to disturb and reduce the convenience of IUU fishing. For example, the subsidy aspect in the professional opportunity perspective might be addressed in combination with control of resources such as the legitimate access to vessels and the perceived risk of detection.

Electronic Reporting for Compliance

Incorrect reporting of fish is emphasized by several scholars as well as law enforcement agencies as one of the important compliance and conformance issues in the fishing industry. This is illustrated by the abbreviation of IUU – Illegal, Unreported, and Unregulated (Petrossian and Pezzella, 2019). As stated by the Norwegian law enforcement agency Økokrim (2022: 28), "it is very likely that some fishermen and companies that receive fish are involved in systematic under and incorrect reporting of fish and shellfish", and "Norwegian fishery resources and their great economic value attract actors who profit from systematic under and misreporting of catches at fish receptions". For example, underreporting of volume is compensated by paying a higher unit price for the registered catch. Another example is misreporting of species that can also be corrected by price. A third example is moving seafood between production units that are owned by the same enterprise. Nobody blows the whistle on wrongdoing when the enterprise uses vulnerable foreign labor, who have poor living quarters, and who are exposed to unjustified deduction in wages as well as termination in violation of working environment acts. The trade in illegally caught fish often takes place in the shadow economy by ignoring customs agencies and tax authorities.

Petrossian and Pezzella (2019: 122) referred to unreported fishing that "pertains to misreporting catches to relevant national authorities or regional fisheries management organizations, in violation of the national and international regulations". Sumaila et al. (2006: 696) argued that the expected benefits from unreported fishing far exceed the expected cost of being detected:

> For an assumed 1 in 5 chance of being apprehended, our calculations show that reported fines for the vessels apprehended will have to be increased by 24 times for the expected cost to be at least as much as the expected benefits.

To restore compliance and conformance, a potential avenue is introduction of electronic reporting in the fishing industry. For example, a new program on CatchID was introduced in Norway, where the goal is for new technological solutions to be used on board fishing and catching vessels to ensure correct registration of the resource extraction (Fiskeridirektoratet, 2021):

> With the help of the new technological solutions, the program aims to move the resource registration as close as possible to the resource extraction itself, preferably already in the catch equipment, when the catch is taken on board or during production on board. There is also a stated a goal of the program that, with the help of new technological solutions, fishermen should be able to move away from non-verifiable self-reporting of catches to automated registration of resource extraction and direct quota settlement, where verifiable data is transferred to relevant authorities in real time from third-party technology. Such a modernization of the resource registration will reduce the scope for breaches of fisheries legislation and reduce the incentive for dishonest actors who try to obtain unjustified financial gain based on the community's resources. As a consequence, compliance will increase.

Electronic reporting in fisheries was studied by Helmond et al. (2020). They looked at electronic monitoring consisting of various activity sensors and cameras positioned on vessels to remotely record fishing activity and catches. They reviewed 100 electronic monitoring trials and 12 fully implemented programs. Electronic monitoring was predominantly implemented in Canada and the United States. Electronic monitoring systems typically consist of various activity sensors with cameras that register catch, computer software that document catch, and positioning communication that register where the catch occurred. The data recorded can be reviewed at a later stage by actors in the value chain of the fishing industry as well as public authorities.

In our perspective of convenience theory, it is interesting to discuss which of the convenience propositions might be influenced by electronic reporting. Figure 4.3 indicates that electronic monitoring can reduce the convenient access to commit crime, and it can reduce the extent of chaos from lack of control and guardianship. By electronic reporting, potential offenders no longer have legitimate access to systems where they can report whatever they

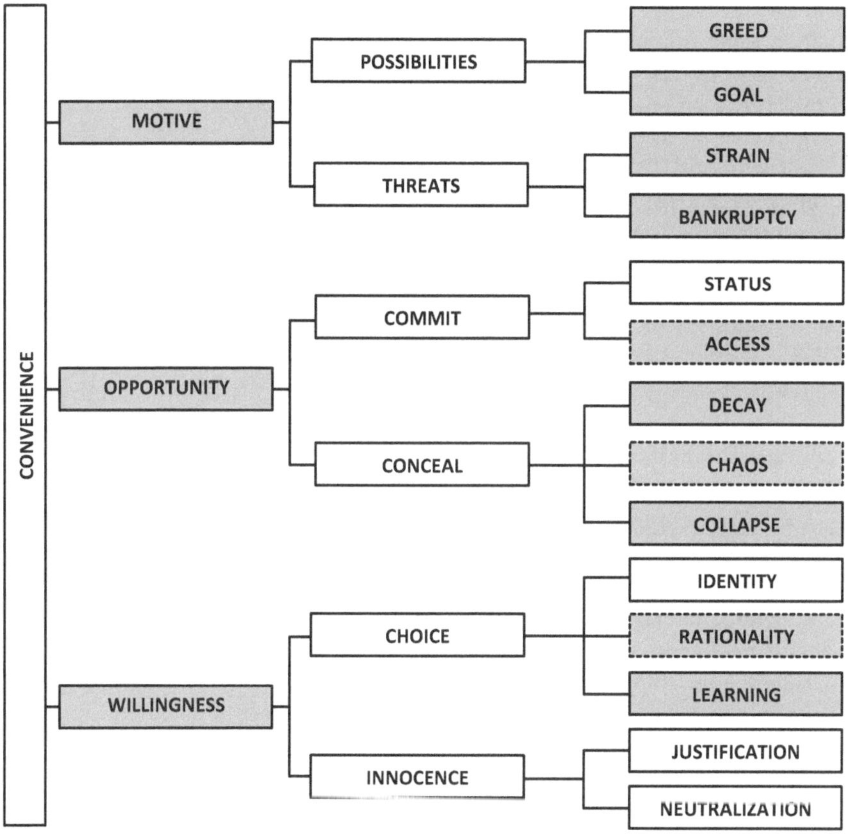

Figure 4.3 Change in convenience propositions for electronic reporting

choose. Rather, access is made less convenient as potential offenders must enter their computer systems to correct numbers that have already been registered and transferred automatically. The resource of registering catch has changed to a less convenient resource of changing already registered and published catch. The opportunity structure for potential offenders has thus changed (Benson and Simpson, 2018).

Electronic reporting can reduce the extent of chaos from lack of control and guardianship as external control entities become recipients of raw data from the various vessels. Generally, guardianship is supervision that may prevent crime by the presence of individuals and systems that are capable and willing to detect and react to wrongdoing. Electronic reporting improves oversight for control and guardianship. While social control is based on attachment, commitment, involvement, and belief, control of facts is based on analyses and reviews. As long as guardians do not become offenders (Chan and Gibbs, 2022), electronic monitoring creates a distance and potential independence between offender and controller (Helmond et al., 2020). In the perspective of principal and agent (Bosse and Phillips, 2016), it might be argued that the receiver on land of data from a vessel on sea enables reduction in the agency problem of the principal not knowing what the agent is doing.

Helmond et al. (2020: 180) found that electronic monitoring caused "greater compliance with rules and regulations in recording". By electronic monitoring, avoidance of misreporting is possible, such as when "fishers under-report problematic interactions with by-catch and quota-limited or 'choke' species" (Helmond et al., 2020: 163). However, in their SWOT (Strengths-Weaknesses-Opportunities-Threats) analysis of electronic monitoring, there were a number of issues that might in fact threaten the expected reduction in crime convenience. For example, sensors and cameras can be manipulated by turning them off or not keeping them clean. There is a difficulty of digitally distinguishing similar-looking species in mixed catches. Furthermore, the installation of equipment onboard vessels might create an impression of control that can make agencies that are normally responsible for reviews, reluctant to control numbers that have been recorded digitally. Furthermore, as emphasized by Vince et al. (2021: 522), fisheries management agencies often allow fishers to disable their transmission systems such as the Automatic Identification System (AIS) while fishing in order to avoid revealing their fishing location to competitors, and "this has led to misinterpretation of a lack of AIS transmission as an indication of illegal activity". The AIS sends information about vessel movement, the vessel itself, and the voyage.

One kind of fraud is non-reporting of fish that is dumped back into the ocean and not brought onshore for production. Both Helmond et al. (2020) and Moncrief-Cox et al. (2020) argued that fish discard on sea is of a significant magnitude. By only reporting what the vessel ends up delivering at the harbor rather than reporting the whole catch on sea, the fraudulent behavior enables the fisher to catch fish beyond the licensed volume since discarded fish is not part of the calculation. This fraudulent activity not only enables the fisher to make illegitimate profit. It also threatens the national and international management of seafood stocks in the oceans. Therefore, electronic reporting onboard the vessel as fish is extracted from the sea will reduce the convenient opportunity structure for concealing fish volumes that are later dumped back into the ocean. The discard composition can later be computed in the system.

Another deviation that can be captured by electronic monitoring is bycatch information where all catch sorting occurs on deck (Moncrief-Cox et al., 2020). Bycatch information is important not only for protected species but also for other types of fish and seabirds (Helmond et al., 2020).

Increased risk of detection by electronic reporting and monitoring (Vince et al., 2021) changes the rationality equation for potential offenders. Fish fraud is a rational choice where advantages exceed disadvantages. Detection is one of the disadvantages. When the perceived risk of detection increases, then fraud becomes a less rational choice. This is indicated in Figure 4.3, where the extent of willingness based on choice decreases. Because the economic model implies that crime can be a rational choice, the crime rate will be lower where potential offenders subjectively perceive the risk of detection to be greater, and where the punishment is stricter (Pratt and Cullen, 2005). Rational choice theorists have taken a position that assumes that the standard economic theory of individual preferences will determine whether crime is committed. The lesser benefits of crime and the greater costs of crime, the less attractive it is to commit criminal acts. According to Berghoff and Spiekermann (2018: 293), potential white-collar offenders "act on cost-benefit calculations involving the expected utility, the likelihood of being caught, and punishment costs".

According to Vince et al. (2021: 522), two other technological tools that are considered useful in addressing illegal fishing include blockchain technology and DNA forensics:

> Both can be used to aid catch documentation schemes (CDS) and to increase traceability. A blockchain is essentially a digital log-book used to record transactions and can be distributed, verified and is irreversible. This traceability approach is appealing as it aims to increase seafood transparency, allowing a consumer to trace a fish from sea to plate, and hence to track whether the supply chain is legal, ethical and/or sustainable. While piloted in multiple instances, to date there has not been large-scale uptake of the approach. Genetic tools are also increasingly being used in an effort to decrease fraud or seafood mislabeling/misidentification, particularly for high value product such as tuna. Recent work, however, suggests that using genetic approaches to identify mislabeling (and potential illegal fishing associated with catch) has limited broad scale applicability, as it is skewed towards particular taxa and geographies. A recent global meta-analysis suggests that mislabeling rates are not statistically different across supply chain locations, products or countries.

Generally, introduction of digital solutions to problems depends on a number of factors to be successful. First of all, fishers as users of technology have to feel comfortable with the technology to be willing to apply it in efficient and effective ways. They need to feel in control of the technology, and not that the technology controls them. They certainly need to perceive that nobody is conducting surveillance by means of the technology on their vessels. Furthermore, everyone connected to the technology needs to understand that the primary activity is to catch fish, while operating a computer system is just another secondary activity in the fishing industry.

References

Aguilera, R.V. and Vadera, A.K. (2008). The dark side of authority: Antecedents, mechanisms, and outcomes of organizational corruption, *Journal of Business Ethics*, 77, 431–449.

Asting, C. and Gottschalk, P. (2022). Attorney fraud in the law firm: A case study of crime convenience theory and crime signal detection theory, *Deviant Behavior*, published online doi: 10.1080/01639625.2022.2071657.

Ballesteros, H.M., Rodriguez-Rodriguez, G., Ferreiro-Seoane, F.J. and Martinez-Cabrera, H. (2021). The fewer insider poachers, the more normative compliance: Clues for managing poaching in the shellfish sector, *Deviant Behavior*, 42 (6), 747–761.

Benson, M.L. and Simpson, S.S. (2018). *White-Collar Crime: An Opportunity Perspective*, Third Edition, Routledge, New York, NY.

Berghoff, H. (2018). "Organised irresponsibility?" The Siemens corruption scandal of the 1990s and 2000s, *Business History*, 60 (3), 423–445.

Berghoff, H. and Spiekermann, U. (2018). Shady business: On the history of white-collar crime, *Business History*, 60 (3), 289–304.

Bernat, I. and Whyte, D. (2020). State-corporate crimes, in: Rorie, M.L. (editor), *The Handbook of White-Collar Crime*, Wiley & Sons, Hoboken, NJ, chapter 9, pages 191–208.

Bjarnadóttir, S.M. (2020). *Iceland's Involvement in Bribes and Corruption in Namibia's Fishing Industry – Discourse Analysis of the Media*, master thesis in culture communication and globalization, September 15, Aalborg University, Denmark.

Boghossian, J. and Marques, J.C. (2019). Saving the Canadian fur industry's hide: Government's strategic use of private authority to constrain radical activism, *Organization Studies*, 40 (8), 1241–1268.

Bosse, D.A. and Phillips, R.A. (2016). Agency theory and bounded self-interest, *Academy of Management Review*, 41 (2), 276–297.

Braaten, C.N. and Vaughn, M.S. (2019). Convenience theory of cryptocurrency crime: A content analysis of U.S. federal court decisions, *Deviant Behavior*, published online https://doi.org/10.1080/01639625.2019.1706706.

Chan, F. and Gibbs, C. (2020). Integrated theories of white-collar and corporate crime, in: Rorie, M.L. (editor), *The Handbook of White-Collar Crime*, Wiley & Sons, Hoboken, NJ, chapter 13, pages 191–208.

Chan, F. and Gibbs, C. (2022). When guardians become offenders: Understanding guardian capability through the lens of corporate crime, *Criminology*, 1–21, published online doi: 10.1111/1745-9125.12300.

Chen, Y. and Moosmayer, D.C. (2020). When guilt is not enough: Interdependent self-construal as moderator of the relationship between guilt and ethical consumption in a Confucian context, *Journal of Business Ethics*, 161, 551–572.

Ciric, J. (2022). Namibia requests Interpol's aid in extraditing former Samherji executives, *Iceland Review*, www.icelandreview.com, retrieved February 21.

Cotterill, J. (2019). Two Namibian ministers resign in Icelandic fishing scandal, *Financial Times*, www.ft.com, retrieved November 14.

Dearden, T.E. and Gottschalk, P. (2020). Gender and white-collar crime: Convenience in target selection, *Deviant Behavior*, 1–9, published online doi: 10.1080/01639625.2020.1756428.

Desmond, S.A., Rorie, M. and Sohoni, T. (2022). Working for God: Religion and occupational crime and deviance, *Deviant Behavior*, published online doi: 10.1080/01639625.2021.2022968.

Eberlein, B. (2019). Who fills the global governance gap? Rethinking the roles of business and government in global governance, *Organization Studies*, 40 (8), 1125–1146.

Elvestad, C. and Kvalvik, I. (2015). Implementing the EU-IUU regulation: Enhancing flag state performance through trade measures, *Ocean Development & International Law*, 46, 241–255.

Fiskeridirektoratet. (2021). Hva er FangstID-programmet? (What is the CatchID program?), *Fiskeridirektoratet* (Norwegian directorate of fisheries), www.fiskeridir.no.

Gallic, B. (2008). The use of trade measures against illicit fishing: Economic and legal considerations, *Ecological Economics*, 64, 858–866.

Gallic, B. and Cox, A. (2006). An economic analysis of illegal, unreported and unregulated (IUU) fishing: Key drivers and possible solutions, *Marine Policy*, 30, 689–695.

Goncharov, I. and Peter, C.D. (2019). Does reporting transparency affect industry coordination? Evidence from the duration of international cartels, *The Accounting Review*, 94 (3), 149–175.

Gottschalk, P. (2017). Convenience in white-collar crime: Introducing a core concept, *Deviant Behavior*, 38 (5), 605–619.

Gottschalk, P. (2022). Trusted chief executives in convenient white-collar crime, *Crime & Delinquency*, published online doi: 10.1177/00111287221104737.

Gottschalk, P. and Gunnesdal, L. (2018). *White-Collar Crime in the Shadow Economy: Lack of Detection, Investigation, and Conviction compared to Social Security Fraud*, Palgrave Pivot, Palgrave Macmillan, Springer Publishing, London, UK.

Hansen, L.L. (2020). Review of the book "convenience triangle in white-collar crime: Case studies of fraud examinations", *Choice Connect*, vol. 57, no. 5, Association of College and Research Libraries, Middletown, CT.

Helmond, A.T.M. van, Mortensen, L.O., Plet-Hansen, K.S., Ulrich, C., Needle, C.L., Oesterwind, D., Kindt-Larsen, L., Catchpole, T., Mangi, S., Zimmermann, C., Olesen, H.J., Bailey, N., Bergsson, H., Dalskov, J., Elson, J., Hosken, M., Peterson, L., McElderry, H., Ruiz, J., Pierre, J.P., Dykstra, C. and Poos, J.J. (2020). Electronic monitoring in fisheries: Lessons from global experiences and future opportunities, *Fish and Fisheries*, 21, 162–189.

Horn, K.S. (2016). Krever millioner av fiskebåtreder i Båtsfjord (Claims millions of fishing boat owner in Båtsfjord), Norwegian public broadcasting *NRK*, www.nrk.no, retrieved October 31.

Kakkar, H., Sivanathan, N. and Globel, M.S. (2020). Fall from grace: The role of dominance and prestige in punishment of high-status actors, *Academy of Management Journal*, 63 (2), 530–553.

Kang, E. and Thosuwanchot, N. (2017). An application of Durkheim's four categories of suicide to organizational crimes, *Deviant Behavior*, 38 (5), 493–513.

Kao, S.M. (2015). International actions against IUU fishing and the adoption of national plans of action, *Ocean Development & International Law*, 46, 2–16.

Kibar, O. (2020). Varsleren (The whistleblower), daily Norwegian business newspaper *Dagens Næringsliv*, Saturday, August 8, pages 32–37.

Kim, H.J. (2019). Inducing state compliance with international fisheries law: Lessons from two case studies concerning the Republic of Korea's IUU fishing, *International Environmental Agreements: Politics, Law & Economics*, 19, 631–645.

Kleinfeld, J. (2019). Anatomy of a Bribe: A deep dive into an underworld of corruption, *News Organization Al Jazeera*, www.aljazeera.com, retrieved December 1.

Kleinfeld, J. (2021). Namibian president caught in new fishing corruption allegations, *News Organization Al Jazeera*, www.aljazeera.com, retrieved April 2.

Lehman, D.W., Cooil, B. and Ramanujam, R. (2020). The effects of rule complexity on organizational noncompliance and remediation: Evidence from restaurant health inspections, *Journal of Management*, 46 (8), 1436–1468.

Moncrief-Cox, H.E., Carlson, J.K., Norris, G.S., Wealti, M.C., Deacy, B.M. and Scott-Denton, E. (2020). Development of video electronic monitoring systems to record

smalltooth sawfish, pristis pectinata, interactions in the shrimp trawl fisheries of the southeastern United States, with application to other protected species and large bycatches, *Marine Fisheries Review*, 82 (3–4), 1–8.
Obodaru, O. (2017). Forgone, but not forgotten: Toward a theory of forgone professional identities, *Academy of Management Journal*, 60 (2), 523–553.
Oka, R. (2021). Introducing an anthropology of convenience, *Economic Anthropology*, 8 (2), 188–207.
Økokrim. (2022). *Økokrims trusselvurdering 2022 (Økokrim's threat assessment 2022)*, Norwegian National Authority for Investigation and Prosecution of Economic and Environmental Crime, Oslo, Norway, 68 pages.
Petrocelli, M., Piquero, A.R. and Smith, M.R. (2003). Conflict theory and racial profiling: An empirical analysis of police traffic stop data, *Journal of Criminal Justice*, 31 (1), 1–11.
Petrossian, G. and Pezzella, F.S. (2019). IUU fishing and seafood fraud: Using crime script analysis to inform intervention, *The Annals of the American Academy*, 679, September, 121–139.
Pontell, H.N., Ghazi-Tehrani, A.K. and Burton, B. (2020). White-collar and corporate crime in China, in: Rorie, M.L. (editor), *The Handbook of White-Collar Crime*, Wiley & Sons, Hoboken, NJ, chapter 22, pages 347–362.
Pratt, T.C. and Cullen, F.T. (2005). Assessing macro-level predictors and theories of crime: A meta-analysis, *Crime and Justice*, 32, 373–450.
Qu, J. (2021). The challenge against economic regulation ethics under the Covid-19 epidemic: An analysis of unethical behavior of convenience, *Converter Magazine*, 2021 (5), 74–79.
Rodriguez, P., Uhlenbruck, K. and Eden, L. (2005). Government corruption and the entry strategies of multinationals, *Academy of Management Review*, 30 (2), 383–396.
Rorie, M. and West, M. (2022). Can 'focused deterrence' produce more effective ethics codes? An experimental study, *Journal of White Collar and Corporate Crime*, 3 (1), 33–45.
Rothe, D.L. and Medley, C. (2020). Beyond state and state-corporate crime typologies: The symbiotic nature, harm, and victimization of crimes of the powerful and their continuation, in: Rorie, M. (editor), *The Handbook of White-Collar Crime*, John Wiley & Sons, Hoboken, NJ, chapter 6, pages 81–94.
Rønneberg, K. (2022). Havet er i ferd med å tømmes for sjødyr (The Ocean Is About to Be Emptied of Sea Creatures), daily Norwegian newspaper *Aftenposten*, Monday, July 4, page 12.
Sajko, M., Boone, C. and Buyl, T. (2021). CEO greed, corporate social responsibility, and organizational resilience to systemic shocks, *Journal of Management*, 47 (4), 957–992.
Samherji. (2019). *Samherji CEO Steps Aside While Investigations Are Ongoing*, www.samherji.is, published November 14 by margret@samherji.is.
Schoen, J.L., DeSimone, J.A., Meyer, R.D., Schnure, K.A. and LeBreton, J.M. (2021). Identifying, defining, and measuring justification mechanisms: The implicit biases underlying individual differences, *Journal of Management*, 47 (3), 716–744.
Schweitzer, M.E., Ordonez, L. and Douma, B. (2004). Goal setting as a motivator of unethical behavior, *Academy of Management Journal*, 47 (3), 422–432.
Seljan, H., Kjartansson, A. and Drengsson, S.A. (2019). What Samherji wanted hidden, Kveikur at *RUV*, public broadcasting on Iceland, www.ruv.is/kveikur/fishrot/fishrot.
Serdy, A. (2017). Pacta Tertiis and regional fisheries management mechanisms: The IUU fishing concept as an illegitimate short-cut to a legitimate goal, *Ocean Development & International Law*, 48 (3–4), 345–364.
Stadler, W.A. and Gottschalk, P. (2022). Testing convenience theory for white-collar crime: Perceptions of potential offenders and non-offenders, *Deviant Behavior*, 43 (7), 804–820.

Sterri, A. and Borge, K. (2022). *How Can an Auditor Prevent and Detect White-Collar Crime? A Convenience Theory Approach*, Master of science in business economics thesis, BI Norwegian Business School, Oslo, Norway, 124 pages.

Sumaila, U.R., Alder, J. and Keith, H. (2006). Global scope and economics of illegal fishing, *Marine Policy*, 30, 696–703.

Sundström, M. and Radon, A. (2015). Utilizing the concept of convenience as a business opportunity in emerging markets, *Organizations and Markets in Emerging Economies*, 6 (2), 7–21.

Thaxton, S. and Agnew, R. (2018). When criminal coping is likely: An examination of conditioning effects in general strain theory, *Journal of Quantitative Criminology*, 34, 887–920.

Vasiu, V.I. (2021). Convenience triangle in white-collar crime: Case studies of fraud examinations, *Criminal Law and Criminal Justice Books*, Rutgers, the State University of New Jersey, May, www.clcjbooks.rutgers.edu.

Vasiu, V.I. and Podgor, E.S. (2019). Organizational opportunity and deviant behavior: Convenience in white-collar crime, *Criminal Law and Criminal Justice Books*, Rutgers, the State University of New Jersey, July, www.clcjbooks.rutgers.edu.

Vince, J., Hardesty, B.D. and Wilcox, C. (2021). Progress and challenges in eliminating illegal fishing, *Fish and Fisheries*, 22, 518–531.

Welsh, D.T., Ordonez, L.D., Snyder, D.G. and Christian, M.S. (2014). The slippery slope: How small ethical transgressions pave the way for larger future transgressions, *Journal of Applied Psychology*, 100 (1), 114–127.

Williams, M.L., Levi, M., Burnap, P. and Gundur, R.V. (2019). Under the corporate radar: Examining insider business cybercrime victimization through an application of routine activities theory, *Deviant Behavior*, 40 (9), 1119–1131.

Wood, J. and Alleyne, E. (2010). Street gang theory and research: Where are we now and where do we go from here? *Aggression and Violent Behavior*, 15, 100–111.

5 COVID-19 Creative Non-Compliance

Creative non-compliance can refer to conveniently complying with the spirit of the law and not with the letter of the law under the COVID-19 lockdown restrictions. Convenience theory is an emerging theoretical perspective to explain the phenomenon of white-collar crime. This chapter presents a one-sided theoretical study of convenience themes that emerged for white-collar offenders during the COVID-19 pandemic by abuse of governments' emergency-support packages for business enterprises. Special motives, special opportunities, and special willingness for deviant behavior in abuse of financial aid occurred during the pandemic. Stronger motives – both based on possibilities and threats – are discussed. The opportunity was mainly rooted in rule complexity linked to external lack of control and guardianship. The willingness has many convenience themes including rationality, learning, justification, and neutralization. The one-sided approach of white-collar crime enablers during the pandemic in abuse of public funding needs to be supplemented by discussion of white-collar crime barriers during the pandemic in future research.

The COVID-19 pandemic was a public health emergency of international concern starting in 2020. The pandemic "led governments around the world to take drastic action and implement a wide range of proactive and reactive measures to limit the spread of the disease" (Payne et al., 2021: 1). There were travel restrictions and border controls, quarantine requirements for those infected, social isolation and distancing requirements for almost everyone, and the closure of various services, businesses, and educational facilities. The new situation globally created convenient opportunities for criminals (Kennedy et al., 2021: 494):

> From the very beginning of the Covid-19 crisis, criminals sought to take advantage of the lack of information available regarding the virus, misinformation coming from official and unofficial sources, and disinformation spread via the internet and social media channels.

While some offenders completely ignored laws, other offenders practiced creative non-compliance that can refer to conveniently complying with the spirit

DOI: 10.4324/9781003379249-7

of the law and not with the letter of the law under the COVID-19 lockdown restrictions (Meers et al., 2021: 1):

> Instead of seeking to avoid the principles behind restrictions, participants instead rationalized their conduct as falling within the law's underpinning purpose, even if they thought their actions breached the strict meaning of the regulations themselves. Put another way, participants justified their non-compliance as within the "spirit of the law" if not the "letter of the law".

When the corona virus COVID-19 spread to Norway, the country closed down most sectors on March 12, 2020. The wealthy Norwegian state provided financial compensation to businesses as well as individuals. Some explored and exploited the compensation arrangements because they found it convenient. They had a convenient motive, a convenient opportunity, as well as a convenient willingness for deviant behavior. The convenient motive was the fear of bankruptcy despite receipt of some legitimate compensation from the state. The convenient motive was also greed, to be able to climb the hierarchy of needs. The convenient opportunity was the lack of controls and guardianship as the state based its payments on trust to be able to provide financial support quickly to victims of the close-down already in April 2020. The convenient willingness was the attribution of guilt to the state that had closed down the economy and the society. The convenient willingness was also the assumption that a number of other people and businesses did abuse the financial compensation arrangements as well. Already after a month into the pandemic, the Norwegian national authority for investigation and prosecution of economic and environmental crime detected COVID-19-related fraud (Langved and Klevstrand, 2020).

This kind of wrongdoing is in line with the theory of convenience suggesting that a strong motive, an attractive opportunity, and a high-level willingness for deviant behavior increase the likelihood of misconduct and crime. COVID-19-related fraud schemes were detected all over the world (e.g., Kennedy et al., 2021).

This chapter addresses the following research question: *What kind of special motives, special opportunities, and special willingness for deviant behavior by white-collar offenders in abuse of financial support packages occurred during the COVID-19 pandemic?*

This chapter maintains that the concept of convenience may help understand the wrongdoing at the top of organizations. The purpose of the chapter is to provide a theoretical foundation for future research based on a multi-dimensional explanation of white-collar offending. This perspective, which is composed of three interrelated themes of motivation, opportunity, and willingness, suggests that individuals more likely to commit white-collar crime are differently oriented to convenience as a factor in the choice to engage in illegal behavior. Individuals become more oriented toward convenience as the motive becomes stronger, as the opportunity improves, and as the willingness to engage in deviant behavior becomes more intense. Thus, perception of convenience should differ between those who view white-collar crime as more acceptable and those who view it as less acceptable.

Variety of COVID-19 Frauds

A variety of COVID-19 frauds developed quickly during the pandemic, including fraud schemes that did not target public financial support packages. Kennedy et al. (2021) studied frauds that targeted consumers and that were related in some way to the virus. They looked at sale and distribution of fake virus-related products such as counterfeit testing kits, some of which were destined for healthcare facilities. Fake preventive medicines and treatments against the virus were marketed to consumers. Counterfeit versions of legitimate goods essential to health and safety infiltrated the legitimate supply chain. Some virus-related scams did not involve products or services, but rather attempts to make consumers turn over personal information or money without ever receiving anything in return.

In our perspective of white-collar abuse of financial support packages, two examples from the United States and Norway, respectively, can illustrate the issues. A California couple was sentenced for US$20 million in COVID-19 fraud, where they had abused the government support package of emergency and relief loans for threatened businesses (Løvik, 2021). The couple had created fictive companies with fake payment checks and income statements in 151 loan applications (Hernandez, 2021):

> A California couple was sentenced to prison for illegally obtaining more that $20 million in Covid-19 relief funds – but authorities need to catch them first. Richard Ayvazyan, 43, was sentenced to 17 years behind bars and his wife, 37-year-old Marietta Terabelian, received a six-year sentence in federal prison on Monday for conspiracy, bank fraud and money laundering, according to the Department of Justice. The two are on the run from authorities and were sentenced in absentia. Federal officials said they cut off their tracking bracelets on August 29, federal officials said. During the sentencing, US District Judge Stephen V. Wilson said he could not recall a fraud case conducted in such a "callous, intentional way without any regard for the law". Wilson described Ayvazyan as "an endemic, cold-hearted fraudster with no regard for the law" and someone who "views fraud as an achievement". The judge also sentenced Ayvazyan's brother, Artur, 41, to five years in prison. On June 25, a federal jury found Richard Ayvazyan, Artur Ayvazyan and Terabelian guilty of one count of conspiracy to commit bank fraud and wire fraud, 11 counts of wire fraud, eight counts of bank fraud and one count of conspiracy to commit money laundering. Richard Ayvazyan and his brother were also convicted of aggravated identity theft. The FBI is offering a reward of up to $20,000 for information leading to the arrest of Richard Ayvazyan and Terabelian.

By December 2021, the Norwegian police had 80 COVID-19 fraud cases on their table. One of the cases that lead to conviction was a couple who made up a list of cancelled concerts as well as a closed-downed parking garage (Haram, 2021):

> By inflating his own and his spouse's income in a manipulated tax return form, the man in his 50s incorrectly reported millions in turnover in companies that were in reality without operations. In this way, he imposed a sky-high tax burden on himself and his wife, but at the same time he was given the opportunity to take advantage of the corona support schemes that the state launched in April 2020. The convicted man in his 50ies registered several companies in different districts to make control difficult. A recent ruling from the Oslo district court states: Despite the fact that "the frauds do not have a very professional character", the convict, by establishing different companies in different tax regions, has tried to "minimize the risk of being exposed/arousing suspicion". Through several companies, he tried to get the Cultural Council to pay out more than NOK 13 million as a result of canceled concerts. He did the same to the Norwegian Lotteries Authority, which he tried to defraud for almost six million. A total of 17 applications were sent for compensation for concerts that "there was no reality behind", the Oslo district court writes in the verdict.
>
> First, the convicted has used several different associations and companies to commit economic crime, both in his own and in the name of the spouse. Secondly, the applications have been developed in line with the new requirements that came in the regulations, including requirements for the events to be traceable, says police lawyer Anders Orerød at Økokrim (Norwegian national authority for investigation and prosecution of economic and environmental crime) to VG.

The economic support package in Norway led to a very profitable year 2020 for many companies in the cultural sector such as entertainment groups. Folkvord et al. (2022) found that 57% of the companies that received government funding had better bottom-line results in 2020 than in previous years. Half of those companies that improved their results had their best year ever in 2020.

In Australia, the economic response package for businesses was called "jobkeeper". Australian government's jobkeeper payments helped keep Australians in jobs and supported businesses affected by the significant economic impact of the COVID-19 pandemic (Treasurer, 2022):

> In the first phase of JobKeeper (30 March to 27 September 2020), eligible businesses and not-for-profits were able to receive $1,500 (before tax) per fortnight per employee to cover the cost of wages. During the extension phase of JobKeeper (28 September – 28 March 2021), the payment was tapered and targeted to those businesses that continued to be significantly affected by the economic downturn. Businesses were required to reassess

their eligibility with reference to their actual turnover. In the extension phase the payment was reduced and paid in two rates:

- From 28 September 2020 to 3 January 2021, the payment rate was $1200 per fortnight for employees who worked 20 hours or more a week on average in the reference period and $750 for employees who worked less than 20 hours a week on average in the reference period.
- From 4 January 2021 to 28 March 2021, the payment rate was $1000 per fortnight for employees who worked 20 hours or more a week on average in the reference period and $650 for employees who worked less than 20 hours a week on average in the reference period.

In Norway, the general compensation arrangement for businesses covered 85% of fixed, unavoidable costs in companies that have had a turnover loss of 30% or more, compared to the year 2019. The compensation was dependent on the size of the turnover loss. The compensation was first limited to NOK 4 million and then NOK 7.5 million for a two-month period. If a company was profitable during this period, the company was required to repay some of the compensation received (Regjeringen, 2022).

COVID-19 Fraud Convenience

Convenience theory is an emerging theoretical perspective to explain the phenomenon of white-collar crime where convenience was first introduced as a core concept by Gottschalk (2017). Recently, the theory has been evaluated (e.g., Chan and Gibbs, 2020; Hansen, 2020; Oka, 2021; Vasiu, 2021; Vasiu and Podgor, 2019) and applied by several scholars such as Asting and Gottschalk (2022), Braaten and Vaughn (2019), Dearden and Gottschalk (2020), Desmond et al. (2022), Stadler and Gottschalk (2022), and Qu (2021).

The structural model of convenience theory is illustrated in Figure 5.1. The motive is dichotomous in possibilities and threats, the opportunity is dichotomous in committing crime and concealing crime, and the willingness is dichotomous in choice and innocence. The motive along the convenience dimension of possibilities for individuals might be greed and for organizations the achievement of goals. The motive along the convenience dimension of threats for individuals might be avoidance of strain and for organizations the avoidance of bankruptcy.

High social status and legitimate access to resources make it convenient to commit crime. Organizational decay in the form of institutional deterioration, organizational chaos in the form of lacking overview and guardianship, and market collapse caused by rule complexity, cartels, and crime networks make it convenient to conceal crime.

Willingness can be based on choice or innocence. Choice is a conscious decision to commit crime, while innocence is a perception of lacking a role

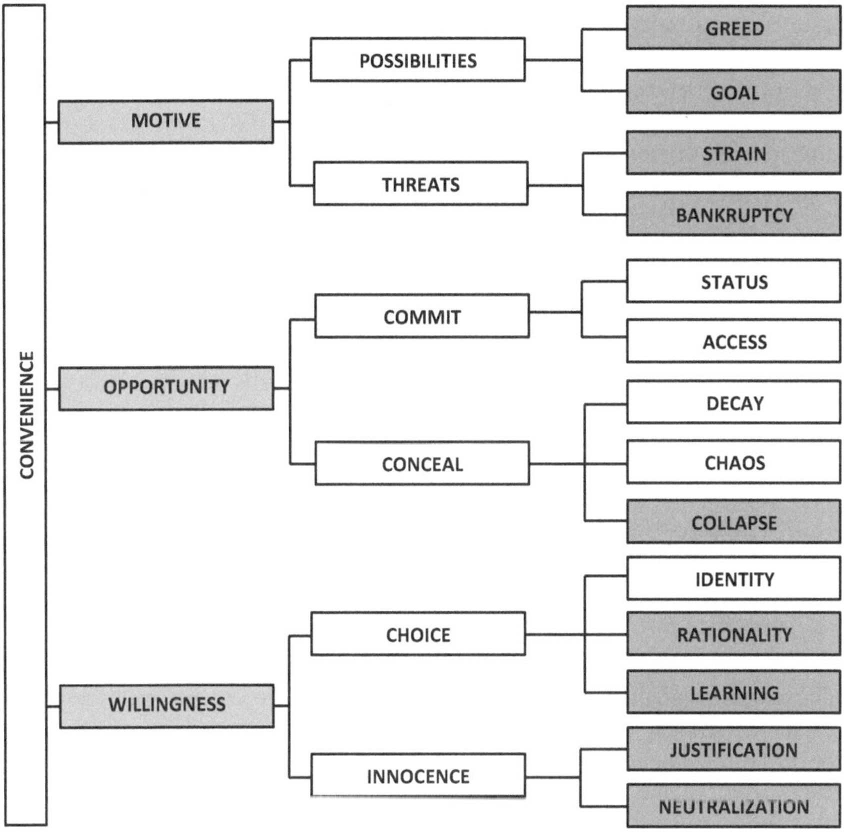

Figure 5.1 Structural model of white-collar crime convenience

in wrongdoing. A conveniently oriented individual in a trusted position with a stronger deviant identity, stronger rational mind, or a stronger differential association has a higher level of willingness to get involved in financial crime. A conveniently oriented individual in a trusted position with a stronger ability to justify wrongdoing or a stronger ability to deny guilt has a higher level of willingness to get involved in financial crime.

There are a total of 14 convenience themes in the structural model of white-collar crime on the right-hand side in Figure 5.1. The theoretical challenge in the following is to identify those themes that are impacted by the COVID-19 pandemic. The theoretically identified convenience themes are marked in gray boxes and discussed in the following. The identified themes represent special motives, special opportunities, and special willingness for deviant behavior by white-collar offenders in abuse of financial support packages that occurred during the COVID-19 pandemic.

Convenient Motive During Pandemic

Some business individuals seized the opportunity for financial gain as a possibility during the pandemic. The greed perspective might derive from a need to restore the perception of equity and equality (Leigh et al., 2010; Cullen et al., 2020)). The equity perspective then as a motive suggests that a person compares his or her outcome during the pandemic to the outcome before the pandemic. The potential reduction in outcome is caused by the state and needs to be compensated. The offender blames the state for having caused reduced freedom to conduct business. While there is no threat to the offender, the offender nevertheless has a motive for fraud to compensate for the unjust restriction treatment by the state.

The greed perspective can also derive from the need to satisfy the desire to help others as social concern (Agnew, 2014). Many suffered losses during the pandemic, and the offender might want to help and thus moving beyond the assumption of simple self-interest. However, as argued by Paternoster et al. (2018), helping others can be a self-interested, rational action.

Some businesses seized the opportunity for financial gain as a possibility during the pandemic to reach ambitious business goals. While the compensation package only intended to make each business stay alive, businesses had their own strategic plans with objectives that needed to be achieved. Goal setting is often perceived in a positive light, meaning that ambitious goals increase performance (Locke and Latham, 2013). The state has created barriers to the achievement of goals. Therefore, the enterprise needs to commit fraud to compensate for the gap in resources to achieve goals. There might be an escalation of commitment to goals where decision-making in the face of negative state restrictions and uncertainty surrounding the likelihood of goal attainment cause even stronger dedication go goals. In many organizations, ends justify means (Campbell and Göritz, 2014).

The pandemic caused strain from uncertainty by lock-down. The strain perspective emphasizes strains and stressors that increase the likelihood of crime, the negative emotions (including anger) resulting from those strains that create pressure for corrective action (Thaxton and Agnew, 2018). Strains are events and conditions that individuals dislike. Strains lead to negative emotions and thereby create pressure for corrective action. Strain triggers negative emotional states such as anger, fear, or depression, with anger being potentially the most criminogenic emotion. Crime is one possible corrective action (Froggio and Agnew, 2007).

An increased fear of falling from a high-status position resulting from the lock-down can cause wrongdoing (Piquero, 2012). The fear of falling perspective suggests that people in leading positions are afraid of the consequences of failure and therefore try to survive in their privileged positions by applying various means. The fear of falling perspective thus suggests that the motivation for financial crime by white-collar offenders is the fear of losing what one has worked so hard to achieve (Benson and Chio, 2020).

The threat of bankruptcy was real as lock-down occurred. Threats are associated with urgency, difficulty, and high stakes (Chattopadhyay et al., 2001). Threats involve a negative situation in which loss is likely and over which one has a fair amount of control. The threat of corporate collapse and bankruptcy might cause exploration and exploitation of illegal avenues to survive, where moral panic can occur (Kang and Thosuwanchot, 2017). The survival of the corporation can become so important that no means come across as unacceptable in the current situation where the state carries the blame.

Both individual and corporate responses to possibilities and threats can result from rational self-interest (Pillay and Kluvers, 2014). During the pandemic, offenders might assume that the risk of detection is low. The rational choice model considers incentives and probability of detection. This applies to both private and professional life. Human behavior finds motivation in the self-centered quest for satisfaction and avoidance of suffering (Hirschi and Gottfredson, 1987). If the individual assesses economic crime as an attractive action in the form of gain now (profit for realization of current ambitions) compared to possible future cost (punishment, isolation, loneliness), and the individual prefers to avoid the use of more time and effort to solve problems preventing realization of ambitions, then convenience theory says that crime will probably occur.

Convenient Opportunity During Pandemic

Some offenders have a status implying that they are almost too big to fail and too powerful to jail (Pontell et al., 2014). Status is an individual's social rank within a formal or informal hierarchy, or the person's relative standing along a valued dimension (Kakkar et al., 2020). In our perspective of special opportunities from the pandemic, there seems to be no convenience issues from status as illustrated in Figure 5.1. Similarly, there seems to be no convenience issues from legitimate access to resources to commit crime (Benson and Simpson, 2018). Furthermore, the pandemic seems to have no influence on organizational decay in the form of institutional deterioration (Barton, 2004; Donk and Molloy, 2008) and no influence on organizational chaos in the form of lacking overview and guardianship (Chan and Gibbs, 2022).

Collapse caused by rule complexity seems to be the only relevant issue in the opportunity structure of concealing wrongdoing as rule complexity prevents compliance. Rule complexity can create a situation where nobody is able to tell whether an action represents a criminal offense (Lehman et al., 2020). It is impossible to understand what is right and what is wrong. Some laws, rules, and regulations are so complex that compliance becomes random, where compliance is the action of complying with laws, rules, and regulations such as the support scheme. The regulatory legal environment is supposed to define the boundaries of appropriate organizational conduct. However, legal complexity is often so extreme that even specialist compliance officers struggle to understand what to recommend to business executives in the organizations. The financial support packages were suddenly introduced as an emergency measure where rules seemed to change frequently regarding issues such as who was entitled and not entitled, what was relevant to get compensated, and how to apply for relief loans and direct subsidies.

It might seem surprising that neither organizational decay in the form of institutional deterioration nor organizational chaos in the form of lacking overview and guardianship are relevant convenience issues in light of the pandemic. The reason is that both issues relate to internal situations in organizations. If convenience theory was extended to include lack of external overview and guardianship in an outside-in perspective, then such convenience themes would become relevant as well as answers to the research question in this chapter.

Convenient Willingness During Pandemic

The extent of deviant identity is a convenience theme that has no connection to the outside situation such as government restrictions on the business. Therefore, this theme is illustrated blank in Figure 5.1. For example, the phenomenon of narcissistic identification with the business (Galvin et al., 2015), where company money seems to be identical to personal money, has nothing to do with government pandemic policies.

The economical dimension of convenience theory applied the rational self-interest motivation. The rational choice approach also applies to the willingness in the behavioral dimension of convenience theory. The rational choice assumption about offending is based on a normative foundation where advantages and disadvantages are subjectively compared (Müller, 2018). When there is no perceived likelihood of detection or punishment, then there is no deterrence effect to prevent offences (Comey, 2009). The economic model of rational self-interest is all about weighing up the pros and cons of alternative courses of action. The pros in favor of fraud were stronger than the cons against fraud for many business enterprises.

Learning to adapt to a new situation was certainly a convenience theme during the pandemic as indicated in Figure 5.1. The offender mind is a result of personal differential association as suggested by Sutherland (1983). The differential association perspective suggests that potential offenders make a choice where they associate with those who agree with them, and distance themselves from those who disagree. This perspective suggests that whether individuals engage in white-collar crime or not depends on their socialization within certain peer groups. In an elite setting, interactions with deviant others promote criminal activity. The essence of differential association is that criminal behavior is learned, and the main part of learning comes from within important personal groups. Exposure to the attitudes of others that either favor or reject turbulent legal codes influences the attitudes of the individual. The individual will go on to commit crime if the person exposes himself or herself more to attitudes that favor law violation than to attitudes that favor abiding the law (Wood and Alleyne, 2010). Learning from others is an active process where a belief quickly settled that others were doing the same during the pandemic.

In a justification, the actor admits responsibility for the act in question but denies its pejorative and negative content (Schoen et al., 2021: 730):

> People use justification mechanisms to protect their sense of self. People who sincerely believe that they are a specific kind of person but routinely demonstrate behaviors that indicate otherwise may avoid cognitive dissonance and maintain their sense of self by using justification mechanisms that allow them to "explain away" their behavior.

The explain-away approach for fraud during the pandemic is convenient since negative life events were caused by the government. The perspective of negative life events suggests that events such as divorce, accident, lack of promotion, and cash problems can cause potential offenders to consider white-collar crime a convenient solution (Engdahl, 2015). As argued by McGloin et al. (2021: 740), "a core tenet of the social sciences is that the actions of others can fundamentally change decision-making and behavior". Innocent justification seems to resonate in many descriptions of offending where group settings incentivize the decision to offend. Group settings can make offending more convenient (i.e., less risky) and also more rewarding. Some are willing to commit crime only if other people started doing so first. People who would otherwise not offend, and people who have a low tendency to offend when alone can have a greater willingness to do so in a group setting. Offending might here be a rational choice that seems convenient to justify.

The final theme in Figure 5.1 is neutralization. It is a matter of lack of or removal of guilt feeling. In fact, white-collar offenders during the pandemic might have felt being victims of government restrictions. There are a number of neutralization techniques suggested by Sykes and Matza (1957) and others that might fit the minds of offenders during the pandemic. First, offenders can refuse damage from the fraud, as they might claim that there was no visible harm for their actions. Similarly, offenders can refuse victim from crime as they might claim that nobody suffered from their actions. Furthermore, offenders might justify crime by higher loyalties as it was according to expectations such as goal achievement.

A final neutralization technique of special interest during the COVID-19 pandemic was the creative non-compliance, where offenders claimed to be complying with the spirit of the law but not with the letter of the law as studied by Meers et al. (2021: 1):

> We characterize this rationalization for rule breaking as "creative non-compliance". This paper outlines this concept and considers the implications of our arguments for the literature on neutralization theory and for studies of compliance under the COVID-19 lockdown restrictions more generally.

As argued by Meers et al. (2021), offenders rationalized their non-compliance with their actions as being entirely consistent with the norms underpinning regulations and not by rejecting the norms. Both rule bending and rule cynicism can make offenders entirely convinced of its legitimacy.

Magnitude of Crime During Pandemic

The COVID-19 pandemic had all kinds of interesting economic impacts that were not all negative. During the pandemic, fewer people went to their regular places to work, and more people stayed at their homes during working hours where they organized various forms of home offices. At daytime then more homes were occupied by residents and the opportunity for property crime like home burglary was reduced for potential offenders. As argued by Rorie et al. (2022), when people spend less time outside their homes, they are less likely to be victimized both personally as well as in terms of property crime like home burglary. In Australia, property crime like home burglary dropped significantly during the pandemic (Payne et al., 2021: 1):

> Drawing upon theories from environmental criminology, this study examines officially recorded property crime rates between March and June 2020 as reported for the state of Queensland, Australia. We use ARIMA modeling techniques to compute 6-month-ahead forecasts of property damage, shop theft, residential burglary, fraud, and motor vehicle theft rates and then compare these forecasts (and their 95% confidence intervals) with the observed data for March through to June. We conclude that, with the exception of fraud, all property offence categories declined significantly.

Similar to this property crime observation, it is imaginable that some aspects of white-collar crime by abuse of financial support packages make offenses less convenient. It is conceivable that there are special motives, special opportunities, and special willingness for compliance by potential white-collar offenders to avoid abuse of financial support packages that occurred during the COVID-19 pandemic. Therefore, it is not obvious that there was a rise in white-collar crime during the pandemic compared to situations before and after the pandemic. It is thus an interesting avenue for future research to study both enablers and barriers to COVID-19 fraud related to government support packages.

This chapter has presented a one-sided theoretical study of convenience themes that emerged for white-collar offenders during the COVID-19 pandemic by abuse of governments' emergency support packages for business enterprises. Special motives, special opportunities, and special willingness for deviant behavior in abuse of financial aid occurred during the pandemic. Stronger motives – based on both possibilities and threats – were identified. The opportunity was mainly rooted in rule complexity linked to external lack of control and guardianship. The willingness has many convenience themes including rationality, learning, justification, and neutralization.

References

Agnew, R. (2014). Social concern and crime: Moving beyond the assumption of simple self-interest, *Criminology*, 52 (1), 1–32.

Asting, C. and Gottschalk, P. (2022). Attorney fraud in the law firm: A case study of crime convenience theory and crime signal detection theory, *Deviant Behavior*, published online doi: 10.1080/01639625.2022.2071657.

Barton, H. (2004). Cultural reformation: A case for intervention within the police service, *International Journal of Human Resources Development and Management*, 4 (2), 191–199.

Benson, M.L. and Chio, H.L. (2020). Who commits occupational crimes, in: Rorie, M. (editor), *The Handbook of White-Collar Crime*, John Wiley & Sons, Hoboken, NJ, chapter 7, pages 97–112.

Benson, M.L. and Simpson, S.S. (2018). *White-Collar Crime: An Opportunity Perspective*, Third Edition, Routledge, New York, NY.

Braaten, C.N. and Vaughn, M.S. (2019). Convenience theory of cryptocurrency crime: A content analysis of U.S. federal court decisions, *Deviant Behavior*, published online https://doi.org/10.1080/01639625.2019.1706706.

Campbell, J.L. and Göritz, A.S. (2014). Culture corrupts! A qualitative study of organizational culture in corrupt organizations, *Journal of Business Ethics*, 120 (3), 291–311.

Chan, F. and Gibbs, C. (2020). Integrated theories of white-collar and corporate crime, in: Rorie, M.L. (editor), *The Handbook of White-Collar Crime*, Wiley & Sons, Hoboken, NJ, chapter 13, pages 191–208.

Chan, F. and Gibbs, C. (2022). When guardians become offenders: Understanding guardian capability through the lens of corporate crime, *Criminology*, 1–21, published online doi: 10.1111/1745-9125.12300.

Chattopadhyay, P., Glick, W.H. and Huber, G.P. (2001). Organizational actions in response to threats and opportunities, *Academy of Management Journal*, 44 (5), 937–955.

Comey, J.B. (2009). Go directly to prison: White collar sentencing after the Sarbanes-Oxley act, *Harvard Law Review*, 122, 1728–1749.

Cullen, F.T., Chouhy, C. and Jonson, C.L. (2020). Public opinion about white-collar crime, in: Rorie, M.L. (editor), *The Handbook of White-Collar Crime*, Wiley & Sons, Hoboken, NJ, chapter 14, pages 211–228.

Dearden, T.E. and Gottschalk, P. (2020). Gender and white-collar crime: Convenience in target selection, *Deviant Behavior*, 1–9, published online doi: 10.1080/01639625.2020.1756428.

Desmond, S.A., Rorie, M. and Sohoni, T. (2022). Working for God: Religion and occupational crime and deviance, *Deviant Behavior*, published online doi: 10.1080/01639625.2021.2022968.

Donk, D.P. and Molloy, E. (2008). From organizing as projects, to projects as organizations, *International Journal of Project Management*, 26, 129–137.

Engdahl, O. (2015). White-collar crime and first-time adult-onset offending: Explorations in the concept of negative life events as turning points, *International Journal of Law, Crime and Justice*, 43 (1), 1–16.

Folkvord, M.S., Eberhard-Gran, L. and Kristiansen, T. (2022). Raja etter VG-avsløring: Ber om mer kontroll av kulturpenger (Raja after VG revelation: Asks for more control of culture money), daily Norwegian newspaper *VG*, www.vg.no, retrieved May 16.

Froggio, G. and Agnew, R. (2007). The relationship between crime and "objective" versus "subjective" strains, *Journal of Criminal Justice*, 35, 81–87.

Galvin, B.M., Lange, D. and Ashforth, B.E. (2015). Narcissistic organizational identification: Seeing oneself as central to the organization's identity, *Academy of Management Review*, 40 (2), 163–181.

Gottschalk, P. (2017). Convenience in white-collar crime: Introducing a core concept, *Deviant Behavior*, 38 (5), 605–619.

Hansen, L.L. (2020). Review of the book "convenience triangle in white-collar crime: Case studies of fraud examinations", *Choice Connect*, vol. 57, no. 5, Association of College and Research Libraries, Middletown, CT.

Haram, O. (2021). Diktet opp konserter og p-hus: Dømt til 3 år og ni måneders fengsel for forsøk på coronasvindel (Invented concerts and car parking: Sentenced to 3 years and nine months in prison for attempted corona fraud), daily Norwegian newspaper *VG*, www.vg.no, retrieved December 23.

Hernandez, M. (2021). California couple sentenced for $20 million in Covid fraud, *New York Post*, www.nypost.com, retrieved November 17.

Hirschi, T. and Gottfredson, M. (1987). Causes of white-collar crime, *Criminology*, 25 (4), 949–974.

Kakkar, H., Sivanathan, N. and Globel, M.S. (2020). Fall from grace: The role of dominance and prestige in punishment of high-status actors, *Academy of Management Journal*, 63 (2), 530–553.

Kang, E. and Thosuwanchot, N. (2017). An application of Durkheim's four categories of suicide to organizational crimes, *Deviant Behavior*, 38 (5), 493–513.

Kennedy, J.P., Rorie, M. and Benson, M.L. (2021). Covid-19 frauds: An exploratory study of victimization during a global crisis, *Criminology & Public Policy*, 20, 493–543.

Langved, Å. and Klevstrand, A. (2020). Økokrims nye trusselvurdering: – Det kan bli misbruk av støtteordninger, tapping av selskaper før konkurs, og for så vidt korrupsjon (Økokrim's (Norwegina national authority for investigation and prosecution of economic and environmental crime) new threat assessment: – There may be abuse of support schemes, bottling of companies before bankruptcy, and also corruption), daily Norwegian business newspaper *Dagens Næringsliv*, www.dn.no, published April 16.

Lehman, D.W., Cooil, B. and Ramanujam, R. (2020). The effects of rule complexity on organizational noncompliance and remediation: Evidence from restaurant health inspections, *Journal of Management*, 46 (8), 1436–1468.

Leigh, A.C., Foote, D.A., Clark, W.R. and Lewis, J.L. (2010). Equity sensitivity: A triadic measure and outcome/input perspectives, *Journal of Managerial Issues*, 22 (3), 286–305.

Locke, E.A. and Latham, G.P. (2013). Goal setting theory: The current state, in: Locke, E.A. and Latham, G.P. (editors), *New Developments in Goal Setting and Task Performance*, Routledge, New York, NY, pages 623–630.

Løvik, V. (2021). Covid-svindel: Ektepar på rømmen: Kuttet av fotlenke (Covid Fraud: Couple on the Run: Cut Off Ankle Brace), daily Norwegian newspaper *Dagbladet*, www.dagbladet.no, retrieved November 18.

McGloin, J.M., Thomas, K.J. and Rowan, Z.R. (2021). Can the group disincentivize offending? Considering opt-out thresholds and decision reversals, *Criminology*, 59, 738–765.

Meers, J., Halliday, S. and Tomlinson, J. (2021). "Creative non-compliance": Complying with the "spirit of the law" not the "letter of the law" under the Covid-19 lockdown restrictions, *Deviant Behavior*, published online doi: 10.1080/01639625.2021.2014286.

Müller, S.M. (2018). Corporate behavior and ecological disaster: Dow chemical and the great lakes mercury crisis, 1970–1972, *Business History*, 60 (3), 399–422.

Oka, R. (2021). Introducing an anthropology of convenience, *Economic Anthropology*, 8 (2), 188–207.

Paternoster, R., Jaynes, C.M. and Wilson, T. (2018). Rational choice theory and interest in the "fortune of others", *Journal of Research in Crime and Delinquency*, 54 (6), 847–868.

Payne, J.L., Morgan, A. and Piquero, A.R. (2021). Exploring regional variability in the short-term impact of Covic-19 on property crime in Queensland, Australia, *Crime Science*, 10 (7), published online doi: 10.1186/s40163-020-00136-3, 20 pages.

Pillay, S. and Kluvers, R. (2014). An institutional theory perspective on corruption: The case of a developing democracy, *Financial Accountability & Management*, 30 (1), 95–119.

Piquero, N.L. (2012). The only thing we have to fear is fear itself: Investigating the relationship between fear of falling and white-collar crime, *Crime and Delinquency*, 58 (3), 362–379.

Pontell, H.N., Black, W.K. and Geis, G. (2014). Too big to fail, too powerful to jail? On the absence of criminal prosecutions after the 2008 financial meltdown, *Crime, Law and Social Change*, 61 (1), 1–13.

Qu, J. (2021). The challenge against economic regulation ethics under the Covid-19 epidemic: An analysis of unethical behavior of convenience, *Converter Magazine*, 2021 (5), 74–79.

Regjeringen. (2022). *Støtteordninger for næringsliv og kultur (Support Schemes for Business and Culture)*, Norwegian government page www.regjeringen.no.

Rorie, M., Park, S. and West, M.P. (2022). Do structural choice theory and the 'risky lifestyles' perspectives predict immunity as well as victimization? A test using zero-inflated mixed-effect SEM analyses of adolescent victimizations in South Korea, *International Review of Victimology*, published online doi: 10.1177/02697580211057330.

Schoen, J.L., DeSimone, J.A., Meyer, R.D., Schnure, K.A. and LeBreton, J.M. (2021). Identifying, defining, and measuring justification mechanisms: The implicit biases underlying individual differences, *Journal of Management*, 47 (3), 716–744.

Stadler, W.A. and Gottschalk, P. (2022). Testing convenience theory for white-collar crime: Perceptions of potential offenders and non-offenders, *Deviant Behavior*, 43 (7), 804–820.

Sutherland, E.H. (1983). *White Collar Crime – The Uncut Version*, Yale University Press, New Haven, CT.

Sykes, G. and Matza, D. (1957). Techniques of neutralization: A theory of delinquency, *American Sociological Review*, 22 (6), 664–670.

Thaxton, S. and Agnew, R. (2018). When criminal coping is likely: An examination of conditioning effects in general strain theory, *Journal of Quantitative Criminology*, 34, 887–920.

Treasurer. (2022). *JobKeeper Payment*, Australian Government, The Treasury, www.treasury.gov.au/coronavirus/jobkeeper.

Vasiu, V.I. (2021). Convenience triangle in white-collar crime: Case studies of fraud examinations, *Criminal Law and Criminal Justice Books*, Rutgers, the State University of New Jersey, May, www.clcjbooks.rutgers.edu.

Vasiu, V.I. and Podgor, E.S. (2019). Organizational opportunity and deviant behavior: Convenience in white-collar crime, *Criminal Law and Criminal Justice Books*, Rutgers, the State University of New Jersey, July, www.clcjbooks.rutgers.edu.

Wood, J. and Alleyne, E. (2010). Street gang theory and research: Where are we now and where do we go from here? *Aggression and Violent Behavior*, 15, 100–111.

6 Stigma or Competition Effect

It is an interesting research issue whether competitors lose or gain when an industry peer is hit by a scandal such as white-collar and corporate crime. Traditionally, it is assumed that the negative stigma effect is more common among others in the same industry rather than the positive competition effect where non-accused firms gain from the accused firm's loss. Recent research has suggested a U-shaped relationship where increasing product market overlap first causes a stigma effect and then causes a competition effect. On the basis of seven cases from seven different countries, this chapter suggests that the U-shape might be influenced by the local extent of white-collar and corporate crime. Specifically, this chapter suggests the following hypothesis for future research: The product market overlap between a non-accused firm and an accused industry peer will exhibit a U-shaped effect on the non-accused firm's market depending on the extent of product market overlap, where the negative stigma effect will be stronger in countries characterized by more corruption and other forms of white-collar and corporate crime, while the positive competition effect will be stronger in countries characterized by less corruption and other forms of white-collar and corporate crime.

When Telia in Sweden was hit by a corporate scandal (Schoultz and Flyghed, 2021), did the local telecommunication industry suffer? When Danske Bank in Denmark was hit by several scandals (Bruun Hjejle, 2018; Plesner, 2020), did the local banking sector suffer? When Volkswagen in Germany was hit by a scandal (Jung and Sharon, 2019), did the local automobile industry suffer? When Wirecard in Germany was hit by a scandal (Storbeck, 2021), did the local finance sector suffer? This list might be much longer, but the point should be obvious: Does an industry and thus competitors suffer of negative consequences when an industry peer is hit by a scandal? Or does suspected wrongdoing by an industry peer represent a competitive advantage for others in the local industry?

These questions are important to address in research since traditionally, as argued by Naumovska and Lavie, 2021: 1130), "research on misconduct suggests that accusations against industry peers generate negative consequences for non-accused firms". Researchers have thus suggested a stigma effect that

DOI: 10.4324/9781003379249-8

generates a negative spillover, whereby other companies in the accused company's industry suffer market loss following the accusation.

Therefore, Naumovska and Lavie (2021: 1131) introduced a counterargument, "predicting a positive spillover to non-accused firms following an accusation against their industry peer". Alleged wrongdoing ascribed to a competitor can improve the competitive position of competing corporations in the same industry. Non-accused corporations can benefit from the revelation of financial misconduct by an industry peer. Major customers might not only consider, but actually carry out a switch of their business to other companies. Then one firm's loss is its competitor's gain.

Naumovska and Lavie (2021: 1134) theorized the stigma effect versus the competition effect by suggesting that

> a non-accused firm that exhibits greater product market overlap with an accused peer will be perceived as more similar to it and thus more likely than other firms to be assigned to the same industry category as the accused peer".

Their research first suggested a growing negative spillover to non-accused firms at increasing product market overlap. Then they changed their suggestion to a U-shaped relationship (Naumovska and Lavie (2021: 1137):

> The product market overlap between a non-accused firm and an accused industry peer will exhibit a U-shaped effect on the non-accused firm's stock market valuation, with the expected stock market valuation first becoming more negative as the product market overlap increases and then becoming more positive with further increases in product market overlap.

This chapter is concerned with the empirical side of the stigma effect versus the competition effect. Corporate scandals are frequently investigated by fraud examiners, and this chapter reviews a convenience sample of investigation reports to identify relevant effects. In our perspective of corporate crime consequences, the presented research is exploratory to review whether one firm's loss is its competitor's loss or gain.

Corporate Crises and Scandals

Scandals are disruptive publicity of misconduct (Dewan and Jensen, 2020) and publicized instances of transgression that run counter to social norms (Hearit, 2006; Whyte, 2016). Scandals typically result in condemnation and discredit and other consequences such as bad press, disengagement of key constituencies, the severance of network ties, and decrease in performance (Piazza and Jourdan, 2018). A scandal can be an act of elite deviance that might include financial, physical, and morally harmful behavior committed by privileged members in society.

A crisis causing a scandal can be a fundamental threat to the organization, characterized by particular ambiguity of cause, effect, and means of resolution (Bundy and Pfarrer, 2015; König et al., 2020). A crisis is an unexpected, publicly known, and harmful event that is associated with uncertainty. Most corporate crises originate from failures within the organization. Scholars denote that organizational crises require timely responses (König et al., 2020). For example, when the Siemens corruption scandal in Germany emerged in the public, top management attempted to blame lower level managers (Berghoff, 2018: 423):

> At first the company defended itself with set phrases like "mishaps of individuals" and isolated offenses committed by a "gang" of criminals, or "This is not Siemens".

According to Greer and McLaughlin (2017), existing research indicates that scandals can have a corrosive impact on the reputational standing, credibility, and legitimacy of organizations. Scandals thus iterate crises for involved organizations, executives, and offenders.

Benson (2019) argued that corporate responses to criminal allegations usually involve attempts to either deny any wrongdoing or employ neutralizations as a way to explain their activities:

> Typically, it is the officers and directors of the firm who attempt to justify the corporation's actions to the public, the media, their shareholders, and if necessary, even before the court. These exercises in corporate self-defense are aimed at protecting the corporation's image and legitimacy and belong to a broader category of offender neutralizations and denials. Furthermore, these corporate neutralizations and denials of harm and wrongdoing can be allowed and aided by state actors, for example, through allowing a firm to pay a hefty fine, yet admits to no wrongdoing or through enabling/allowing corporate harm via de-regulation.

As argued by Kim et al. (2009), traditional approaches to trust repair by the corporation that has lost trust by scandals include apologies, denials, promises, excuses, reparations, legalistic remedies, and no response at all. However, as argued by Bundy and Pfarrer (2015), the effectiveness of such accounts is depending on the match or mismatch between situational attribution of trust-reducing incidents and the chosen trust-repair message. An account is a form of speech for explanations of negative events that the corporation wants to communicate. An account is a statement made to explain unanticipated or untoward behavior (Scott and Lyman, 1968).

Situational attribution of responsibility for a scandal is assigned to the trustee by the trustor. When situational attribution is low, then the corporate response might be more defensive. When the situational attribution is high, then the corporate response might be more accommodative. While a defensive response accepts no or little responsibility for an incident, an accommodative response acknowledges the corporation's causal role in the incident. Denials and excuses are examples of defensive responses, while apologies and promises are examples of accommodative responses.

By scapegoating, the responsibility for the act or event is transferred from the corporation to one or a few public figures, such as dismissed senior company executives or lower level managers. A scapegoat is a person who is blamed for the wrongdoings, mistakes, or faults of others, in this case the wrongdoings of top management. For example when hit by a scandal, Astellas in Japan applied the procedure of scapegoating (Mulinari et al., 2021: 75):

> According to Astellas Europe, "the email indicated that there was a conscious decision by one individual" . . ., but that "as an organization" Astellas had been completely unaware of the email up until this point. Hence, the company submitted there "was no dishonesty or deliberate attempt to mislead" – except by this single rogue employee. Astellas Europe also stated that, "immediate action" had been taken to address the conduct of this senior member of staff.

As this quote illustrates, corporate offenders can use crisis intervention in the form of accounts to spread the blame and thereby potentially minimize their own negative consequences (Gottschalk and Benson, 2020).

Effects on Non-Accused Firms

Naumovska and Lavie (2021) studied stigma effects versus competition effects on non-accused firms when an industry peer is accused of financial misconduct. Stigma effects refer to negative consequences for non-accused firms from accusations against industry peers. Competition effects refer to benefits for non-accused firms that compete with these peers. The research analyzed investors' shareholdings and stock market returns of non-accused firms in the United States. A reduced stock market valuation indicates stigma effects, while an increased stock market valuation indicates competition effects.

Naumovska and Lavie (2021: 1159) thus distinguished between "stigma by association" versus "gain by misfortune":

> An industry peer's financial misconduct can generate either positive or negative spillovers to non-accused firms. Understanding these spillovers calls attention to the underlying mechanisms. Our theory discerns two mechanisms: the stigma effect, which generates negative spillover, and the competition effect, which yields positive spillover. Prior research has mostly underscored the stigma effect, paying almost no attention to the competition effect. Our study is the first to simultaneously consider the stigma and competition effects ascribed by financial misconduct within an industry, and thus it sheds new light on the relative prevalence of these conflicting effects and the resulting net spillover that they generate to non-accused firms. . . .

> On average, investors negatively assess non-accused firms in the accused peer's industry, suggesting that the stigma effect dominates the competition effect. Yet we find that the net effect of stigma versus competition varies depending on the market overlap between each non-accused firm and its accused peer. The negative spillover increases with product market overlap, but beyond a certain level it gives way to positive spillover attributed to the intensifying competition effect.

The study found that the accused peer's closest competitors will mainly benefit from the competition effect and suffer less from the stigma effect. The accused peer's customers will switch to other firms in the same market that offer comparable products. It is a matter of substitution, where a non-accused firm can substitute an accused firm's products. The non-accused firm has an opportunity to capitalize on the market lost by its direct competitor following accusations against that industry peer (Naumovska and Lavie, 2021: 1135):

> The greater the market overlap between the non-accused firm and its peer, the stronger the competition effect that creates positive spillover to firms that can enhance their competitive position vis-à-vis that peer.

The extent of product market overlap was defined in the study in terms of both factual and perceived overlap. The study suggested a U-shaped relationship between stock market valuation and product market overlap: A low product market overlap reduces stock market valuation, while a high product market overlap increases stock market valuation.

Fraud Investigation Reports

Fraud examiners from law firms and accounting firms are typically hired by private and public organizations to investigate suspicions of white-collar and corporate crime (King, 2020, 2021; Meerts, 2020). At the end of their inquiry, a report is produced and given to the client organization as their property. Unfortunately for researchers, most clients keep reports secret (Gottschalk and Tcherni-Buzzeo, 2017). Only a few reports are publicly available, and they are often hard to find. Via Internet searches, we were able to identify and retrieve a small sample of seven reports from seven different countries written in English. Each report was evidence of a corporate scandal.

Media coverage of each scandal indicated whether others in the same industry had suffered or gained from the scandal of the industry peer. Via Internet searches and specific searches in newspapers such as the *Financial Times*, it was possible to find evidence of both stigma effects and competition effects of the various scandals. Scandals have become a prized news commodity that validates the professional watchdog conception of investigative journalism (Barak, 2007; Zavyalova et al., 2012).

The sample of investigation reports by fraud examiners is listed in Table 6.1. The first entry is concerned with the Danish bank Danske Bank that had

Table 6.1 Investigation reports by fraud examiners

Accused Firm	*Market Overlap*	*Non-Accused Firms*
Danske Bank (Bruun Hjejle, 2018) in Denmark	Strong product market overlap with other banks	***Competition effect*** of bank customers leaving Danske Bank in protest out of lack of trust (Olsen, 2019)
Hurtigruten Cruises (Wiersholm, 2020) in Norway	Weak product market overlap with other cruise lines	***Stigma effect*** by avoiding cruise ships in general (CDC, 2021)
Mercy Corps (Smith, 2020) in Congo	Strong product market overlap with other aid organizations	***Stigma effect*** as people lose faith and trust in humanitarian work (Larsen, 2021)
Swedbank (Clifford Chance, 2020) in Sweden	Strong product market overlap with other banks	***Competition effect*** of bank customers leaving Swedbank in protest out of lack of trust (Asplid, 2019)
Unibank (Kroll, 2017) in Moldova	Strong product market overlap with other banks	***Stigma effect*** by avoiding investments in Moldovan banks (Buckley, 2018)
Wells Fargo (Shearman Sterling, 2017) Community Bank in the United States	Strong product market overlap with other banks	***Competition effect*** of bank customers leaving Wells Fargo (Gray, 2016)
Wirecard (KPMG, 2020) banking in Germany	Strong product market overlap with other banks	***Competition effect*** from Wirecard collapse that made customers switch bank (Nestler, 2020)

money laundering issues (Bruun Hjejle, 2018). The Danish newspaper *Berlingske* reported that Danske Bank lost thousands of customers in the aftermath of the money laundering scandal in Estonia (Olsen 2019). There was a competition effect since the customers left Danske Bank for other Danish banks that had the same and similar products. There is a strong market overlap with other banks that caused a competition effect of bank customers leaving Danske Bank in protest out of lack of trust.

The second entry is concerned with the Norwegian cruise line Hurtigruten Cruises. In the aftermath of the COVID-19 outbreak on a cruise ship operated by Hurtigruten (Wiersholm, 2020), cruise ship travel during COVID-19 received increased attention (CDC, 2021):

> The chance of getting Covid-19 on cruise ships is high because the virus spreads easily between people in close quarters aboard ships.

Thus, a stigma effect occurred where all cruise lines suffered from the detected threat of virus outbreak aboard Hurtigruten ships as well as other cruise ships (Rose and Street, 2021).

The third entry is concerned with the charity Mercy Corps. The international non-government organization (NGO) experienced a scam in the Democratic Republic of Congo (DRC). The scam involved corrupt aid workers, business owners, and community leaders (Kleinfeld, 2020):

> Together they zeroed in on the humanitarian sector's flagship rapid response programs – the main mechanism for helping displaced people in Congo, where hundreds of millions of dollars of foreign aid are spent every year.

Some US$636,000 was lost by Mercy Corps and partners in just a few months. It was estimated that the charity had lost US$6 million in about two years. Kleinfeld (2020) describes the modus operandi in some of the wrongdoing:

> When a conflict or natural disaster occurred, aid groups would receive reports from local community leaders that exaggerated the number of people who had fled their homes. Businesspeople would then pay kickbacks to corrupt aid workers to register hundreds of additional people for cash support who were not actually displaced. The merchants would then receive the aid payments and share with the local leaders. Of the nineteen Mercy Corps aid workers alleged to be involved in the scam, some were using the extra cash to buy new cars, Armani glasses, and iPhones, according to several of their colleagues who spoke to The New Humanitarian (TNH). One even started building a hotel, colleagues said.

The investigation by Smith (2020) strengthened people's skepticism toward foreign aid. Skeptics believe that most of the money never arrives at their destinations. Instead, foreign aid money ends up in the pockets of over-administered aid organizations as well as in the pockets of local corrupt businesspeople. There was thus a stigma effect harming not only Mercy Corps but also other organizations in the same industry such as the Red Cross. People lose faith and trust in humanitarian work (Larsen, 2021).

Swedbank in Sweden is the fourth accused firm in the table. Similar to Danske Bank in Denmark, Swedbank ignored money laundering issues in their Eastern European operations. Swedbank carried out bank transactions of more than €37 billion (about US$40 billion) with a high risk for money laundering over a five-year period according to private policing in terms of an internal investigation by fraud examiners from law firm Clifford Chance (2020). The investigation report suggests that the Swedish bank actively targeted high-risk individuals in the Baltic region and points to failings from both top management and the board (Milne, 2020). Birgitte Bonnesen was the chief executive officer (CEO) at Swedbank. She had to leave the position in 2019 (Makortoff, 2019). When Clifford Chance (2020) presented their report of investigation, the new Swedbank board decided to withdraw her final compensation of 26 million Swedish kroner (US$2.7 million). At the same time, Swedbank accepted a fine of 4 billion Swedish kroner (US$408 million) from the Swedish finance inspection (Johannessen and Christensen, 2020). Similar to Danske Bank in Denmark, customers switched banks, so there was a competition effect in Sweden (Asplid, 2019).

The fifth entry is also concerned with a bank scandal in Moldova that might be compared to the bank scandals in Denmark and Sweden. However, as indicated in the table, there was a stigma effect rather than a competition effect in the Moldovan case (Buckley, 2018). People did not only lose trust in the involved bank Unibank; they also lost trust in the banking sector in Moldova. One reason was that a few more banks were involved in the scandal with Unibank (Kroll, 2017). Another reason was that the National Bank of Moldova seemed to lack control with local banks. The *New York Times* reported in October 2015 that Moldova

> was rocked this year by the discovery that $1 billion had fraudulently siphoned from Moldova's banking system over a period of years, a huge amount for an impoverished country whose entire economic output is only about $8 billion a year".
>
> (Nechepurenko, 2015)

The *Financial Times* reported in January 2016 that "until the fraud came to light last year, Moldova was considered a rare success in the EU's campaign to build bridges to post-Soviet states" (Seddon, 2016).

Regarding the sixth entry in Table 6.1, Shichor and Heeren (2021: 99) described concerted ignorance at Wells Fargo in the United States:

> Management expectations of making profits through lower level employees, without being interested in how the results are achieved, can be characterized as "concerted ignorance" which is a general way of covering up when open discussion of certain practices or policies would threaten the solidarity and cohesion in an organization.

Shichor and Heeren (2021) found that concerted ignorance was created by an organizational emphasis on decentralization. Concerted ignorance was promoted by the common interest of limiting the knowledge each member of the organization obtains about other members of the organization. After the investigation of the scandal by Shearman Sterling (2017), a competition effect of bank customers leaving Wells Fargo occurred (Gray, 2016).

The final entry in Table 6.1 is concerned with Wirecard in Germany. Chancellor Angela Merkel in Germany had to explain herself about helping Wirecard accused of a billion-dollar fraud. The creditors of Wirecard were left with a loss of €3 billion. Merkel had to explain how she could vouch for the bankrupt company (Kagge, 2021). The payment company Wirecard, which was hailed as one of Germany's rare technology successes, collapsed into insolvency in the summer of 2020 after revealing that €2 billion in cash did not exist (Storbeck, 2021; Storbeck and Morris, 2021). A few months before the collapse, fraud examiners from KPMG (2020) conducted an internal investigation at Wirecard where Markus Braun was the CEO. After the collapse, a competition effect occurred (Nestler, 2020).

In the list of cases, corporate accounts had various elements of crisis communication to minimize corporate harm. Both Scandinavian banks dismissed their chief executives to attribute blame to them (Milne and Binham, 2018; Milne, 2020). At Hurtigruten Cruises, the medical doctor onboard the ship was blamed (CDC, 2021). At Mercy Corps, the investigated corruption was attempted attributed to the bribers rather than the bribed (Kleinfeld, 2020). In Moldova, a prominent politician fled the country and received the blame (Buckley, 2018). At Wells Fargo's Community Bank, the retired chief executive was blamed (Shichor and Heeren, 2021). At Wirecard, management blamed auditors for alleging misconduct before the bankruptcy and the public prosecution of the chief executive (Storbeck, 2021).

Peer Product Market Overlap

According to Naumovska and Lavie (2021), the stigma versus the competition effect on non-accused firms when an industry peer is accused of financial misconduct is dependent on the product market overlap between the non-accused firm and its accused peer. They suggested that the negative stigma effect will be more severe with greater extent of market overlap up to a point. Beyond that point, the competition effect will be stronger than the stigma effect, thus causing a U-shaped relationship between the market valuation of a non-accused firm and the product market overlap with the accused firm. Their research found support for this U-shaped prediction in the US software industry based on investors' shareholdings and stock market returns of non-accused firms.

We applied the same kind of theorizing to our convenience sample of seven accused organizations in seven different countries. Six out of seven cases are characterized by strong product market overlap. Five out of those six agree with the competition effect. One case seems to have a better fit with the stigma effect as banks in Moldova generally lost trust because of the fraud at Unibank. A potential explanation might be the greater extent of white-collar and corporate crime generally in Moldova as evidenced by that country's rank on the corruption index by Transparency International. While Moldova ranks 115, Denmark ranks 1, Norway ranks 7, Congo ranks 165 (and the Democratic Republic of Congo ranks 180), Sweden ranks 3, the United States of America ranks 25, and Germany ranks 9. We return below to the low rank of Congo. The interesting deviation by Moldova might both be caused by the fact that more than one bank in the country was involved in the scandal, and that Moldova is considered a corrupt country based on the corruption perceptions index. While investors in Denmark, Sweden, and Germany switched financial institution away from Danske Bank, Swedbank, and Wirecard to non-accused banks locally, it seems that investors left all banks in Moldova.

The only case characterized by relatively weak product market overlap is cruise lines. We argue that Hurtigruten Cruises is different from other cruise lines in terms of the adventure offered. While other cruise lines may operate in holiday waters of warm weather, cosmopolitan cities, and paradise islands, Hurtigruten Cruises operates in exploratory waters in the north to see ice bears, reindeer, and whales in cold waters. Even among other cruise lines there might be weak product market overlap as indicated by their pricing strategies, where some trips are inexpensive with low standard, while others are exotic with extreme luxury and prices accordingly. Thus, the low product market overlap in the cruise industry might explain the stigma effect being stronger than the competition effect.

The final case of Congo is concerned with strong product market overlap among NGOs in the business of foreign aid. We suggest a strong product market overlap as both private donors and governments do not necessarily distinguish between various aid organizations. For example, in Norway, it seems to be quite random whether you financially support Norwegian Red Cross, Norwegian People's Aid, Norwegian Refugee Council, Strømme Foundation, Care Norway, or any other of the numerous aid organizations. Strong product market overlap should – according to Naumovska and Lavie (2021) – result in a competition effect stronger than the stigma effect. However, it seems that donors lose faith in the efficiency and effectiveness of aid organizations when one aid organization, such as Mercy Corps, is hit by a scandal. A potential reason is the extent of white-collar crime and corporate crime already present in countries that receive foreign aid. Development aid funds might seem to disappear within bureaucratic and inefficient NGOs as well as corrupt local destinations.

On the basis of the small and convenient sample of countries in this study, we suggest an extension of the theoretical perspective by Naumovska and Lavie (2021), where the local situation is taken into account. Specifically, based on our conclusion regarding Moldova and Congo, we suggest that non-accused firms will suffer from a stigma effect rather than a competition effect to a greater extent in countries characterized by high levels of white-collar and corporate crime. Formulated as a research hypothesis for future research, we suggest the following angle: *The product market overlap between a non-accused firm and an accused industry peer will exhibit a U-shaped effect on the non-accused firm's market depending on the extent of product market overlap, where the negative stigma effect will be stronger in countries characterized by more corruption and other forms of white-collar and corporate crime, while the positive competition effect will be stronger in countries characterized by less corruption and other forms of white-collar and corporate crime.*

There are a number of limitations in this research that might open up avenues for future research. First of all, the sample size is so small that it is not at all sufficient to make any generalizations based on the results. Second, there was only one person's interpretation where multiple researchers should have reviewed both investigation reports and media coverage. Third, there is very little evidence to suggest that country-level variables are impacting effects. Fourth, the impact of accounts on the extent of stigma and competition effects is left open. Finally, there is no way to determine how large the stigma and the competition effects were in the seven cases as this would require a study of the media outlets where articles about scandals appeared.

In conclusion, based on recent research regarding whether competitors lose or gain when an industry peer is hit by a scandal, this chapter has contributed to an extension of previous theorizing. While the relationship between the extent of product market overlap and stigma versus competition effects is supported, anecdotal evidence suggests that the stigma effect will be stronger and more persistent in nations with more corruption and other forms of white-collar and corporate crime. On the basis of exploratory research in this chapter, the following hypothesis is formulated for future research: The product market overlap between a non-accused firm and an accused industry peer will exhibit a U-shaped effect on the non-accused firm's market depending on the extent of product market overlap, where the negative stigma effect will be stronger in countries characterized by more corruption and other forms of white-collar and corporate crime, while the positive competition effect will be stronger in countries characterized by less corruption and other forms of white-collar and corporate crime.

References

Asplid, Å. (2019). Swedbank-kund: "Väldigt obehagligt" (Swedbank Customer: Very Unpleasant), Swedish business journal *Dina Penger*, www.expressen.se, retrieved December 13.

Barak, G. (2007). Doing newsmaking criminology from within the academy, *Theoretical Criminology*, 11 (2), 191–207.

Benson, M.L. (2019). The neutralization of corporate crime: Organizational and state-facilitated denials of corporate harm and wrongdoing, *Journal of White Collar and Corporate Crime*, https://ascdwcc.org/journal-of-white-collar-and-corporate-crime/, retrieved April 2.

Berghoff, H. (2018). "Organised irresponsibility?" The Siemens corruption scandal of the 1990s and 2000s, *Business History*, 60 (3), 423–445.

Bruun Hjejle. (2018). *Report on the Non-Resident Portfolio at Danske Bank's Estonian branch*, report of investigation, law firm Bruun Hjejle, Copenhagen, Denmark, 87 pages.

Buckley, N. (2018). Latvia: A banking scandal on the Baltic, *Financial Times*, www.ft.com, retrieved February 23.

Bundy, J. and Pfarrer, M.D. (2015). A burden of responsibility: The role of social approval at the onset of a crisis, *Academy of Management Review*, 40 (3), 345–369.

CDC. (2021). Cruise ship travel during Covid-19, *Centers for Disease Control and Prevention*, www.cdc.gov, retrieved November 1.

Clifford Chance. (2020). *Report of Investigation on Swedbank*, report of investigation, law firm Clifford Chance, Washington, DC, 218 pages.

Dewan, Y. and Jensen, M. (2020). Catching the big fish: The role of scandals in making status a liability, *Academy of Management Journal*, 63 (5), 1652–1678.

Gottschalk, P. and Benson, M.L. (2020). The evolution of corporate accounts of scandals from exposure to investigation, *British Journal of Criminology*, 60, 949–969.

Gottschalk, P. and Tcherni-Buzzeo, M. (2017). Reasons for gaps in crime reporting: The case of white-collar criminals investigated by private fraud examiners in Norway, *Deviant Behavior*, 38 (3), 267–281.

Gray, A. (2016). Wells Fargo loses status as world's most valuable bank, *Financial Times*, www.ft.com, retrieved September 14.

Greer, C. and McLaughlin, E. (2017). Theorizing institutional scandal and the regulatory state, *Theoretical Criminology*, 21 (2), 112–132.

Hearit, K.M. (2006). *Crisis Management by Apology: Corporate Responses to Allegations of Wrongdoing*, Lawrence Erlbaum Associates, Mahwah, NJ.

Johannessen, S.Ø. and Christensen, J. (2020). Swedbank vil ikke betale sluttpakke til toppsjef som måtte gå av etter hvitvaskingsskandale (Swedbank Will Not Pay Final Package to Top Executive Who Had to Leave After Money Laundering Scandal), daily Norwegian business newspaper *Dagens Næringsliv*, www.dn.no, retrieved March 23.

Jung, J.C. and Sharon, E. (2019). The Volkswagen emissions scandal and its aftermath, *Global Business & Organizational Excellence*, 38 (4), 6–15.

Kagge, G. (2021). Merkel må forklare seg om hjelp til selskap anklaget for milliardsvindel (Merkel Must Explain Herself About Help to Companies Accused of Billion Fraud), daily Norwegian newspaper *Aftenposten*, Thursday, April 22, page 24.

Kim, P.H., Dirks, K.T. and Cooper, C.D. (2009). The repair of trust: A dynamic bilateral perspective and multilevel conceptualization, *Academy of Management Review*, 34 (3), 401–422.

King, M. (2020). Private investigation into economic crime: Regulation of a multidisciplinary field, *Journal of Applied Security Research*, published online doi: 10.1080/19361610.2020.1832018.

King, M. (2021). Profiting from a tainted trade: Private investigators' views on the popular culture glamorization of their trade, *Journal of Criminological Research Policy and Practice*, 7 (2), 112–125.

Kleinfeld, P. (2020). Congo aid scam triggers sector-wide alarm, *The New Humanitarian*, www.thenewhumanitarian.org, retrieved June 11.

König, A., Graf-Vlachy, L., Bundy, J. and Little, L.M. (2020). A blessing and a curse: How CEOs' trait empathy affects their management of organizational crisis, *Academy of Management Review*, 45 (1), 130–153.

KPMG. (2020). *Report Concerning the Independent Special Investigation at Wirecard AG*, April 27, audit firm KPMG, Munich, Germany, 74 pages.

Kroll. (2017). *Project Tenor II, Summary Report, Report Prepared for The National Bank of Moldova, Report of Investigation*, 58 pages, audit firm Kroll, London, UK. (2016: Project Tenor – Scoping Phase, 84 pages. 2018: Project Tenor II, Confidential Working Papers Part I to the Detailed Report, Detailed tracing analysis, 60 pages. 2018: Project Tenor II – Confidential working papers – Part II, Evidence Packs – Funds traced to: Ilan Shor, Alexandr Macloivici and Olga Bondarciuc. 2018: Project Tenor II – Detailed Report, Report Prepared for The National Bank of Moldova, 154 pages).

Larsen, O.J. (2021). Tidligere bistandstopp: -Bistand virker ikke (Former Aid Executive: Aid Does Not Work), Norwegian broadcasting corporation *NRK*, www.nrk.no, retrieved December 13.

Makortoff, K. (2019). Swedbank chief sacked amid money laundering scandal, *The Guardian*, www.theguardian.com, retrieved March 28.

Meerts, C. (2020). Corporate investigations: Beyond notions of public-private relations, *Journal of Contemporary Criminal Justice*, 36 (1), 86–100.

Milne, R. (2020). Swedbank failings on E37bn of transactions revealed in report, *Financial Times*, www.ft.com, retrieved March 23.

Milne, R. and Binham, C. (2018). Danske Bank chief Thomas Borgen quits over money laundering scandal, *Financial Times*, www.ft.com, retrieved September 19.

Mulinari, S., Davis, C. and Ozieranski, P. (2021). Failure of responsive regulation? Pharmaceutical marketing, corporate impression management and off-label promotion of enzalutamide in Europe, *Journal of White Collar and Corporate Crime*, 2 (2), 69–80.

Naumovska, I. and Lavie, D. (2021). When an industry peer is accused of financial misconduct: Stigma versus competition effects on non-accused firms, *Administrative Science Quarterly*, 66 (4), 1130–1172.

Nechepurenko, I. (2015). Moldova parliament dismisses government amid bank scandal, *The New York Times*, www.nytimes.com, retrieved October 29.

Nestler, F. (2020). Kunden auf der Flucht (Customers on the run), daily German newspaper *Frankfurter Allgemeine Zeitung*, www.faz.net, retrieved June 24.

Olsen, S.M. (2019). Danske Bank mister tusindvis af kunder – men topchef venter prop i flugten (Danske Bank loses thousands of customers – but the top manager is expecting a plug in the outlet), daily Danish newspaper *Berlingske*, www.berlingske.dk, retrieved April 30.

Piazza, A. and Jourdan, J. (2018). When the dust settles: The consequences of scandals for organizational competition, *Academy of Management Journal*, 61 (1), 165–190.

Plesner. (2020). *Response to DFSA-letter: Anmodning om redegørelse om Danske Bank A/S' gældsinddrivelsessystem (Response to DFSA Letter: Request for Account Concerning Danske Bank Inc.'s Debt Collection System)*, investigation report by Danske Bank, law firm Plesner, Copenhagen, Denmark, 120 pages.

Rose, A. and Street, F. (2021). 48 test positive for Covid on world's biggest cruise ship, *CNN*, www.cnn.com, retrieved December 21.

Schoultz, I. and Flyghed, J. (2021). Performing unbelonging in court: Observations from a transnational corporate bribery trial – A dramaturgical approach, *Crime, Law and Social Change*, published online doi: 10.1007/s10611-021-09990-x.

Scott, M.B. and Lyman, S.M. (1968). Accounts, *American Sociological Review*, 33 (1), 46–62.

Seddon, M. (2016). Outrage over Moldova bank scandal threatens reforms, *Financial Times*, www.ft.com, retrieved January 26.

Shearman Sterling. (2017). Independent Directors of the Board of Wells Fargo & Company: Sales Practices Investigation Report, Community Bank, Report of investigation, 113 pages, law firm *Shearman Sterling*, San Francisco, CA.

Shichor, D. and Heeren, J.W. (2021). Reflecting on corporate crime and control: The Wells Fargo banking saga, *Journal of White Collar and Corporate Crime*, 2 (2), 97–108.

Smith. (2020). *Operational Review of Exposure to Corrupt Practices in Humanitarian Aid Implementation Mechanisms in the DRC*, Adam Smith International, www.reliefweb.int, written by N. Henze, F. Grünewald and S. Parmar, published in July.

Storbeck, O. (2021). Prosecutors delayed arrest warrant for Wirecard's Jan Marsalek, *Financial Times*, www.ft.com, retrieved January 29.

Storbeck, O. and Morris, S. (2021). BaFin files insider trading complaint against Deutsche Bank board member, *Financial Times*, www.ft.com, retrieved April 19.

Whyte, D. (2016). It's common sense, stupid! Corporate crime and techniques of neutralization in the automobile industry, *Crime, Law and Social Change*, 66 (2), 165–181.

Wiersholm. (2020). *Granskingsrapport: Utbrudd av covid-19 på Hurtigruten-skipet MS Roald Amundsen 17.-31. juli 2020 (Investigation Report: Outbreak of Covid-19 on Hurtigruten Ship MS Roald Amundsen July 17–31, 2020*), law firm Wiersholm, Oslo, Norway, 51 pages.

Zavyalova, A., Pfarrer, M.D., Reger, R.K. and Shapiro, D.L. (2012). Managing the message: The effects of firm actions and industry spillovers on media coverage following wrongdoing, *Academy of Management Journal*, 55 (5), 1079–1101.

Part II

Compliance Control

7 Corporate Social License to Operate

Traditionally, white-collar and corporate crime research has focused on the role of the criminal justice system in prosecuting and punishing offenders and offenses. The frequent lack of prosecution and punishment has been explained by various theoretical perspectives that reflect the legal license to operate. However, the emerging perspective of the social license to operate (SLO) illustrates punishment at violations that can cause termination of executives, market loss, and other serious harm to individuals and firms. This chapter presents three case studies where fraud examiners reviewed the legal license, when the social license was ignored. There is an interesting avenue here for future white-collar and corporate crime research in distinguishing between punishment from violations of the legal license and punishment from violations of the SLO.

Surprisingly often, fraud examiners conclude with misconduct but no crime in their internal investigations of suspected white-collar and corporate offenses (Gottschalk, 2016, 2020, 2021). Fraud examiners are in the business of reconstructing past events and sequences of events when there are allegations and suspicions of financial crime such as corruption and embezzlement (King, 2012, 2020, 2021; Meerts, 2020, 2021). Investigation conclusions of misconduct but no crime implies that the client organizations did not violate the legal license to operate. The legal license refers to laws that describe wrongdoing and punishment (Haines et al., 2022; Sale, 2021).

However, fraud examiners often identify misconduct and wrongdoing that represents violations of the SLO. Rather than punishment by the criminal justice systems, violations of the social license from wrongdoing lead to punishment by the local community and relevant stakeholders, where such punishment seems to grow in importance for accused enterprises (Baba et al., 2021; Haines et al., 2022; Hurst et al., 2020; Sale, 2021). Therefore – even when fraud examiners find that the legal license was obviously not violated – accused enterprises tend to change their business practice as a response to organized criticism to avoid harm to the business.

This chapter reviews fraud investigation reports and their consequences to provide insights into violations of the SLO. The current research is important, as the emerging stream of social license literature can illustrate that although white-collar and corporate crime suspicions tend to avoid the attention of

DOI: 10.4324/9781003379249-10

the criminal justice system (Gottschalk and Gunnesdal, 2018; Gottschalk and Tcherni-Buzzeo, 2017), there are nevertheless consequences for offenders from external reactions that can harm and potentially threaten enterprise existence. In fact, the threat of sanctions from powerful stakeholders might in the future become more frightening than the threat of traditional criminal prosecution.

Characteristics of the Social License

The social license refers to "the acceptance or approval by the local – if not indigenous – communities and stakeholders of a business enterprise's operations or projects in a certain area" (Saenz, 2019: 297). The social license is "the set of demands and expectations held by local stakeholders and broader society about how a business should operate", and "a license is then said to be granted if the business is deemed to have met these demands and expectations – and thus is viewed as being socially acceptable" (Hurst et al., 2020: 1). The social license is "a social construction to which various stakeholders contributes" (Baba et al., 2021: 248). The social license is an expression "often used in the context of a possible disapproval of their activities, when such disapproval may result in resistance that could harm business interests", and the term "refers to mainly tacit consent on the part of society toward the activities of the business" (Demuijnck and Fasterling, 2016: 675). According to Rooney et al. (2014: 209), a social license refers to "an informal agreement that is granted by communities and relevant stakeholders to an organization or industry working in the local area":

> Organizations holding a social license may not even recognize they have one. However, when a social license is removed it becomes obvious to all, incurring both human and economic costs that sometimes can be irreparable.

Haines et al. (2022: 184) examined "how social control in the form of community pressure might be used to control corporate harm and shape business conduct in a more socially responsible direction". They suggested a social license to civilize, control, or repel corporate activity. They defined a social license as acceptance of a business or business activity within a particular community. The social license adds to the legal license to operate business activities. The social license is predominantly centered on social permission for business activity, where the media, social movements, and citizen watchdogs exert pressure, demand change, and bring enterprises to account. The social license is a visible manifestation of a commitment to corporate social responsibility regarding agreement between company and community in business operations. Similarly, Sale (2021) defined social license as the acceptance of business or organization by the relevant communities and stakeholders, and Cui et al. (2016: 775) referred to the SLO as "a community's acceptance or approval of a specific company project or of the entire company's ongoing operations in the community". Melé and

Armengou (2016) referred to social license as the acceptance of the expansion of profit-seeking business that can affect community life.

The rise of social media, nongovernment organizations, as well as the knowledge level among citizens has led to the strengthening of stakeholder demands (Panda and Sangle, 2019: 1085):

> As a result, firms often find themselves in conflicts. The cost of these conflicts for the firm is the opportunity cost of future projects due to loss of reputation, and for the stakeholders, it is the loss of opportunities, both social and economic, that could been brought by the projects. The tension between firms and stakeholders creates a dynamic environment where following compliance is not enough and social acceptance is equally important as government licenses. Such an acceptance is termed as 'social license to operate' (SLO). SLO exists when a project is seen as having the broad, ongoing approval and acceptance of society to conduct its activities.

The value of a social license lies in both the defensive and the offensive dimensions. The defensive dimension is concerned with avoiding criticism and obstacles in business activities from skeptical representatives of the community. Executives do not like bad press and activist campaigns, and they want to avoid consumer reactions. Companies do not want critical attention from various supervisory authorities, and they avoid becoming negative topics in municipal committees and government agencies. Companies want a social license that can "prevent demonstrations, boycotts, shutdowns, negative publicity, and the increases in regulation that are a hallmark of publicness" (Sale, 2021: 820). The defensive dimension is a matter of violation of the license or even loss of the license. Such circumstances "can lead to serious delays and costs for organizations, reduced market access, boycotts or protests, community anger, increased regulations, loss of reputation, and, in extreme instances, the failure of a project, organization and/or industry" (Hurst et al., 2020: 1). For example in the Netherlands, the loss of the SLO caused Groningen gas to stop its operations making substantial volumes of gas being left in the ground (Beukel and Geuns, 2019).

The offensive dimension of social license value is concerned with benefits and advantages in business activities from supportive and enthusiastic representatives of the community. Executives do like favorable press, and they enjoy consumers' expression of satisfaction. Companies want positive attention – or no attention – from various supervisory authorities, and they avoid becoming topics in municipal committees and government agencies, unless they are called upon as resources to solve state problems. As a resource, an enterprise can be an enabler of solutions preferred by politicians that they cannot accomplish without the help of the enterprise. Ideally as a resource, the enterprise has unique expertise in the field that can be applied to solve problems perceived challenging in the community. The value of social dimension in the offensive dimension includes "the generation of legitimacy, trust, and credibility among stakeholders; improved corporate reputation; long-term business success; ongoing access to resources; improved market competitiveness; strengthened stakeholder relationships; and positive effects on employees" (Hurst et al. 2020: 1).

Danish Bestseller in Myanmar

The first fraud investigation report to be reviewed here was written by Danish law firm Offersen Christoffersen for the company Bestseller that operated 2,700 branded chain stores across 38 markets worldwide, and their products were sold in 15,000 multi-brand and department stores. In 2022, the junta executed four democracy activists (Nystuen, 2022). Some of the Bestseller garments were produced in Myanmar also after the military coup in the country. Bestseller faced serious criticism (Einarsdottir, 2021) including negative comments from the Danish foreign minister (Ritzau, 2021):

> The military is in power in Myanmar. According to the UN report, factories that Bestseller uses are effectively owned by the military. Two of the factories used by Danish clothing giant Bestseller in Myanmar in recent years are cooperating with the military in the country, according to a UN report. And this could have consequences, Denmark's foreign minister Jeppe Kofod told the newspaper. He is greatly exasperated by the cooperation.
>
> – I would like to make it quite clear that I think it is highly problematic if Bestseller chooses to have clothes produced in factories controlled by the military dictatorship in Myanmar, according to the UN, he told the newspaper.

Bestseller also faced serious criticism from the clothing and fashion industry that could harm the company's outlets and their brands (Einarsdottir, 2021):

> Bestseller receives criticism for alleged military connections in crisis-stricken Myanmar. The Danish fashion giant Bestseller is once again in bad weather. This time it is due to their connections in crisis-hit Myanmar. Bestseller, which owns about twenty fashion brands such as Vero Moda, Only and Jack & Jones, produces at three factories in the industrial zone Ngwe Pinlae outside the city of Yangon. A report from 2019 to the UN Human Rights Council points out that the zone is controlled by the industrial conglomerate Myanmar Economic Holdings Limited (MEHL). Their owners consist of the military and individuals in the military leadership, among them chief of staff Min Aung Hlaing who is mainly responsible for the recent bloody attacks on civilians in the country where over 700 people have been killed, writes Fashion Forum.

However, Bestseller kept its legal license to operate as the fraud examiners made an assessment that the company did not violate any sanctions against the Myanmar regime. In fact, the fraud examiners made the recommendation of continuing procurements in Myanmar because of employment and thus income for poor local citizens (Larsen, 2021; Reed and Nilsson, 2021). The report by Christoffersen and Mikkelsen (2021) was obviously not sufficient to regain the social license since global and local unions were still skeptical to business activities in Myanmar. The only relevant attempt to regain the license seemed to be by not placing new orders in Myanmar. The argument that poor workers and their families would suffer income loss was contradicted by the argument that the well-being of garment workers in the country was not guaranteed.

The report by Christoffersen and Mikkelsen (2021) that asserted legal license and attempted to achieve social license was published on May 10, 2021. Since the attempt failed, Bestseller announced August 27 in the same year that they had stopped their business in Myanmar already, and that they would place no new orders (Bestseller, 2021):

> Following the announcement from IndustryALL Global Union and their Myanmar affiliate, the Industrial Workers Federation of Myanmar (IWEM), Bestseller will not place new orders in the country until an impact assessment and dialogue with experts, NGOs, trade unions and other relevant stakeholders with a clear focus on the wellbeing of garment workers in Myanmar has been conducted.

Because of the criticism, Bestseller was "among the companies that froze orders from the south-east Asian country because of human rights concerns and civil unrest" (Reed and Nilsson, 2021). The following year, Bestseller had still suspended their business in Myanmar (Reed, 2022):

> In garments, multinational companies such as H&M, Bestseller and Primark brought in supply-chain investors and created jobs, mostly women, during Myanmar's decade of democratic transition, which ended with a coup. While some have suspended their Myanmar operations, others are quietly still buying.

The EU imposed "sanctions against almost two dozen Myanmar government and military officials as well as a state-backed oil and gas group" (Meixler and Creery, 2022). Bestseller headquartered in Denmark did indeed want to resume business in Myanmar again (Larsen, 2021), but regaining the social license was more important to the firm (Reed and Nilsson, 2021).

In recent decades, the military in Myanmar has gained control over many business enterprises in the country. They control large parts of the land where private citizens, hotel owners, and business executives have to pay substantial fees for renting property (Wikan, 2022).

Social Housing by Obos in Norway

The second fraud investigation report to be reviewed here was written by audit firm KPMG for the cooperative Obos that is Norway's largest housing developer. Obos engages in the development and sale of homes and properties as well as property management and real estate brokerage. Obos is a cooperative member organization with half a million members. The cooperative was established in 1929 to provide a solution to housing shortages for low-income families in the capital of Oslo. After World War II, Obos played an important role of building apartment blocks on the eastside of Oslo. The rich people live on the west side of Oslo, while the less fortunate live on the eastside of the city center. Apartments were affordable for poor families as Obos required minimal deposits and favorable loans (Oesterud, 2016). To be qualified to buy the most attractive Obos apartments, buyers had to document membership for several decades when moving into the 1950s, 1960s, and 1970s. There was a strong social profile in all Obos operations that granted management both a legal and an SLO (Holm, 2021).

The social license was violated by management when they started to build extremely expensive apartments and sold apartment buildings to landlords (Jacobsen, 2020; Lorch-Falch and Tomter, 2021). Members reacted to the deviations, but discovered that they had no saying. They wrote newspaper articles about the change away from the basic vision and mission of the cooperative (Holm, 2021; Stang, 2021). Members argued that Obos had lost its soul (Hegtun, 2021). The revolt included demonstrations in front of the Obos headquarters with the demand from members that the cooperative is ours (Sørgjeld, 2021). The revolt leader requested that the chief executive be removed from his position (Lorch-Falch et al., 2021). Some protesters suggested that executives suffered from megalomania that refers to a mental disorder characterized by an excessive increase in attention to one's own person (Lundgaard and Sørgjeld, 2021). Protesters disliked the comradely tone between elite members who supposedly negotiated with each other (Lorch-Falch and Tomter, 2021).

As a reaction to the criticism, the Obos board hired fraud examiners from KPMG (2021) to review the allegations. However, similar to the Bestseller investigation, fraud examiners only reviewed whether or not the legal license had been violated. The examiners concluded that the recent transactions with rich people did not violate rules and regulations at Obos since it constituted only a minor part of the overall business.

Revolt leaders in the Obos membership were not happy with the legal review. Member allegations of social license violations by Obos management in their operations were still concerned with four issues:

1. The mission and vision of Obos are to secure pleasant and affordable housing for members of the cooperative. They should build ordinary homes for ordinary people. It was a violation of the cooperative purpose to sell two complete residential buildings with many apartments to a landlord whose business purpose is to make money on renting the apartments to tenants.
2. The sales price achieved in the anti-purpose transaction was below market value as estimated by Norwegian kroner per square meter. Obos thus suffered a loss compared to selling each apartment separately to its members.

The giveaway price and the following loss seemed caused in close personal relationships between individuals on the seller and the buyer sides, as exemplified later.

3. There was a close relationship and comradely tone between the CEO at Obos and the representative of the buyer causing impartiality in connection with the sale of the apartment blocks. The two privileged persons communicated directly with each other about the transaction with minor involvement of governance bodies at Obos.
4. There was also a close relationship between the executive vice president in charge of housing development at Obos and the relevant family members who invested in the purchase of the apartment blocks. The vice president's impartiality was not at all trustworthy, and he was too late removed from his involvement in the transaction.

One of the community revolt leaders posted on his blog why the social license was lost as the aforementioned issues illustrate that Obos is no longer a member-governed cooperative institution. He mentioned a number of incidents in addition to those listed earlier, such as favoring employees in the Obos organization at the expense of other members, demonstrating arrogant executive behavior, and granting hunting rights to privileged individuals. The revolt leader wrote that the members are the true owners of the cooperative (Larsen, 2021):

> Obos is owned by the members. The members exercise their corporate governance through the general assembly meeting and the elected general meeting representatives. Put at the forefront are the board and administration who are servants of the owners. More nuanced, we can state that the board and administration must ensure that they act in accordance with the owners' wishes. In this context, several of the above issues are relevant: The reason why they have created attention and engagement is obviously that they are perceived as controversial. It could have been okay if the positions taken were rooted in the members, but they were not.

It was obvious that Obos management intended never again to repeat the criticized transactions. Furthermore, member involvement was enhanced by establishing a new organizational structure that would give members a real chance of influence. A democratization process started in 2022. Furthermore, company representatives learned that an a priori assertion of their legal right to manage properties freely would be met by anger and defiance. Relying on their legal rights was seen as arrogant and likely to lead to another member uproar.

To offer ordinary homes to ordinary people while the prices in the capital Oslo were still very high and often a barrier to entry, Obos introduced a new financial model caused by the member revolt. According to the new model, Obos offers members the option of buying half of the apartment and rent the other half from Obos. Over time, the member has the option of increasing ownership share from 50% by down payments to Obos at the discretion of the owner's financial situation (Lundgaard, 2022).

Icelandic Samherji Fishing in Namibia

The third fraud investigation report to be reviewed here was written by law firm Wikborg Rein for the seafood company Samherji on Iceland (Kibar, 2020a, 2020b). According to a whistleblower, Samherji had bribed government officials to obtain fishing rights on the west coast of Namibia (Cotterill, 2019; Kleinfeld, 2019, 2020, 2021; Menges, 2020). While Samherji denied disclosure of the complete investigation report, they admitted that corruption had taken place. However, their initial account was that a bad apple in the organization locally was responsible without any knowledge or involvement on the part of company (Samherji, 2019a, 2019b, 2020a, 2020b). Thereby the firm attempted to keep the legal license (Seljan et al., 2019). The legal license was challenged when Namibian officials requested Samherji executives to appear in court to be prosecuted for the corruption together with local government ministers (Ciric, 2022).

The late apology statement by Samherji (2021) was probably not enough for regaining the SLO. Media reports had emphasized reputation damage not only to the company but also to Iceland (Bjarnadóttir, 2020: 34):

> Prime minister, Katrin Jakobsdóttir, said to Mbl "that if allegations against Samherji are substantiated, it is a matter of great concern for the Icelandic economy and shame for Samherji. The issue can affect the nation as a whole". In the same article, it is stated that Iceland was placed on the grey list of the FATF, an international working group on measures against money laundering and terrorist financing, almost a month ago. Katrin says then that being on the list is disappointing and that she has concerns about our reputation but states that Samherji's case "is not descriptive of Icelandic society as a whole".

According to Reuters (2019), Samherji had transferred more than US$70 million through a shell company in the tax haven Marshall Islands from 2011 to 2018. Samherji transferred the money through bank accounts in DNB Norway. The bank's largest shareholder is the Norwegian state, which holds 34% stake in the bank (Reuters, 2019):

> The money consisted partly of proceeds from Samherji's questionable and possibly unlawful operations in Namibia where the company bribes officials to get secure access to fishing quotas. The company in the Marshall Islands was used to pay salaries to the crews of Samherji's factory trawlers. These trawlers fished horse mackerel in Mauritania, Morocco, and Namibia.

It would indeed be a challenge for Samherji to regain its SLO. The national reputation problem added to the challenge. Stakeholders abroad might remember the banking collapse in Iceland, where greedy Icelanders were in the lead roles. The Panama Papers revealed that wealthy Icelanders had the world record in the number of offshore accounts relative to the number of citizens (Bjarnadóttir, 2020).

Shortcomings of Legal Perspectives

All three case studies help illustrate the shortcomings of only legal perspectives in the work of fraud examiners when conducting internal investigations for client organizations. Bestseller headquartered in Denmark was dependent on the SLO and therefore terminated its business in Myanmar. Obos in Norway was dependent on member acceptance and will therefore avoid deviance from their basic idea of social housing. Samherji in Iceland was dependent on local acceptance by the government as well as citizens in the country and therefore made an apology for corruption, although without accepting the blame.

Anecdotal evidence from these three investigation reports illustrates the emerging perspective of the SLO becoming important. It seems not sufficient anymore for acceptance of business practice simply based on legal perspectives. In knowledge societies such as Denmark, Norway, and Iceland, citizens do not trust the criminal justice system to the extent that all forms of wrongdoing are covered in statutes, and that all incidents of wrongdoing are prosecuted. In a criminological perspective, crime is defined by two characteristics. The first is that an incident is wrong. The second is that an incident should be punished. Crime is then wrongdoing that requires punishment, while law is statutory principles, which may or may not cover the specific wrongdoing. In this line of reasoning, Friedrichs (2020: 19) mentioned humanistic definition of crime:

> A humanistic definition of crime focuses on demonstrable harm, more often than not coming from powerful elements of society, rather than legal status as the basis for something being designated a crime.

Perceived seriousness has been studied as a factor that can influence the involvement or lack of involvement of the criminal justice system in cases of white-collar and corporate crime. For example, Cullen et al. (2020) studied public opinion about white-collar crime, and they found public willingness to punish white-collar offenders. However, they found that public opinion about inflicting punishment on white-collar criminals varies depending on clarity of culpability, typical harm, violation of trust, and need to show equity. Sources of authority for assessing violations of the SLO can, however, apply different criteria when determining the seriousness of wrongdoing.

There are important implications of perspectives presented in this chapter for future fraud examinations as well as corporate crime research. Fraud examiners might look beyond legal issues when conducting internal investigations in client organizations, as the reasons for harm and punishment might be found in social issues. Similarly, corporate crime research might consider punishment beyond the criminal justice system of prison and fine by looking at executive terminations and changes in business practices.

In conclusion, studies as well as examinations of white-collar and corporate crime tend to apply the legal definition of crime where corporate escape from allegations and accusations is assumed if there is no involvement of the criminal justice system. The emerging perspective of a SLO tells a different story. As illustrated by three case studies in this chapter, violations of the social license do have consequences. There is an interesting avenue here for future white-collar and corporate crime research in distinguishing between punishment from violations of the legal license and punishment from violations of the SLO where perceived seriousness can be introduced as an important factor.

References

Baba, S., Hemissi, O., Berrahou, Z. and Traiki, C. (2021). The spatiotemporal dimension of the social license to operate: The case of a landfill facility in Algeria, *Management International – Mi*, 25 (4), 247–266.

Bestseller. (2021). *Not Placing New Orders in Myanmar*, Bestseller, www.bestseller.com, retrieved August 27.

Beukel, J. and Geuns, L. (2019). *Groningen Gas: The Loss of a Social License to Operate*, Hague Centre for Strategic Studies, the Netherlands.

Bjarnadóttir, S.M. (2020). *Iceland's Involvement in Bribes and Corruption in Namibia's Fishing Industry – Discourse Analysis of the Media*, master thesis in culture communication and globalization, September 15, Aalborg University, Denmark.

Christoffersen, J. and Mikkelsen, M.S. (2021). *Redegjørelse: Bestseller A/S' samfundsansvar i Myanmar (Statement: Bestseller Ltd.'s Social Responsibility in Myanmar)*, law firm Offersen Christoffersen, Copenhagen, Denmark, 122 pages, May 10.

Ciric, J. (2022). Namibia requests Interpol's aid in extraditing former Samherji executives, *Iceland Review*, www.icelandreview.com, retrieved February 21.

Cotterill, J. (2019). Two Namibian ministers resign in Icelandic fishing scandal, *Financial Times*, www.ft.com, retrieved November 14.

Cui, J., Jo, H. and Velasquez, M.G. (2016). Community religion, employees, and the social license to operate, *Journal of Business Ethics*, 136, 775–807.

Cullen, F.T., Chouhy, C. and Jonson, C.L. (2020). Public opinion about white-collar crime, in: Rorie, M.L. (editor), *The Handbook of White-Collar Crime*, Wiley & Sons, Hoboken, NJ, chapter 14, pages 211–228.

Demuijnck, G. and Fasterling, B. (2016). The social license to operate, *Journal of Business Ethics*, 136, 675–685.

Einarsdottir, I.E. (2021). Bestseller får kritikk for påståtte militærforbindelser i kriserammede Myanmar (Bestseller receives criticism for alleged military connections in Crisis-Stricken Myanmar), Fashion industry magazine *Melk & Honning*, www.melkoghonning.no, retrieved April 20.

Friedrichs, D.O. (2020). White collar crime: Definitional debates and the case for a typological approach, in: Rorie, M. (editor), *The Handbook of White-Collar Crime*, John Wiley & Sons, Hoboken, NJ, chapter 2, pages 16–31.

Gottschalk, P. (2016). Private policing of financial crime: Key issues in the investigation business in Norway, *European Journal of Policing Studies*, 3 (3), 292–314.

Gottschalk, P. (2020). Private policing of white-collar crime: Case studies of internal investigations by fraud examiners, *Police Practice and Research*, 21 (6), 717–738.

Gottschalk, P. (2021). *Private Policing of Economic Crime – Case Studies of Internal Investigations by Fraud Examiners*, Routledge, London, UK.

Gottschalk, P. and Gunnesdal, L. (2018). *White-Collar Crime in the Shadow Economy: Lack of Detection, Investigation, and Conviction compared to Social Security Fraud*, Palgrave Pivot, Palgrave Macmillan, Springer Publishing, London, UK.

Gottschalk, P. and Tcherni-Buzzeo, M. (2017). Reasons for gaps in crime reporting: The case of white-collar criminals investigated by private fraud examiners in Norway, *Deviant Behavior*, 38 (3), 267–281.

Haines, F., Bice, S., Einfeld, C. and Sullivan, H. (2022). Countering corporate power through social control: What does a social license offer? *The British Journal of Criminology*, 62, 184–199.

Hegtun, H. (2021). Granskere har gått inn i PC-en og telefonen hans. "Helt greit", sier presset Obos-sjef (Investigators Have Entered the PC and His Phone. "Quit All Right", Says the Pressured Obos Boss), weekly magazine *A-magasinet*, www.aftenposten.no, retrieved June 12.

Holm, E.D. (2021). Er Obos løsningen eller problemet? (Is Obos the Solution or the Problem?), daily Norwegian newspaper *Aftenposten*, www.aftenposten.no, retrieved June 21.

Hurst, B., Johnston, K.A. and Lane, A.B. (2020). Engaging for a social license to operate, *Public Relations Review*, 40, published online doi: 10.1016/j.pubrev.2020.101931.

Jacobsen, S. (2020). Har solgt 182 leiligheter for 936 millioner (Have Sold 182 Apartments for 936 Million), daily Norwegian business newspaper *Finansavisen*, www.finansavisen.no, retrieved December 3.

Kibar, O. (2020a). Varsleren (The whistleblower), daily Norwegian business newspaper *Dagens Næringsliv*, Saturday, August 8, pages 32–37.

Kibar, O. (2020b). Både ryddet opp for og gransket fiskerikjempe (Both Cleaned Up and Investigated Fishing Giant), daily Norwegian business newspaper *Dagens Næringsliv*, Tuesday, September 1, pages 18–19.

King, M. (2012). The contemporary role of private investigators in Australia, *Criminal Justice Matters*, 89 (1), 12–14.

King, M. (2020). Financial fraud investigative interviewing – Corporate investigators' beliefs and practices: A qualitative inquiry, *Journal of Financial Crime*, published online 10.1108/JFC-08-2020-0158.

King, M. (2021). Profiting from a tainted trade: Private investigators' views on the popular culture glamorization of their trade, *Journal of Criminological Research Policy and Practice*, published online doi: 10.1108/JCRPP-07-2020-0050.

Kleinfeld, J. (2019). Anatomy of a bribe: A deep dive into an underworld of corruption, news organization *Al Jazeera*, www.aljazeera.com, retrieved December 1.

Kleinfeld, J. (2020). Corruption allegations in Namibian 5G deal with Huawei, news organization *Al Jazeera*, www.aljazeera.com, retrieved July 15.

Kleinfeld, J. (2021). Namibian president caught in new fishing corruption allegations, news organization *Al Jazeera*, www.aljazeera.com, retrieved April 2.

KPMG. (2021). *Ulven-transaksjonen – Granskingsrapport til styret i Obos (The Ulven Transaction – Investigation Report to the Board at Obos)*, law firm KPMG, Oslo, Norway, 34 pages.

Larsen, B.E. (2021). Noen betraktninger før Obos' generalforsamling 2021 (Some Considerations Before Obos' General Assembly 2021), *Benjamin E. Larsen's blog*, www.benjaminlarsen.net, retrieved June 19.

Lorch-Falch, S. and Tomter, L. (2021). Slaget om Obos (The battle of Obos), public Norwegian broadcasting corporation, *NRK*, www.nrk.no, retrieved June 22.

Lorch-Falch, S., Tomter, L. and Engebretsen, D.K. (2021). Obos-opprøret tapte kamp om maktseter (The Obos Uprising Lost the Battle for Seats), Norwegian public broadcasting *NRK*, www.nrk.no, retrieved June 22.

Lundgaard, H. (2022). Hun hadde ikke sjanse til å kjøpe leilighet. Nå skal flere tusen få samme muligheten (She Had No Chance of Buying an Apartment. Now Several Thousand Will Have the Same Opportunity), daily Norwegian newspaper *Aftenposten*, Thursday, February 24, page 6.

Lundgaard, H. and Sørgjeld, C. (2021). Milliardene renner inn i Obos-kassen. Men mer enn 80 prosent kommer ikke fra boligbygging (The billions are floating into the Obos cash register. But more than 80 percent do not come from housing construction), daily Norwegian newspaper *Aftenposten*, www.aftenposten.no, retrieved June 21.

Meerts, C. (2020). Corporate investigations: Beyond notions of public-private relations, *Journal of Contemporary Criminal Justice*, 36 (1), 86–100.

Meerts, C. (2021). Struggles in cooperation: Public-private relations in the investigation of internal financial crime in the Netherlands, in: Lord, N., Inzelt, E., Huisman, W. and Faria, R. (editors), *European White-Collar Crime: Exploring the Nature of European Realities*, Bristol University Press, Bristol, UK.

Meixler, E. and Creery, J. (2022). EU targets Myanmar's lucrative energy sector in latest sanctions, *Financial Times*, www.ft.com, retrieved February 22.

Melé, D. and Armengou, J. (2016). Moral legitimacy in controversial projects and its relationships with social license to operate: A case study, *Journal of Business Ethics*, 136, 729–742.

Menges, W. (2020). Fishrot lawyer fights to stay on as executor, *The Namibian*, www.namibian.com, retrieved August 6.

Nystuen, M.M. (2022). Demokratiforkjempere henrettet av Myanmars militærjunta (Pro-democracy activists executed by Myanmar's military junta, daily Norwegian newspaper *Aftenposten*, Tuesday, July 26, page 10.

Oesterud, T.I. (2016). The prices for OBOS housing in Oslo increased by 11.5 percent, *Norway Today*, www.norwaytoday.info, retrieved April 1.

Panda, S.S. and Sangle, S. (2019). An exploratory study to investigate the relationship between social license to operate and sustainable development strategies, *Sustainable Development*, 27, 1085–1095.

Reed, J. (2022). Stay or go: The dilemma for multinationals in Myanmar, *Financial Times*, www.ft.com, retrieved January 25.

Reed, J. and Nilsson, P. (2021). H&M and Primark resume Myanmar orders for first time since coup, *Financial Times*, www.ft.com, retrieved May 21.

Reuters. (2019). Norway's DNB investigates allegedly improper Samherji payments to Namibia, *Under Current News*, www.undercurrentnews.com, retrieved November 15.

Ritzau. (2021). Kofod fortørnet over Bestsellers brug af fabrikker i Myanmar (Kofod upset over Bestseller's use of factories in Myanmar), Danish broadcasting *TV2*, www.nyheder.tv2.dk, retrieved April 18.

Rooney, D., Leach, J. and Ashworth, P. (2014). Doing the social in social license, *Social Epistemology*, 28 (3–4), 209–218.

Saenz, C. (2019). Building legitimacy and trust between a mining company and a community to earn social license to operate: A Peruvian case study, *Corporate Social Responsibility and Environmental Management*, 26 (2), 296–306.

Sale, H.A. (2021). The corporate purpose of social license, *Sothern California Law Review*, 94 (4), 785–842.

Samherji. (2019a). *Statement from Samherji: Press release*, www.samherji.is, retrieved November 11 by margret@samherji.is.
Samherji. (2019b). *Samherji CEO Steps Aside While Investigations Are Ongoing*, www.samherji.is, retrieved November 14 by margret@samherji.is.
Samherji. (2020a). *Samherji's Namibia Investigation Finalized*, Samherji ice fresh seafood, website www.samherji.is/en/moya/news/samherjis-namibia-investigation-finalized, Akureyri, Iceland, published by margret@samherji.is.
Samherji. (2020b). *Fees for Quotas Were in Line With Market Prices in Namibia*, Samherji seafood, www.samherji.is, retrieved September 25 by Margrét Ólafsdóttir, margret@samherji.is.
Samherji. (2021). *Statement and Apology From Samherji*, Samherji seafood, www.samherji.is, retrieved June 22.
Seljan, H., Kjartansson, A. and Drengsson, S.A. (2019). What Samherji wanted hidden, Kveikur at *RUV*, public broadcasting on Iceland, www.ruv.is/kveikur/fishrot/fishrot.
Stang, F. (2021). Obos saboterer sitt eget samfunnsoppdrag (Obos sabotages its own social mission), daily Norwegian newspaper *Aftenposten*, www.aftenposten.no, retrieved June 21.
Sørgjeld, C. (2021). På utsiden demonstrerte Obos-opprøret. På innsiden ble de nedstemt (On the outside, the Obos demonstration revolted. On the inside, they were voted down), daily Norwegian newspaper *Aftenposten*, www.aftenposten.no, retrieved June 22.
Wikan, V.S. (2022). Norge fordømte kuppet i Myanmar. Så brukte de millioner på svartelistet hotel (Norway condemned the coup in Myanmar. Then they spent millions on blacklisted hotels), daily Norwegian newspaper *Aftenposten*, Wednesday, August 17, page 6.

8 Bottom-Up Corporate Control

Traditionally, control in organizations is concerned with top-down approaches, where executives attempt to direct their employees to align their work with organizational objectives. This chapter addresses the challenge of directing executives to align their work with laws, rules, and ethics. Various bottom-up approaches are explored based on the theory of convenience. The bottom-up approaches to executive compliance focus on organizational measures to make white-collar crime less convenient for potential offenders. Bottom-up control refers to the manner in which organizational members can use different types of control mechanisms – such as whistleblowing, transparency, resource access, or culture – to monitor, measure, and evaluate executives' avoidance of deviant behaviors and influence them toward achieving the organization's goals in efficient and effective ways.

Traditionally, control was all about executives attempt to direct their employees' attention, behaviors, and performance to align with the organization's goals and objectives. More recently, the control perspective has extended to include customization and transmutation of control mechanisms, where transmutation captures the idea that organizational units implement control regimes that are different from the mandated control mechanism from management (Chown, 2020: 711):

> Researchers are now beginning to bring these literatures together, marrying the top-down managerial perspective with the lived experiences of employees throughout the organization.

This book takes a new approach by turning the challenge of control upside down as it focuses on control of executives who find white-collar crime convenient. The bottom-up approach to executive compliance focuses on organizational measures to make white-collar crime less convenient for potential offenders. Compliance refers to obeying the formal rules and regulations in force at a given time and place (Durand et al., 2019).

Control is concerned with a negative discrepancy between the desired and current state of affairs. Control mechanisms attempt to reduce the discrepancy through adaptive action in the form of behavioral reactions (Direnzo and Greenhaus, 2011). Control mechanisms attempt to influence and manage

DOI: 10.4324/9781003379249-11

the process, content, and outcome of work (Kownatzki et al., 2013). Control involves processes of negotiation in which various strategies are developed to produce particular outcomes. Control is therefore a dynamic process that regulates behavior through a set of modes, rules, or strategies (Gill, 2019).

Corporate white-collar crime control is mainly focused on attempts to prevent, detect, and reduce negative discrepancy between desired and current state of executive affairs. Control attempts to influence the process of work in normative ways. Control targets executive behavior to ensure that executive individuals perform tasks in a legitimate manner. As argued by Kownatzki et al. (2013), behavior control relies on subjective, organizationally relevant criteria to assess executive activity and measures performance in the context of long-term progress toward the development of a particular way of doing things. Behavior control not only provides checks and balances for executive performance, but also provides a common vocabulary that facilitates dialogue among stakeholders and fosters the creation of ambitious behavioral norms. When behavior rather that outcome is the focus, controls may provide a buffer for external short-term pressures.

Within an organization, struggles are about conceptions of control (Yue et al., 2013). Control mechanisms have to satisfy a number of requirements to be successful, such as fairness perceived by controlled individuals (Long et al., 2011). Social control is based on attachment, commitment, involvement, and belief, where a control mechanism is informal punishment in the appearance of shaming (Amry and Meliala, 2021).

At its core, top-down control refers to the manner in which "an organization's managers can use different types of control mechanisms – such as financial incentives, performance management, or culture – to monitor, measure, and evaluate workers' behaviors and influence them toward achieving the organization's goals in efficient and effective ways" (Chown, 2020: 713). Similarly at its core, bottom-up control refers to the manner in which organizational members can use different types of control mechanisms – such as whistleblowing, transparency, resource access, or culture – to monitor, measure, and evaluate executives' avoidance of deviant behaviors and influence them toward achieving the organization's goals in efficient and effective ways. While the hierarchical structure remains with executives at the top of the organization in charge of the business, bottom-up control is a matter of stakeholder involvement in compliance. While top-down control is often a formal and rigid system, bottom-up control can be an informal and flexible system.

When noticing wrongdoing at the top of the organization, improvisation might be a key capability for organizational members. Capability is the ability to perform (Paruchuri et al., 2021). Improvisation refers to the spontaneous process by which planning and execution happen at the same time (Mannucci et al., 2021). Rather than following formal reporting lines to people who are not trustworthy, improvisation is a matter of spontaneous action in response to unanticipated occurrences, in which individuals find a way to manage the unexpected problem.

The theoretical perspective introduced in this chapter to discuss a bottom-up approach to executive deviance is crime convenience (Asting and Gottschalk, 2022; Braaten and Vaughn, 2019; Dearden and Gottschalk, 2020; Stadler and Gottschalk, 2022). Reducing crime convenience is a matter of disturbing financial motives based on possibilities and threats, disturbing organizational opportunities to commit and conceal crime, and disturbing willingness for deviant behavior.

First in this chapter, the challenge of controlling chief executive officers is discussed. Next in this chapter, the perspective of crime convenience is introduced, followed by a discussion of bottom-up approaches to executive status, resource access, organizational deterioration, lack of guardianship and control, and criminal market forces as convenience themes in the organizational opportunity structure.

Chief Executive Offenders

Research has documented the failure of the traditional top-down approach to executive compliance, in particular control of chief executive officers (Bosse and Phillips, 2006; Galvin et al., 2015; Khanna et al., 2015; Pillay and Kluvers, 2014; Williams, 2008; Zahra, 2005; Zhu and Chen, 2015).

Some CEOs will employ illegal or objectionable means in striving to reach goals. This type of behavior is not necessarily different from the behavior of others in positions of power and authority (e.g., politicians, officers of universities, church officials, heads of major philanthropies), but the degrees of freedom enjoyed by many CEOs make the CEO position nevertheless very special in terms of convenience. For example, a CEO may conveniently cheat and defraud owners (Khanna et al., 2015; Williams, 2008; Zahra et al., 2005) because there is lack of oversight and guardianship in the agency relationship (Bosse and Phillips, 2016; Pillay and Kluvers, 2014).

While there is considerable variance in narcissistic tendencies across CEOs, many CEOs have narcissistic personality traits such as self-focus, self-admiration, a sense of entitlement, and a sense of superiority (Zhu and Chen, 2015: 35):

> Narcissistic CEOs tend to favor bold actions, such as large acquisitions, that attract attention. They are less responsive than other CEOs to objective indicators of their performance and more responsive to social praise. For instance, while narcissistic CEOs tend to aggressively adopt technological discontinuities, they are especially likely to do so when such behavior is expected to garner attention and admiration from external audiences.

Galvin et al. (2015: 163) found that some CEOs suffer from narcissistic identification with the organization:

> It is not uncommon to learn of individuals in positions of power and responsibility, especially CEOs, who exploit and undermine their organizations

> for personal gain. A circumstance not well explained in the literature, however, is that some of those individuals may highly identify with their organizations, meaning that they see little difference between their identity and the organization's identity – between their interests and the organization's interest. This presents a paradox, because organizational identification typically is not noted for its adverse consequences on the organization.

The CEO is the only person at that top hierarchical level in the organization. Below the CEO, there are a number of executives at the same hierarchical level. Above the CEO, there are a number of board members at the same hierarchical level. However, the CEO is alone at his or her level. The CEO is supposed to face control by the board, but the board only meets occasionally to discuss business cases. Executives below the CEO are typically appointed by the CEO and typically loyal to the CEO (Bendiktsson, 2010; Bigley and Wiersma, 2002; Chatterjee and Pollock, 2017; Chen and Nadkarni, 2017; Davidson et al., 2019; Gamache and McNamara, 2019; Gangloff et al., 2016; Khanna et al., 2015; König et al., 2020; McClelland et al., 2010; Schnatterly et al., 2018; Shen, 2003; Zhu and Chen, 2015).

The board of directors is typically incapable of controlling chief executive activities (Ghannam et al., 2019). Examples of former CEOs as white-collar crime convicts include Thomas Middelhoff at Alcantor in Germany, Boris Benulic at Kraft & Kultur in Sweden, Hisao Tanaka at Toshiba Corporation in Japan, Are Blomhoff at Betanien Foundation in Norway, and Trond Kristoffersen at Finance Credit in Norway – in addition to all the well-known names in the United States.

Control of executives is necessary to ensure the legitimate success and survival of organizations. As argued by Gill (2019), there are two important conceptual dimensions that draw together insights from studies of control and resistance in the workplace. The dimension of compatibility considers executives' subjective experiences of the fit between their personhood and modes of control, where alignment can inspire fulfillment and misalignment can prompt suffering and deviant behavior. The dimension of coherence considers executives' perception of the consistency between modes, which can be fragmented or unified to reinforce organizationally prescribed compliance and ethics, where "ethics is not equivalent to laws" (Dion, 2019: 836).

Offender Crime Convenience

White-collar crime is financial crime based on the social and occupational position of the offender committed by a person of respectability and high social influence in the course of the offender's occupation (Sutherland, 1939, 1983). This offender-based definition emphasizes some combination of the actor's high social status, power, and respectability as the key features of white-collar crime (Benson et al., 2021) as well as the violation of stakeholder trust (Sohoni and Rorie, 2021).

The deviant behavior by white-collar offenders can be explained by the theory of convenience that suggests a triangle of financial motive, organizational opportunity, and personal willingness (Asting and Gottschalk, 2022; Braaten and Vaughn, 2019; Dearden and Gottschalk, 2020; Stadler and Gottschalk, 2022). Convenience is savings in time and effort, reduced pain and strain, and other factors that make a certain path or choice attractive. Convenience is the state of being able to proceed with something with little effort or difficulty, avoiding pain and strain (Collier and Kimes, 2012; Mai and Olsen, 2016; Sundström and Radon, 2015).

How privileged individuals in the elite think and feel about time and effort varies. Chen and Nadkarni (2017: 34) found that many CEOs can be characterized by time urgency where they have the feeling of being chronically hurried:

> Time urgency is a relatively stable trait. Time-urgent people are acutely aware of the passage of time and feel chronically hurried. They often create aggressive internal deadlines and use them as markers of the timely completion of team tasks. They regularly check work progress, increase others' awareness of the remaining time, and motivate others to accomplish commitments within the allotted time.

Convenience is a concept that was theoretically mainly associated with efficiency in time savings. Today, convenience is associated with a number of other characteristics, such as reduced effort and reduced pain. Convenience is linked to terms such as fast, easy, and safe. Convenience says something about attractiveness and accessibility. A convenient individual is not necessarily neither bad nor lazy. On the contrary, the person can be seen as smart and rational (Sundström and Radon, 2015).

Convenience orientation is conceptualized as the value that individuals and organizations place on actions with inherent characteristics of saving time and effort as well as avoiding strain and pain. Convenience orientation can be considered a value-like construct that influences behavior and decision-making. Mai and Olsen (2016) measured convenience orientation in terms of a desire to spend as little time as possible on the task, in terms of an attitude that the less effort needed the better, as well as in terms of a consideration that it is a waste of time to spend long hours on the task. Convenience orientation toward illegal actions increases as negative attitudes toward legal actions increase. The basic elements in convenience orientation are the individual attitudes toward the saving of time, effort and discomfort in the planning, action and achievement of goals. Generally, convenience orientation is the degree to which an individual or a group of individuals are inclined to save time and effort to reach goals.

Convenience orientation refers to a person's or persons' general preference for convenient maneuvers. A convenience-oriented person is one who seeks to accomplish a task in the shortest time with the least expenditure of human energy (Berry et al., 2002; Farquhar and Rowley, 2009).

Convenience in the decision-making process is not only concerned with one alternative being more convenient than another alternative. Convenience is also concerned with the extent to which an individual collects information about more alternatives and collects more information about each alternative. Market research indicates that consumers tend to make buying decisions based on little information about few alternatives (Sundström and Radon, 2015). A similar process can be explored for white-collar crime where the individual avoids the effort of collecting more information about more alternatives that might have led to a non-criminal rather than a criminal solution to a challenge or problem.

It is not the actual convenience that is important in convenience theory. Rather, it is the perceived, expected, and assumed convenience that influences choice of action. Berry et al. (2002) make this distinction explicit by conceptualizing convenience as individuals time and effort perceptions related to an action. White-collar criminals probably vary in their perceived convenience of their actions. Low expected convenience can be one of the reasons why not more members of the elite commit white-collar offenses.

A combination of motive, opportunity, and willingness determines the extent of white-collar crime convenience as illustrated in the structural model in Figure 8.1. There are a total of 14 convenience themes on the right-hand side in the figure. Corporate white-collar crime control is concerned with the five organizational opportunity themes of status, access, decay, chaos, and collapse.

In the financial motive dimension, profit might be a goal in itself or an enabler to exploit possibilities and to avoid threats. Possibilities and threats exist both for individual members of the organization and for the organization as a whole. It is convenient to exploit possibilities and to avoid threats by financial means.

In the organizational opportunity dimension, convenience can exist both to commit white-collar crime and to conceal white-collar crime. Offenders have high social status in privileged positions, and they have legitimate access to crime resources. Disorganized institutional deterioration causes decay, lack of oversight and guardianship cause chaos, while criminal market structures cause collapse.

The personal willingness for deviant behavior focuses on offender choice and perceived innocence. The choice of crime can be caused by deviant identity, rational consideration, or learning from others. Justification and neutralization cause the perceived innocence at crime. Identity, rationality, learning, justification, and neutralization all contribute to making white-collar crime action a convenient behavior for offenders.

This chapter will concentrate on the opportunity dimension of convenience theory to discuss bottom-up approaches to executive deviance convenience.

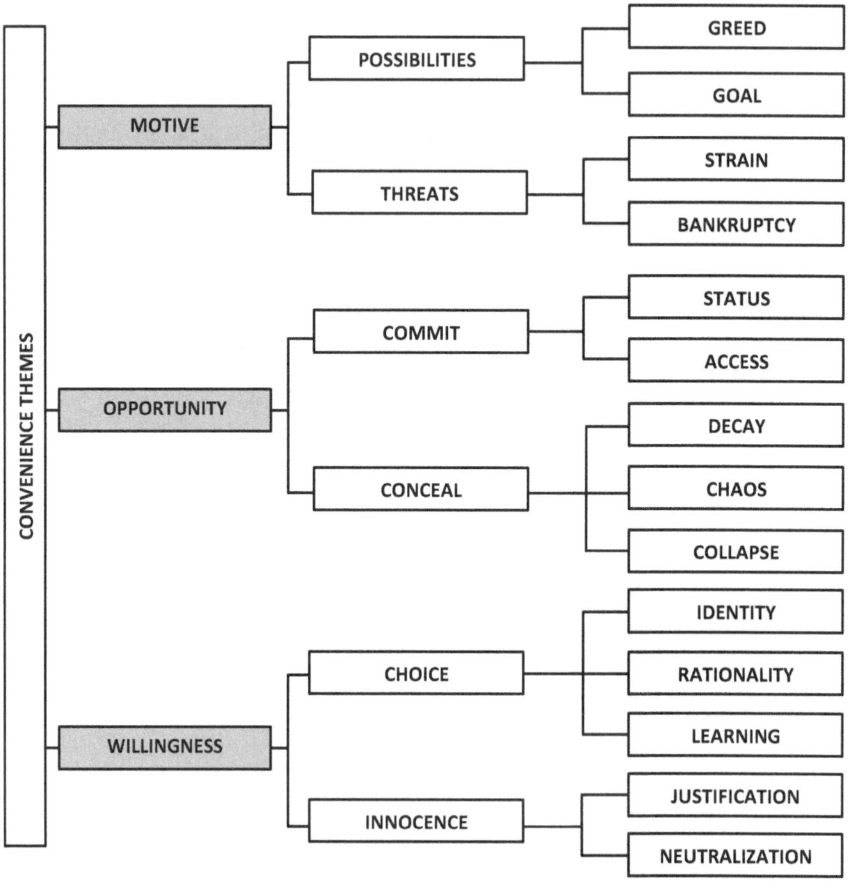

Figure 8.1 Structural model of convenience propositions

Offender Status Convenience

Corporate executive status is the first convenience theme in Figure 8.1 for organizational opportunity along the axis of committing white-collar crime. The perspective here is to discuss how a bottom-up approach to executive compliance can disturb and reduce the extent of white-collar crime convenience from executive status. A bottom-up approach might involve disclosure of executive language, removal of powerful people, detection of misleading attribution, disregard of offender humor, and correction of power inequality.

Status is an individual's social rank within a formal or informal hierarchy, or the person's relative standing along a valued social dimension. Status is the extent to which an individual is respected and admired by others, and status is the outcome of a subjective assessment process (McClean et al., 2018). High-status individuals enjoy greater respect and deference from, as well as power and influence over, those who are positioned lower in the social hierarchy (Kakkar et al., 2020).

Executive status can allow executive language that nobody understands. For example, one might suggest that elite members are considered too big to fail and too powerful to jail (Pontell et al., 2014), and there is power inequality between the elite and others (Patel and Cooper, 2014). Therefore, subordinates tend to accept executive language that they do not really understand (Ferraro et al., 2005), and they get distracted from observing deviant behavior by offender humor (Yam et al., 2018). A consequence of strange language and offender humor might be an acceptance of blame game by misleading attribution to others (Eberly et al., 2011).

Executives may reinforce a culture of financial crime by ignoring criminal actions and otherwise facilitate unethical behavior. At the same time, they try to distance and disassociate themselves from criminal actions (Pontell et al., 2021: 9):

> High status corporate criminals often go to great lengths to distance themselves from the crimes committed by their subordinates and to hide any incriminating evidence of their role in the decisions that authorized those criminal acts.

Misleading attribution of blame to subordinates by executives is both a matter of detection and reaction (Eberly et al., 2011). Generally, attribution is concerned with how individuals make judgments about responsibility (Piening et al., 2020: 335):

> Attributions of responsibility involve a series of yes-no judgments in which individuals first determine whether a negative event has been caused by internal or external factors. If the event is attributed to internal causes, the process continues to determine whether the cause was controllable or not, whereas in case of external causality, the organization cannot be held responsible, so the process stops.

When the Siemens corruption scandal emerged in the public, top management attempted to blame lower level managers (Berghoff, 2018: 423):

> At first the company defended itself with set phrases like "mishaps of individuals" and isolated offenses committed by a "gang" of criminals, or "This is not Siemens".

Bottom-up detection of misleading attribution can cause self-conscious emotions of guilt and shame among potential and actual white-collar offenders, making deviance less convenient (Zhong and Robinson, 2021: 1439):

> These are painful emotions that individuals experience when they perceive their actions have violated a standard, prompting a negative evaluation of

> their behavior in the case of guilt or a negative evaluation of their global self in the case of shame. Prior studies have revealed that many forms of wrongdoing can beget guilt and/or shame, including transgressions, cheating, psychological aggression, ostracism, lying and deception, and unethical behavior.

A bottom-up approach to executive deviance is to avoid acceptance of executive language that people do not really understand (Ferraro et al., 2005) and avoid distraction from observing deviant behavior by offender humor (Yam et al., 2018). A consequence of ignorance of strange language and offender humor might be detection of the blame game by misleading attribution to others (Eberly et al., 2011). Furthermore, leaders with an aggressive humor might practice morally ambiguous leadership (Dion, 2020), where their ambiguity can become vulnerable to bottom-up criticism.

Resource Access Convenience

Legitimate access to resources is the second convenience theme in Figure 8.1. A white-collar offender has typically legitimate and convenient access to resources to commit crime (Füss and Hecker, 2008; Huisman and Erp, 2013; Lange, 2008; Pinto et al., 2008; Reyns, 2013). A resource is an enabler applied and used to satisfy human and organizational needs. A resource has utility and limited availability. According to Petrocelli et al. (2003), access to resources equates access to power. Other organizational members are losers in the competition for resources (Wheelock et al., 2011).

The threat of dismissal following corporate scandals limits corporate involvement in executive destiny. Even when the executive is not necessarily to blame, the executive is a potential scapegoat that the organization deprives of access to resources (Gottschalk and Benson, 2020). Dismissal occurs instantly, where the former privileged individual has no access anymore to defense attorneys, documents, or colleagues. The corporation has to survive at the expense of an executive (Ghannam et al., 2019).

A bottom-up approach to disturbing and reducing access to resources might be a matter of restrictions on access to systems, disclosure of entrepreneurialism, review of specialized access, and limits to strategic resources.

While executive access to premises and systems has to be monitored, customization and transmutation are needed to ensure that control mechanisms achieve the intended control outcomes based on executives' own assessment of their management challenges (Chown, 2020). As mentioned in the introduction, transmutation captures the idea that organizational units including management implement control regimes that are different from the mandated and general control mechanism of the organization. While there is no more need for trust regarding executive work versus others' work in an organization, control mechanisms implemented in management need to ensure intended control outcomes.

Berghoff and Spiekermann (2018: 291) argued that all economic transactions depend on a certain degree of trust, without which transaction costs would simply be too high for economic activity:

> White-collar criminals abuse the good faith of various stakeholders, from customers to the general public, from shareholders to the authorities. Therefore, white-collar crime often coincides with the breach of trust.

High social status in privileged positions is sometimes associated with entrepreneurship, where an entrepreneurial individual can create opportunities for deviant behavior (Ramoglou and Tsang, 2016). The entrepreneurship perspective emphasizes that entrepreneurs discover and create innovative and entrepreneurial opportunities (Smith, 2009; Tonoyan et al., 2010; Welter et al., 2017). Criminal entrepreneurs actualize illegal opportunities in the shadow economy (Mc Elwee and Smith, 2015). Scheaf and Wood (2021: 2) found that entrepreneurial fraud has stimulated a wide array of research related to white-collar crime, where they provided the following definition of entrepreneurial fraud:

> Enterprising individuals (alone or in groups) deceiving stakeholders by sharing statements about their identity, individual capabilities, elements of new market offerings, and/or new venture activities that they know to be false in order to obtain something of value.

Access to strategic resources need to be monitored. Strategic resources are characterized by being valuable (application of the resource provides desired outcome), unique (very few have access to the resource), not imitable (resource cannot be copied), not transferrable (resource cannot be released from context), combinable with other resources (results in better outcome), exploitable (possible to apply in criminal activities), and not substitutable (cannot be replaced by a different resource).

Organization Deterioration Convenience

Decay in the form of institutional deterioration is the third convenience theme in Figure 8.1. An institution is a system of interrelated formal and informal elements – rules, guidelines, norms, traditions, beliefs – governing relationships between institutional members within which members pursue their mutual interests (Győry, 2020). Institutional deterioration can occur conveniently as a result of external legitimacy where deviance is the norm (Rodriguez et al., 2005). Executive deviance enacted at institutional deterioration is dependent on a number of factors. For example, in the case of government corruption for multinational enterprises in host countries, both pervasiveness and arbitrariness are important factors. Pervasiveness is the average firm's likelihood of encountering bribery, while arbitrariness is the inherent degree of ambiguity associated with corrupt transactions in a given nation or state (Rodriguez et al., 2005).

Pinto et al. (2008: 686) define the beneficiary of corruption as the actor deriving direct and primary benefit from the action: "For example, even if individuals can benefit financially from corruption on behalf of the organization (e.g., through bonuses or high prices for their stocks), the organization is still the primary and direct financial beneficiary".

Bottom-up approaches to disturb white-collar crime convenience in times of institutional deterioration include transparency in deterioration, replacement of disorganization, detection of crime signals, transparency in accounting, corporate social responsibility (CSR), and sharing of audit reports.

Transparency is understood as conditions that make it relatively easy for observers to accurately evaluate phenomena of interest (Haack et al., 2021) since the phenomena occur in a setting with elaborate reporting procedures (Sorour et al., 2021). Internal transparency refers to the possibility for and ability of organizational members to know what is going on in the organization (Maas and Yin, 2021: 4):

> Organizations can manage the level of transparency through policies to actively distribute information among managers and employees, or alternatively, policies to deliberately suppress information flows. Examples of the former type include intranet webpages, newsletters, meetings, and publicly accessible databases. To illustrate, some organizations actively disseminate information about managers by making the managers' work calendar visible to everyone in the firm.

The institutional perspective considers the processes by which structures, including schemes; rules; norms; and routines become established as authoritative guidelines for social behavior. Triggers of institutional adaption include political, cultural, and social influences. Behavioral patterns supported by norms, values, and expectations lead to cultural influence. A desire to equal others implies social influence. Normative institutional pressure is concerned with conformity, where deviance and nonconformity are disliked, disapproved, or even dismissed (Witt et al., 2021).

Training in crime signal detection is a matter of separating real signals from noise signals. The perspective of crime signal detection suggests that there is often too much interference and noise for white-collar crime to reach the attention of observers. There are four possibilities in the decision matrix of the observer of potential misconduct and crime (Karim and Siegel, 1998: 368):

- The observer notices a noise when it is a signal (called a miss).
- The observer notices a signal when it is a signal (called a hit).
- The observer notices a noise when it is a noise (called a correct identification).
- The observer notices a signal when it is a noise (called a false alarm).

The observer needs to decide concerning the event and classify it as either a signal or a noise. In an organizational context, where less powerful individuals may suspect powerful individuals, the less powerful will conveniently prefer to think of the event as a noise signal rather than as a crime signal. The perspective of crime signal detection holds that the observation of a stimulus depends on both the intensity of the stimulus and the physical and psychological state of the observer.

A bottom-up approach to prevention and detection of white-collar crime is increased transparency in accounting. The discourse and rituals of transparency, account-giving, and verification are central to corporate governance (Mehrpouya and Salles-Djelic, 2019: 13):

> Transparency has been a normative shell through which financial accounting and audit standards have been pushed around the world. Under the contemporary governance paradigm, financial disclosure regimes are an important dimension of what it means to make organizations, states and individuals transparent and accountable. Champions of transparency, such as the former head of the IMF, Michel Camdessus, describe transparency as the "golden rule" of the new international financial system, "absolutely central to the task of civilizing globalization". Transparency implies unhindered access to information for the public. However, the definition of the public, targets and beneficiaries of transparency, along with associated programs and technologies, has been contested and has evolved through time.

As stated earlier, disorganized institutional deterioration in combination with lack of CSR cause both internal and external collapses. The introduction and improvement in corporate social responsibility might represent a bottom-up approach by employees who are concerned with the legitimacy of current business practices. If the reputation and the legitimacy of the business practice deteriorate, then key personnel with an ethical orientation might leave the organization and cause decline in business performance as a consequence of employee turnover. Legitimacy relates to the perception that the organization is operating in a desirable and appropriate way that is consistent with a broader system of norms, values, and beliefs (Sorour et al., 2021).

The bottom-up approach might focus on the signaling effect of CSR, where signals are observable actions that a firm takes to provide information to stakeholders about its unobservable intentions and capabilities (Jardine et al., 2020: 851):

> Specifically, the activities that serve as CSR signals indicate that a firm is willing and able to act with a long-term vision and to take into account the interests of different stakeholders. For example, by hiring a female board member (an observable action), a firm can signal to job seekers that it is both willing and able (its unobservable intentions and capabilities) to

> support women in their careers. Similarly, by engaging in CSR activities (an observable action), a firm can signal to governments that it would be a trustworthy partner (an unobservable intention) for a government procurement contract.

Bottom-up approaches to both transparency and CSR can foster a mutual reinforcing effect between the two approaches. Transparency can foster the substantive adoption of CSR, while CSR to be trustworthy requires transparency. The bottom-up call for a condition under which it is relatively easy for external observers to accurately determine the degree to which a practice is implemented forces and enables an organization to explore, embrace, and eventually enact the behavioral prescriptions enshrined in CSR policies and principles (Haack et al., 2021).

Since cover-ups allow problematic behavior to continue and often escalate causing additional damage, it is important for insiders to create a punishment regime in the best interest of the organization. An element of such a punishment regime might be to leak stories to the police and to the press. Application of negative consequences for involved individual executives might easily make the organization distance and disassociate itself from the offenders and thereby avoid harming organizational reputation. This bottom-up approach represents a reversal of the common top-down approach where leaders reinforce a culture of financial crime by ignoring criminal actions and otherwise facilitate unethical behavior. At the same time, they try to distance and disassociate themselves from criminal actions (Pontell et al., 2021: 9):

> High status corporate criminals often go to great lengths to distance themselves from the crimes committed by their subordinates and to hide any incriminating evidence of their role in the decisions that authorized those criminal acts.

As illustrated by the above perspectives, CSR requires substance to be trustworthy in terms of transparency and social capital when an executive scandal hits the organization. Furthermore, a bottom-up approach to CSR has to replace window dressing by documented actions against actual misconduct events. Window dressing is the discrepancy between the outside positive presentation of an enterprise and the real negative situation within the enterprise.

Role Agency Convenience

The agency perspective suggests that a principal is often unable to control an agent who does work for the principal. The agency perspective assumes narrow self-interest among both principals and agents. The interests of principal and agent tend to diverge, they may have different risk willingness or risk aversion, there is knowledge asymmetry between the two parties, and the principal has imperfect information about the agent's contribution (Bosse and Phillips, 2016; Chrisman et al., 2007; Pillay and Kluvers, 2014; Williams, 2008).

Lack of whistleblowing is an important part of the opportunity structure for white-collar crime. When people notice wrongdoing in the organization, they are reluctant to report it because of perceived retaliation threats. As argued by Keil et al. (2010), costs tend to exceed benefits for individual whistleblowers. In addition, as argued by Bussmann et al. (2018), employees in societies characterized by collectivist values are reluctant to blow the whistle on others. In the bottom-up approach of whistleblowing to address suspicions of white-collar crime, it is important for whistleblowers and their allies to avoid conspiracy theories. Sometimes executives, board members, and shareholders might seem to enter into a conspiracy without doing so. The thought of conspiracy can emerge as whistleblowers receive no feedback regarding their notices, and when whistleblowers experience reluctance to talk to them about perceived wrongdoing. Whistleblowers can then easily fall into the trap of considering management and others involved in a conspiracy to conceal wrongdoing and make whistleblowers subject to retaliation, reprisal, and refuting.

As evidenced by many internal investigation reports by fraud examiners after white-collar crime scandals, internal auditors, external auditors, compliance committees, and other internal and external control units do not function properly (e.g., Bruun Hjejle, 2018; Clifford Chance, 2020; Deloitte, 2015, 2017; Mannheimer Swartling, 2016; Shearman Sterling, 2017). Oversight and control functions tend to be formal units without any insights into the substance of business activities. They tend to review procedures rather than transactions within procedures. Therefore, ineffective control functions are often an important part of the opportunity structure for white-collar crime.

Rule Complexity Convenience

Rule complexity can create a situation where nobody is able to tell whether an action represented a criminal offense. It is impossible to understand what is right and what is wrong. Some laws, rules, and regulations are so complex that compliance becomes random, where compliance is the action of complying with laws, rules, and regulations. The regulatory legal environment is supposed to define the boundaries of appropriate organizational conduct. However, legal complexity is often so extreme that even specialist compliance officers struggle to understand what to recommend to business executives in the organizations (Lehman et al., 2020).

Cartels are associations of independent corporations in the same industry that strive to reduce competition. When competitors join forces in controlling a market, then excluded competitors as well as customers of the cartel participants become victims (Freiberg, 2020; Goncharov and Peter, 2019; Nielsen, 2003). A bottom-up approach to executive deviance among cartel members would be to blow the whistle on white-collar crime. An alternative is the outside-in approach where outsiders notice and report wrongdoing. For example, customers may notice that the prices are extremely high, or they may notice that some vendors are reluctant to provide supplies since there are other vendors assigned to those customers by the cartel agreement.

Outside-In Approaches

Bottom-up approaches can align with outside-in approaches to executive deviance convenience. Outside-in approaches should be recognized as supplements to control of white-collar crime. Outside organizations, there are various professionals who can either help white-collar offenders commit and conceal crime, or they can help prevent and detect white-collar individuals in organizations. Lawyers can report suspicious transactions on client accounts, certified accountants as well as auditors can blow the whistle on suspected value assessments, bank officials can react to attempts to use tax havens for corruption payments, and employees in health care can detect wrongdoing in pharmaceutical firms.

Bottom-up approach is matter of people in the organization who prevent potential white-collar offenders from committing financial crime and who detect white-collar offenders having committed financial crime. A different approach in the same line of reasoning is the outside-in approach where outsiders rather than insiders prevent and detect white-collar wrongdoing in the organization. The outside-in approach involves professional service providers such as law firms, accounting firms, auditing firms, real estate agencies, and banks with their lawyers, accountants, auditors, real estate agents, and bank clerks.

Often, the convenience of white-collar crime is dependent on the cooperation with external professionals who may turn a blind eye to potential law violations by and together with their clients. Instead of turning a blind eye, they might indeed help their clients with compliance to avoid misconduct and crime. This chapter discusses the outside-in perspective of corporate control of white-collar offenses as it influences crime convenience such as lawyers, auditors, accountants, real estate agents, and health care workers. Many other external helpers can contribute to an outside-in effort of prevention and detection. An example is the art market where money laundering and fraud take place (Oosterman et al., 2021).

In an outside-in perspective, knowledgeable lawyers and law firms based on integrity and accountability can prevent potential offenses in client organizations, and they can report instances legitimized by the money laundering act in violation of the duty of confidentiality. However, many lawyers and law firms ted to slide on the slippery slope over to the wrong side of the law when there is a profitable client (Økokrim, 2021).

Like certified accountants, certified auditors can give the company legitimacy and can be used to facilitate or commit various forms of financial crime. Økokrim (2021) found that auditors often have chosen to resign from their role at those companies where they have not received sufficient answers to questions. Some auditors are suspected of approving accounts without special control, or they even more actively assist criminals. These auditors are often associated with companies that operate in the gray zone for what is legal. Some auditors accept reporting and being loyal to deviant management (Hurley et al., 2019). In our outside-in perspective, the ideal contribution from auditors would be to deny acceptance of accounts where their queries are not satisfactorily answered and report their findings to the board of directors as well as externally to public authorities.

In our perspective of combatting white-collar crime through outside-in measures, a bank that discovers an attempt at bank fraud should consider reporting it not only to the police but also to the supervisory committee and the compliance officer in the company, where someone made the fraudulent attempt. Since police agencies sometimes lack both competence and capacity to investigate, a more preventive measure would be to let the offender organization know of the attempt.

In the outside-in perspective, OECD (2021: 27) argued that tax authorities can encounter professional enablers across a number of different functions, from those business areas involved in promoting voluntary compliance to those undertaking audits or investigations, through those leading on enforcement activity such as civil penalties and criminal prosecution:

> Lawyers, tax advisors, notaries and accountants are valued gatekeepers to a sound legal and financial system. Their unique sets of skills, together with the professional privileges awarded to them by statutes, put them in a special place within societies. They are experts who are in a position of trust and enjoy certain rights that are not shared by other professions. Jurisdictions should ensure that advisors perform their tasks in accordance with the law, and penalize those few who use their skills, expertise and privileges to design structures with the purpose of breaking the law. This requires that countries have in place a legal framework to support criminal investigators and the justice system in addressing and punishing professional enablers that engage in and facilitate the commission of such crimes.

White-collar crime in the health care sector is growing as individual patients as well as public agencies spend a growing amount of money on health care for themselves and for the population. An example is the pharmaceutical industry, which hands out prizes and awards to medical doctors at hospitals. The awards, prizes, and funding for research do frequently resemble regular bribes. In our perspective of outside-in, pharmaceutical officials not involved in bribing should notify hospitals about corrupt medical doctors.

In conclusion, based on the theory of convenience, this chapter has suggested a number of themes that might reduce the convenience of crime for white-collar offenders. Traditionally, control in organizations is concerned with top-down approaches, where executives attempt to direct their employees to align their work with organizational objectives. This chapter has addressed the challenge of directing executives to align their work with laws, rules, and ethics. Various bottom-up approaches were explored that need further inquiry in future research.

References

Amry, M.A. and Meliala, A. (2021). Lifestyle-related shaming: The significance of reintegrative shaming on drug relapse offenders in Indonesia, *Journal of Social and Political Sciences*, 4 (1), 145–153.

Asting, C. and Gottschalk, P. (2022). Attorney fraud in the law firm: A case study of crime convenience theory and crime signal detection theory, *Deviant Behavior*, published online doi: 10.1080/01639625.2022.2071657.

Bendiktsson, M.O. (2010). The Deviant organization and the bad apple CEO: Ideology and accountability in media coverage of corporate scandals, *Social Forces*, 88 (5), 2189–2216.

Benson, M.L., Feldmeyer, B., Gabbidon, S.L. and Chio, H.L. (2021). Race, ethnicity, and social change: The democratization of middle-class crime, *Criminology*, 59 (1), 10–41.

Berghoff, H. (2018). "Organised irresponsibility?" The Siemens corruption scandal of the 1990s and 2000s, *Business History*, 60 (3), 423–445.

Berghoff, H. and Spiekermann, U. (2018). Shady business: On the history of white-collar crime, *Business History*, 60 (3),, 289–304.

Berry, L.L., Seiders, K. and Grewal, D. (2002). Understanding service convenience, *Journal of Marketing*, 66, 1–17.

Bigley, G.A. and Wiersma, M.F. (2002). New CEOs and corporate strategic refocusing: How experience as heir apparent influences the use of power, *Administrative Science Quarterly*, 47, 707–727.

Bosse, D.A. and Phillips, R.A. (2016). Agency theory and bounded self-interest, *Academy of Management Review*, 41 (2), 276–297.

Braaten, C.N. and Vaughn, M.S. (2019). Convenience theory of cryptocurrency crime: A content analysis of U.S. federal court decisions, *Deviant Behavior*, published online doi: 10.1080/01639625.2019.1706706.

Bruun Hjejle. (2018). *Report on the Non-Resident Portfolio at Danske Bank's Estonian branch*, law firm Bruun Hjejle, Copenhagen, Denmark, 87 pages.

Bussmann, K.D., Niemeczek, A. and Vockrodt, M. (2018). Company culture and prevention of corruption in Germany, China and Russia, *European Journal of Criminology*, 15 (3), 255–277.

Chatterjee, A. and Pollock, T.G. (2017). Master of puppets: How narcissistic CEOs construct their professional worlds, *Academy of Management Review*, 42 (4), 703–725.

Chen, J. and Nadkarni, S. (2017). It's about time! CEOs' temporal dispositions, temporal leadership, and corporate entrepreneurship, *Administrative Science Quarterly*, 62 (1), 31–66.

Chown, J. (2020). The unfolding of control mechanisms inside organizations: Pathways of customization and transmutation, *Administrative Science Quarterly*, 66 (3), 711–752.

Chrisman, J.J., Chua, J.H., Kellermanns, F.W. and Chang, E.P.C. (2007). Are family managers agents or stewards? An exploratory study in privately held family firms, *Journal of Business Research*, 60 (10), 1030–1038.

Clifford Chance. (2020). *Report of Investigation on Swedbank*, law firm Clifford Chance, Washington, DC, 218 pages.

Collier, J.E. and Kimes, S.E. (2012). Only if it is convenient: Understanding how convenience Influences self-service technology evaluation, *Journal of Service Research*, 16 (1), 39–51.

Davidson, R.H., Dey, A. and Smith, A.J. (2019). CEO materialism and corporate social responsibility, *The Accounting Review*, 94 (1), 101–126.

Dearden, T.E. and Gottschalk, P. (2020). Gender and white-collar crime: Convenience in target selection, *Deviant Behavior*, 1–9, published online doi: 10.1080/01639625.2020.1756428.

Deloitte. (2015). *Investigation Report, Summary Version, Independent Investigation Committee for Toshiba Corporation*, audit firm Deloitte, Tokyo, Japan, 90 pages.

Deloitte. (2017). *Investigation Report*, Independent Investigation Committee, by global auditing firm Deloitte, published June 10, Ito, T., Sato, K. and Nishimura, K., www.fujifilmholdings.com/en/pdf/investors/finance/materials/ff_irdata_investigation_001e.pdf, retrieved September 8, 2018, 89 pages.

Dion, M. (2019). A Gadamerian perspective on financial crimes, *Journal of Financial Crime*, 26 (3), 836–860.

Dion, M. (2020). Bribery, extortion and "morally ambiguous" leadership in organizations, *Journal of Financial Crime*, 27 (4), 1027–1046.

Direnzo, M.S. and Greenhaus, J.H. (2011). Job search and voluntary turnover in a boundaryless world: A control theory perspective, *Academy of Management Review*, 36 (3), 567–589.

Durand, R., Hawn, O. and Ioannou, I. (2019). Willing and able: A general model of organizational responses to normative pressures, *Academy of Management Review*, 44 (2), 299–320.

Eberly, M.B., Holley, E.C., Johnson, M.D. and Mitchell, T.R. (2011). Beyond internal and external: A dyadic theory of relational attributions, *Academy of Management Review*, 36 (4), 731–753.

Farquhar, J.D. and Rowley, J. (2009). Convenience: A services perspective, *Marketing Theory*, 9 (4), 425–438.

Ferraro, F., Pfeffer, J. and Sutton, R.I. (2005). Economics language and assumptions: How theories can become self-fulfilling, *Academy of Management Review*, 30 (1), 8–24.

Freiberg, A. (2020). Researching white-collar crime: An Australian perspective, in: Rorie, M.L. (editor), *The Handbook of White-Collar Crime*, Wiley & Sons, Hoboken, NJ, chapter 26, pages 418–436.

Füss, R. and Hecker, A. (2008). Profiling white-collar crime. Evidence from German-speaking countries, *Corporate Ownership & Control*, 5 (4), 149–161.

Galvin, B.M., Lange, D. and Ashforth, B.E. (2015). Narcissistic organizational identification: Seeing oneself as central to the organization's identity, *Academy of Management Review*, 40 (2), 163–181.

Gamache, D.L. and McNamara, G. (2019). Responding to bad press: How CEO temporal focus influences the sensitivity to negative media coverage of acquisitions, *Academy of Management Journal*, 62 (3), 918–943.

Gangloff, K.A., Connelly, B.L. and Shook, C.L. (2016). Of scapegoats and signals: Investor reactions to CEO succession in the aftermath of wrongdoing, *Journal of Management*, 42, 1614–1634.

Ghannam, S., Bugeja, M., Matolcsy, Z.P. and Spiropoulos, H. (2019). Are qualified and experienced outside directors willing to join fraudulent firms and if so, why? *The Accounting Review*, 94 (2), 205–227.

Gill, M.J. (2019). The significance of suffering in organizations: Understanding variation in workers' responses to multiple modes of control, *Academy of Management Review*, 44 (2), 377–404.

Goncharov, I. and Peter, C.D. (2019). Does reporting transparency affect industry coordination? Evidence from the duration of international cartels, *The Accounting Review*, 94 (3), 149–175.

Gottschalk, P. and Benson, M.L. (2020). The evolution of corporate accounts of scandals from exposure to investigation, *British Journal of Criminology*, 60, 949–969.

Gyõry, C. (2020). The institutional context of financial fraud in a post-transition economy: The Quaestor scandal, *European Journal of Criminology*, 17 (1), 31–49.

Haack, P., Martignoni, D. and Schoeneborn, D. (2021). A bait-and-switch model of corporate social responsibility, *Academy of Management Review*, 46 (3), 440–464.

Huisman, W. and Erp, J. (2013). Opportunities for environmental crime, *British Journal of Criminology*, 53, 1178–1200.

Hurley, P.J., Mayhew, B.W. and Obermire, K.M. (2019). Realigning auditors' accountability: Experimental evidence, *The Accounting Review*, 94 (3), 233–250.

Jardine, M.R., Marti, E. and Durand, R. (2020). Why activist hedge funds target socially responsible firms: The reaction costs of signaling corporate social responsibility, *Academy of Management Journal*, 64 (3), 851–872.

Kakkar, H., Sivanathan, N. and Globel, M.S. (2020). Fall from grace: The role of dominance and prestige in punishment of high-status actors, *Academy of Management Journal*, 63 (2), 530–553.

Karim, K.E. and Siegel, P.H. (1998). A signal detection theory approach to analyzing the efficiency and effectiveness of auditing to detect management fraud, *Managerial Auditing Journal*, 13 (6), 367–375.

Keil, M., Tiwana, A., Sainsbury, R. and Sneha, S. (2010). Toward a theory of whistleblowing intentions: A benefit-cost differential perspective, *Decision Sciences*, 41 (4), 787–812.

Khanna, V., Kim, E.H. and Lu, Y. (2015). CEO connectedness and corporate fraud, *The Journal of Finance*, 70, 1203–1252.

Kownatzki, M., Walter, J., Floyd, S.W. and Lechner, C. (2013). Corporate control and the speed of strategic business unit decision making, *Academy of Management Journal*, 56 (5), 1295–1324.

König, A., Graf-Vlachy, L., Bundy, J. and Little, L.M. (2020). A blessing and a curse: How CEOs' trait empathy affects their management of organizational crises, *Academy of Management Review*, 45 (1), 130–153.

Lange, D. (2008). A multidimensional conceptualization of organizational corruption control, *Academy of Management Journal*, 33 (3), 710–729.

Lehman, D.W., Cooil, B. and Ramanujam, R. (2020). The effects of rule complexity on organizational noncompliance and remediation: Evidence from restaurant health inspections, *Journal of Management*, 46 (8), 1436–1468.

Long, C.P., Bendersky, C. and Morrill, C. (2011). Fairness monitoring: Linking managerial controls and fairness judgments in organizations, *Academy of Management Review*, 54 (5), 1045–1068.

Maas, V.S. and Yin, H. (2021). Finding partners in crime? How transparency about managers' behavior affects employee collusion, *Accounting, Organizations, and Society*, published online doi: 10.106/j.aos.2021.101293.

Mai, H.T.X. and Olsen, S.O. (2016). Consumer participation in self-production: The role of control mechanisms, convenience orientation, and moral obligation, *Journal of Marketing Theory and Practice*, 24 (2), 209–223.

Mannheimer Swartling. (2016). *Report on Investigation of Nordea Private Banking in Relation to Offshore Structures*, law firm Mannheimer Swartling, Stockholm, Sweden, 42 pages.

Mannucci, P.V., Orazi, D.C. and Valck, K. (2021). Developing improvisation skills: The influence of individual orientations, *Administrative Science Quarterly*, 66 (3), 612–658.

McClean, E.J., Martin, S.R., Emich, K.J. and Woodruff, T. (2018). The social consequences of voice: An examination of voice type and gender on status and subsequent leader emergence, *Academy of Management Journal*, 61 (5), 1869–1891.

McClelland, P.L., Liang, X. and Barker, V.L. (2010). CEO commitment to the status quo: Replication and extension using content analysis, *Journal of Management*, 36 (5), 1251–1277.

McElwee, G. and Smith, R. (2015). Towards a Nuanced Typology of Illegal Entrepreneurship: A Theoretical and Conceptual Overview, in: McElwee, G. and Smith, R. (editors), *Exploring Criminal and Illegal Enterprise: New Perspectives on Research, Policy & Practice: Contemporary Issues in Entrepreneurship Research Volume 5*, Emerald, Bingley.

Mehrpouya, A. and Salles-Djelic, M.L. (2019). Seeing like the market; Exploring the mutual rise of transparency and accounting in transnational economic and market governance, *Accounting, Organizations and Society*, 76, 12–31.

Nielsen, R.P. (2003). Corruption networks and implications for ethical corruption reform, *Journal of Business Ethics*, 42 (2), 125–149.

OECD. (2021). *Ending the Shell Game: Checking Down on the Professionals Who Enable Tax and White Collar Crimes*, OECD Publishing, Organization for Economic Co-operation and Development, Paris, www.oecd.org, 57 pages.

Økokrim. (2021). *Temarapport: Profesjonelle aktører (Theme Report: Professional Actors)*, Økokrim, Norwegian National Authority for Investigation and Prosecution of Economic and Environmental Crime, Oslo, Norway.

Oosterman, N., Mackenzie, S. and Yates, D. (2021). Regulating the wild west: Symbolic security bubbles and white collar crime in the art market, *Journal of White Collar and Corporate Crime*, published online doi: 10.1177/2631309X211035724.

Paruchuri, S., Han, J.H. and Prakash, P. (2021). Salient expectations? Incongruence across capability and integrity signals and investor reactions to organizational misconduct, *Academy of Management Journal*, 64 (2), 562–586.

Patel, P.C. and Cooper, D. (2014). Structural power equality between family and nonfamily TMT members and the performance of family firms, *Academy of Management Journal*, 57 (6), 1624–1649.

Petrocelli, M., Piquero, A.R. and Smith, M.R. (2003). Conflict theory and racial profiling: An empirical analysis of police traffic stop data, *Journal of Criminal Justice*, 31 (1), 1–11.

Piening, E.P., Salge, T.O., Antons, D. and Kreiner, G.E. (2020). Standing together or falling apart? Understanding employees' responses to organizational identity threats, *Academy of Management Review*, 45 (2), 325–351.

Pillay, S. and Kluvers, R. (2014). An institutional theory perspective on corruption: The case of a developing democracy, *Financial Accountability & Management*, 30 (1), 95–119.

Pinto, J., Leana, C.R. and Pil, F.K. (2008). Corrupt organizations or organizations of corrupt individuals? Two types of organization-level corruption, *Academy of Management Review*, 33 (3), 685–709.

Pontell, H.N., Black, W.K. and Geis, G. (2014). Too big to fail, too powerful to jail? On the absence of criminal prosecutions after the 2008 financial meltdown, *Crime, Law and Social Change*, 61 (1), 1–13.

Pontell, H.N., Tillman, R. and Ghazi-Tehrani, A.K. (2021). In-your-face Watergate: Neutralizing government lawbreaking and the war against white-collar crime, *Crime, Law and Social Change*, published online doi: 10.1007/s10611-021-09954-1, 19 pages.

Ramoglou, S. and Tsang, E.W.K. (2016). A realist perspective of entrepreneurship: Opportunities as propensities, *Academy of Management Review*, 41, 410–434.

Reyns, B.W. (2013). Online routines and identity theft victimization: Further expanding routine activity theory beyond direct-contact offenses, *Journal of Research in Crime and Delinquency*, 50, 216–238.

Rodriguez, P., Uhlenbruck, K. and Eden, L. (2005). Government corruption and the entry strategies of multinationals, *Academy of Management Review*, 30 (2), 383–396.

Scheaf, D.J. and Wood, M.S. (2021). Entrepreneurial fraud: A multidisciplinary review and synthesized framework, *Entrepreneurship: Theory and Practice*, 1–36, published online doi: 10.1177/0422587211001818.

Schnatterly, K., Gangloff, K.A. and Tuschke, A. (2018). CEO wrongdoing: A review of pressure, opportunity, and rationalization, *Journal of Management*, 44 (6), 2405–2432.

Shearman Sterling. (2017). *Independent Directors of the Board of Wells Fargo & Company: Sales Practices Investigation Report*, law firm Shearman & Sterling, New York, NY, 113 pages.

Shen, W. (2003). The dynamics of the CEO-board relationship: An evolutionary perspective, *Academy of Management Review*, 28 (3), 466–476.

Smith, G. (2009). Citizen oversight of independent police services: Bifurcated accountability, regulation creep, and lessons learning, *Regulation & Governance*, 3, 421–441.

Sohoni, T. and Rorie, M. (2021). The whiteness of white-collar crime in the United States: Examining the role of race in a culture of elite white-collar offending, *Theoretical Criminology*, 25 (1), 66–87.

Sorour, M.K., Boadu, M. and Soobaroyen, T. (2021). The role of corporate social responsibility in organizational identity communication, co-creation and orientation, *Journal of Business Ethics*, 173, 89–108.

Stadler, W.A. and Gottschalk, P. (2022). Testing convenience theory for white-collar crime: Perceptions of potential offenders and non-offenders, *Deviant Behavior*, 43 (7), 804–820.

Sundström, M. and Radon, A. (2015). Utilizing the concept of convenience as a business opportunity in emerging markets, *Organizations and Markets in Emerging Economies*, 6 (2), 7–21.

Sutherland, E.H. (1939). White-collar criminality, *American Sociological Review*, 5 (1), 1–12.

Sutherland, E.H. (1983). *White Collar Crime – The Uncut Version*, Yale University Press, New Haven, CT.

Tonoyan, V., Strohmeyer, R., Habib, M. and Perlitz, M. (2010). Corruption and entrepreneurship: How formal and informal institutions shape small firm behavior in transition and mature market economies, *Entrepreneurship: Theory & Practice*, 34 (5), 803–831.

Welter, F., Baker, T., Audretsch, D.B. and Gartner, W.B. (2017). Everyday entrepreneurship: A call for entrepreneurship research to embrace entrepreneurial diversity, *Entrepreneurship: Theory and Practice*, 41 (3), 323–347.

Wheelock, D., Semukhina, O. and Demidov, N.N. (2011). Perceived group threat and punitive attitudes in Russia and the United States, *British Journal of Criminology*, 51, 937–959.

Williams, J.W. (2008). The lessons of Enron: Media accounts, corporate crimes, and financial markets, *Theoretical Criminology*, 12 (4), 471–499.

Witt, M.A., Fainshmidt, S. and Aguilera, R.V. (2021). Our board, our rules: Nonconformity to global corporate governance norms, *Administrative Science Quarterly*, 1–36, published online doi: 10.1177/00018392211022726.

Yam, K.C., Christian, M.S., Wei, W., Liao, Z. and Nai, J. (2018). The mixed blessing of leader sense of humor: Examining costs and benefits, *Academy of Management Journal*, 61 (1), 348–369.

Yue, L.Q., Luo, J. and Ingram, P. (2013). The failure of private regulation: Elite control and market crises in the Manhattan banking industry, *Administrative Science Quarterly*, 58 (1), 37–68.

Zahra, S.A., Priem, R.L. and Rasheed, A.A. (2005). The antecedents and consequences of top management fraud, *Journal of Management*, 31, 803–828.

Zhong, R. and Robinson, S.L. (2021). What happens to bad actors in organizations? A review of actor-centric outcomes of negative behavior, *Journal of Management*, 47 (6), 1430–1467.

Zhu, D.H. and Chen, G. (2015). CEO narcissism and the impact of prior board experience on corporate strategy, *Administrative Science Quarterly*, 60 (1), 31–65.

9 Auditors Disturbing Crime Convenience

Auditors can disturb crime convenience for white-collar offenders as discussed in this chapter by application of convenience theory. The motive based on both possibilities and threats, the opportunity to both commit and conceal financial crime, as well as the choice of crime might be disturbed by auditors and thereby cause increase in prevention and detection of white-collar offences. Important elements in auditors' disturbance of financial motives are goal and bonus reviews, of organizational opportunities are status ignorance and forensic accounting, and of personal willingness are transparency and professional skepticism. While this chapter details measures that can be applied by auditors to prevent and detect crime, it also illustrates the gap to practice where sometimes auditors are reluctant to intervene and even become crime participants.

Auditors belong to the group of crime service professionals as discussed earlier in the book. Auditors consign legitimacy to companies and are most often associated with economic crime as passive actors. It is typical that in companies where financial crime occurs, both accounting and auditing work are deficient. When studying illegal backdating, Mohliver (2019: 311) found that auditors in professional service firms "assist companies in concealing the adoption of practices that could potentially result in costly sanctions", the firms serve "as key professional experts responsible for auditing financial statements that encompass the backdating practice", and the client–auditor relationship can "lead auditors to prioritize their clients' interests over their legal obligations".

However, auditors are in an essential function when verifying the financial statements and operations of organizations. The independent role of auditors aids users of financial statements and the authorities in assessing information from the companies. Auditors are in unique positions to disturb white-collar crime convenience for potential offenders. Auditors are supposed to obtain satisfactory assurance that the accounts do not contain material misstatements. Furthermore, auditors are supposed to contribute to prevention and detection of fraud. Auditors are expected to perform further review procedures in events of fraud suspicions. Therefore, this chapter addresses the following research question: How can an auditor prevent and detect white-collar crime and disturb crime convenience?

DOI: 10.4324/9781003379249-12

Crime Prevention and Detection

Prevention of white-collar crime implies "stopping potential crimes and harms before they occur" (Lord and Wingerde, 2019: 2). Furthermore, according to Hughes (2003: 85), prevention of crime is "any action or technique by public agencies or private organizations/individuals that aims to reduce the damage caused by potential acts defined as criminal". Lord and Wingerde (2019) argued that little is known about how white-collar crime is carried out, and therefore it is difficult for researchers and practitioners to determine what methods of prevention work.

Detection is the identification of "indicators sufficient to warrant recommending an investigation" (O'Gara, 2004: 169). Detection includes the discovery of committed crime, identification of a suspect, and gathering of evidence of the crime. Crime indicators can "arise as a result of controls established by management, tests conducted by auditors, and other sources both within and outside the organization" (O'Gara, 2004: 169).

The mere presence of an auditor may have a disturbing effect on potential offenders when the auditor asks critical questions. Responses to critical questions will in turn increase the likelihood of detection of actual offenders. If an auditor identifies the risk of material misstatement as a result of fraud, the auditor is required to design special audit procedures based on the assessed risk of material misstatement as a result of the fraud. For example, special audit procedures can include obtaining external confirmation from suppliers and customers, as well as counting cash and reviewing securities. An auditor has thus potentially a significant role in crime prevention and detection.

Audit fees represent boundaries within which auditors can work in terms of time and effort. Suryanto (2014: 28) claimed that an important aspect of auditors reaching their purpose is "the ability to conduct audit works in accordance with auditing standards". With sufficient audit fees, auditors are able to spend enough time to perform their role and responsibility during audits. The amount of time, in turn, will "affect the amount of audit fee to be received or determined" (Suryanto (2014: 37).

Audit fees should be sufficient to review internal controls, require separation of functions, establish managerial controls, and influence whistleblowing effectiveness as suggested by Farrell and Franco (1999: 8) in an effort to prevent and detect white-collar crime: "To combat the problem of fraud, a crucial element in deterring theft is strict internal controls, segregation of duties, and separation of functions". "All professional literature makes it clear that the responsibility of internal controls, proper reporting, and adoption of sound accounting policies rests solely with management" (Farrell and Franco, 1999: 8). Auditors can aid in establishing managerial controls.

Zager et al. (2016: 697) highlighted the auditor's role and responsibilities in the fight against fraud as the auditor is "responsible for obtaining reasonable assurance that the financial statements taken as a while are free from material misstatement, whether caused by fraud or error". They argued that the auditor is responsible for maintaining professional skepticism throughout the audit and for awareness of the potential for management to override controls. They found that the establishment of an appropriate number of audits and internal controls in a company has significant impact on the prevention and detection of fraud, where the number of audits is influenced by the audit fee. The specific measures an auditor can take in curbing white-collar crime are to require and review internal controls, review accounting substance rather than accounting procedures, maintain professional skepticism, and review and control management.

The offender-based perspective in addition to the offense-based perspective is needed to prevent and detect white-collar crime. While financial misstatements represent evidence of wrongdoing, the wrongdoer has to be identified. The offender-based perspective emphasizes characteristics of actors such as social and occupational status, respectability, and power (Friedrichs et al., 2018; Pontell et al., 2014). This offender-based definition emphasizes some combination of the actors' high social status, power, and respectability as the key features of white-collar crime (Benson, 2021). The offense-based definition focuses on the acts of white-collar crime, where distinctions can be made between groups such as fraud, theft, manipulation, and corruption, with a number of subgroups. Offense-based approaches to white-collar crime emphasize the actions and nature of the illegal acts as the defining agent (Galvin et al. 2018; Piquero, 2018). For example, white-collar crime is considered a non-violent offense (Berghoff and Spiekermann, 2018).

Mohliver (2019) discussed potential consequences of auditors reporting white-collar crime suspicions to the criminal justice system. One consequence might be that the harmed client organization switches to a different audit firm. Another consequence might be that auditor integrity and accountability is confirmed in the market for professional services. Combatting white-collar crime implies accepting potential harm from reporting fraud to public authorities and being loyal to the audit task and not to the client.

Hurley et al. (2019: 32) found that "removing auditors' economic accountability to managers and replacing it with . . . accountability to investors significantly increases audit quality". Auditors should not primarily be accountable to the companies they are auditing but rather to companies' current and future investors. Auditors should be independent of management and report to the board of directors or the supervisory board as representative of the owners depending on corporate legal structures in various countries (Alon et al., 2019). It is again emphasized that auditors have to accept potential harm to their business from reporting fraud to public authorities.

One aspect of being skeptical in audit work relates to the frequent high status, sometimes even heroic or superstar status, of the chief executive officer (CEO) in the client organization. Status is an individual's social rank within a formal or informal hierarchy, or the person's relative standing along a valued social dimension. Status is the extent to which an individual is respected and admired by others, and status is the outcome of a subjective assessment process

(McClean et al., 2018). High-status individuals enjoy greater respect and deference from, as well as power and influence over, those who are positioned lower in the social hierarchy (Kakkar et al., 2020.532):

> Status is a property that rests in the eyes of others and is conferred to individuals who are deemed to have a higher rank or social standing in a pecking order based on a mutually valued set of social attributes. Higher social status or rank grants its holder a host of tangible benefits in both professional and personal domains. For instance, high-status actors are sought by groups for advice, are paid higher, receive unsolicited help, and are credited disproportionately in joint tasks. In innumerable ways, our social ecosystem consistently rewards those with high status.

Harvin and Killey (2021) highlighted the potential effect a superstar status of the CEO can have on the auditor. Their study found that superstar status might have a negative impact on the risk assessment that auditors conduct. Auditors can unwittingly or consciously lower the risk assessment as a result of the CEO status. In their study, Harvin and Killey (2021: 502) stressed the importance of professional skepticism, meaning that the auditor "maintains a neutral attitude pertaining to the adequacy of the client's financial statements" while having a "questioning mind and suspension of judgment which indicates neither a trust or distrust of management". Professional skepticism refers to an attitude that includes a questioning mind, being alert to conditions, which may indicate possible misstatements due to error or fraud, and a critical assessment of audit evidence. The recommendation is to ignore the potential superstar status of the CEO and maintain professional skepticism.

Whistleblowers are an important source of information regarding potential wrongdoing. Whistleblowing is the disclosure by an individual in an organization or in society of deviant practices to someone who can do something about it (Bjørkelo et al., 2011). Whistleblowing is an action by employees who believe that their business or colleague(s) are involved in activities of misconduct or crime, cause unnecessary harm, violate human rights, or contribute to otherwise immoral offenses (Mpho, 2017). Whistleblowers stand out as a group of reporters who have made observations and who are willing to disclose what they have observed. However, executives may try to withhold bad news (Bao et al., 2019) and punish whistleblowers by reprisals and retaliation. Even when whistleblowing messages are difficult to understand, and it is complicated to relate to whistleblowers, it is nevertheless important for auditors to take the time to understand the messages.

Another aspect of whistleblowing importance is at potential negligence or wrongdoing on the part of auditors. Alleyne et al. (2013: 11) emphasized whistleblowing as an important measure within audit firms to warn of ignorance and other forms of deviance: "external audit promotes the view that public interest is protected by making corporate managers and their companies accountable". The problem is that auditing firms are pursuing profits, and auditors are pursuing personal income that may harm wider social interests. There is sometimes the need to blow the whistle on colleague auditors who adopt irregular auditing practices and who sometimes even resort to the falsification of audit working papers. Colleague auditors as wrongdoing observers need to "protect the interests of both the public and the profession by blowing the whistle on colleagues who commit wrongdoing" (Alleyne et al., 2013: 10).

Not only whistleblowing messages and whistleblowers can be difficult to understand. Detection by auditors is a matter of being able to distinguish crime signals from noise signals. There is typically interference and noise in crime signals. Misconduct and crime can be hard to detect (Friedrich, 2020), because signals of deviant behavior drown or disappear in noise (Gomulya and Mishina, 2017). Karim and Siegel (1998) defined four possible outcomes in the decision matrix of an observer. First, the observer notices a noise signal when it is a crime signal (called a miss). Second, the observer notices a crime signal when it is a crime signal (called a hit). Third, the observer notices a noise signal when it is a noise signal (called a correct identification). Finally, the observer notices a crime signal when it is a noise signal (called a false alarm). The more relative frequent false alarms and misses occur, the less efficient is the audit. The more relative frequent hits and notifications occur, the more efficient is the audit.

The extent of hits and notifications relative to false alarms and misses is dependent on the auditor's signal alertness, discerning ability, and pattern recognition. Signal alertness is a unique readiness to recognize misconduct opportunities when they exist. Discerning ability is concerned with information-bearing recognition and random recognition that distracts from relevant insights. Pattern recognition is concerned with screening of data elements where the auditor prioritizes among possible types of signals. The focus at pattern recognition is how the auditor places differential value on signals that may come from different senders such as documents, accounts, and individuals. Auditors have to screen by focusing on signals that they believe are highly correlated with unobservable characteristics of interest (Gomulya and Mishina, 2017). Szalma and Hancock (2013) stressed that control functions typically need higher signal alertness, and that such functions need the ability to recognize and interpret patterns in signals.

Herron and Cornell (2021) emphasized creativity in the audit process relating to fraud risk cues. Creativity is the use of imagination and original ideas to create new insights into phenomena. Auditors have to avoid standardization in audit work that harms audit creativity.

Recognition of and responses to fraud cues are often dependent on observer creativity. Bishop (2022) recommended auditors an improvisational style of thinking, a tolerance for unpredictability and uncertainty, and an open-mindedness that is associated with responses to perceived fraud risk cues. To avoid tunnel vision of not seeing anything else but the end of the tunnel, auditors should avoid rigid procedures and documentation requirements of auditing standards and regulatory guidelines in the creative search for deviance and potential offenders. "Auditor creativity is related to the ability to detect and respond to potential fraud in ways that are unlikely to be captured by standardized procedures" (Herron and Cornell, 2021: 324).

Asare et al. (2015) suggested that auditors need to assess management's incentives to commit fraud, management's opportunities to commit fraud, and management's willingness to commit fraud. This is in line with convenience theory that suggests motive, opportunity, and willingness as the three interrelated dimensions for white-collar crime (Gottschalk, 2022). On the basis of auditors' assessments, audit programs have to be modified to fit the threat assessments.

Several scholars reiterate the need for auditors to practice professional skepticism to prevent and detect fraud. For example, Martinez (2022) emphasized discussions with executives to understand their potential deviance, while Schuster (2021) emphasized auditors' understanding of the client businesses and industry. Andrew et al. (2022) highlighted the importance of providing a proper audit opinion that cannot be abused by management to rationalize fraud.

Forensic auditing represents a bottom-up approach to detection of white-collar crime (Baird and Zelin, 2009; Shawver and Clements, 2019; Sonnier et al., 2015). Forensic auditing is an activity that focuses on the gathering, verifying, processing, analyzing, and reporting information within a predefined context in the area of financial irregularities and wrongdoing. Forensic accounting is the tracking and collection of investigative evidence for potential prosecution of financial crime. It is a professional service that is caused by disputes, allegations, and rumors. Forensic auditing refers to examination, review, and evaluation of financial information for use as evidence of wrongdoing by trusted individuals in the organization (Oyerogba, 2021).

Convenience Disturbance Themes

Convenience theory is an emerging theoretical perspective to explain the phenomenon of white-collar crime where convenience was first introduced as a core concept by Gottschalk (2017). Recently, the theory has been reviewed (e.g., Chan and Gibbs, 2020; Hansen, 2020; Oka, 2021; Vasiu, 2021; Vasiu and Podgor, 2019) and applied by several scholars such as Asting and Gottschalk (2022), Braaten and Vaughn (2019), Dearden and Gottschalk (2020), Desmond et al. (2022), Qu (2021), Stadler and Gottschalk (2022), and Sterri and Borge (2022).

A combination of motive, opportunity, and willingness determines the extent of white-collar crime convenience as illustrated in the structural model in Figure 9.1.

In the financial motive dimension, profit might be a goal in itself or an enabler to exploit possibilities and to avoid threats. Possibilities and threats exist both for individual members of the organization and for the organization as a whole. It is convenient to exploit possibilities and to avoid threats by illegitimate financial means (Gottschalk, 2022).

In the organizational opportunity dimension, convenience can exist both to commit white-collar crime and to conceal crime. Offenders have high social status in privileged positions, and they have legitimate access to crime

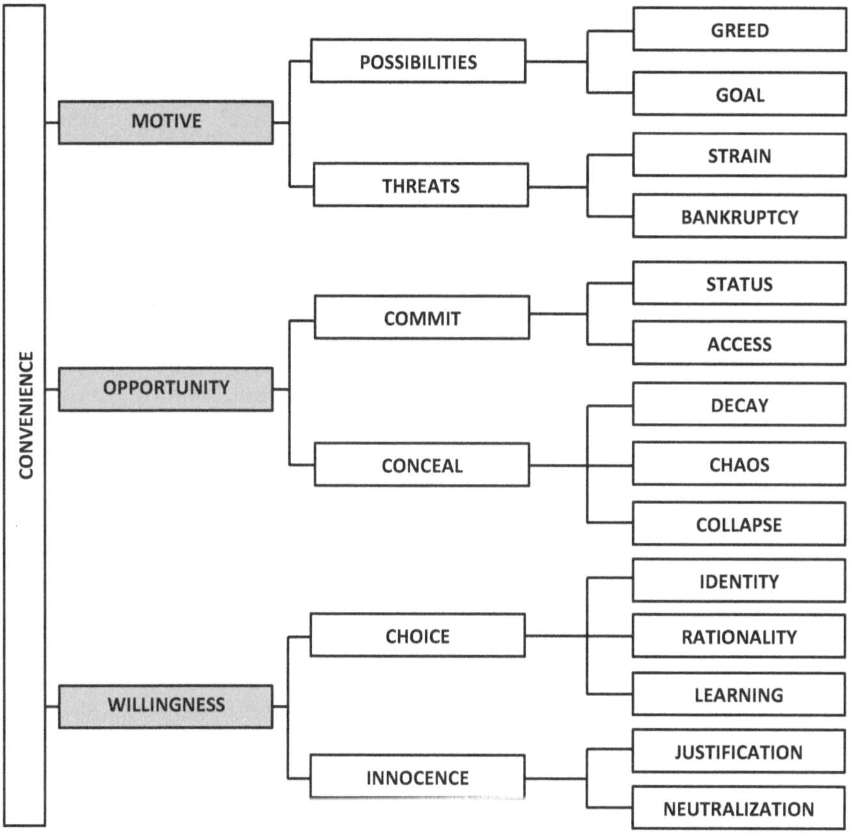

Figure 9.1 Structural model of convenience propositions

resources. Disorganized institutional deterioration causes decay, lack of oversight and guardianship cause chaos, while criminal market structures cause collapse (Gottschalk, 2022).

The personal willingness for deviant behavior focuses on offender choice and perceived innocence. The choice of crime can be caused by deviant identity, rational consideration, or learning from others. Justification and neutralization cause the perceived innocence at crime. Identity, rationality, learning, justification, and neutralization all contribute to making white-collar crime action a convenient behavior for offenders (Gottschalk, 2022).

The convenience triangle for white-collar crime has similarities with the fraud triangle (Cressey, 1972; Wells, 1997), which suggests three conditions for fraud: (1) incentives and pressures, (2) opportunities, and (3) attitudes and rationalization. However, there are three distinct differences. First, convenience is a relative concept, indicating that offenders have the option of alternative actions to reach their goals that do not represent illegitimate behavior. While the fraud triangle suggests that opportunities will stimulate crime, the convenience triangle suggests that relative opportunities will stimulate crime. There is no reason to commit crime, even if there are many opportunities, as long as alternative convenient decisions may lead to the same result. It is the extent of relative convenience, and not the extent of opportunity, that determines whether an offense is attractive. A very conveniently oriented decision maker may resort to illegal activities when legal activities are slightly more stressful. A less conveniently oriented decision maker may try intensely to solve problems and explore opportunities without violating the law.

Second, it is in the organizational setting where offenders have access to resources so that opportunity arises to commit and conceal crime. While the fraud triangle emphasizes opportunity in general, the convenience triangle concentrates on the privileged position that offenders can abuse to commit and conceal crime. There is trust and lack of control, obedience and fear, which create convenient opportunities. The convenient opportunity derives from legitimate access to resources in a trusted position without guardians, where resources are enablers to carry out activities that are not available to others. Opportunity convenience emerges because of an organizational structure and an organizational culture where members of the elite may feel above the law.

Third, a white-collar offender can influence the organizational opportunity over time. Therefore, opportunity in convenience theory is a dynamic rather than a static condition. By collecting decision rights, by controlling information flows, and by authoritarian leadership styles, a potential offender develops an opportunity space that grows over time. Whether intentional or not, the opportunity space changes over time as a reaction to the potential offender's behavior.

Disturbing Motive Convenience

Convenience theory suggests that a strong financial motive based on possibilities and threats is part of the explanation for the phenomenon of white-collar crime occurrence. High-performance goal-oriented companies with lucrative individual bonus schemes are associated with strong financial motives for white-collar crime. Therefore, the role of auditors is to review and assess the realism of financial business goals and the extent of individual bonus schemes. With professional skepticism (Harvin and Killey, 2021; Martinez, 2022; Schuster, 2021; Zager et al., 2016), auditors should report their assessments to the owners or their representatives on the supervisory board or the board of directors depending on the legal structure of companies in various jurisdictions.

Welsh and Ordonez (2014) found that high performance goals cause unethical behavior. Dodge (2009: 15) suggested that tough rivalry among executives make them commit crime to attain goals: "The competitive environment generates pressures on the organization to violate the law in order to attain goals". Goal setting is often perceived in a positive light, meaning that ambitious goals increase performance (Locke and Latham, 2013). However, there is also evidence suggesting that high performance goals can lead to unethical behavior (Schweitzer et al., 2004; Simmons, 2018). Welsh et al. (2020) argued that this is not only because of rewards associated with goal attainment but also because of changing morale reasoning processes related to the goal. As such, high goal commitment facilitates unethical behavior by increasing not only the motivation to achieve the goal but also the motivation to justify doing so by any means necessary (Locatelli et al., 2017). This is known as state morale disagreement, a process through which individuals justify unethical behavior (Moore, 2015) and disengage morally (Theoharakis et al., 2021). It is part of the dark side of ambitious goals where the dark side is an evolutionary, socially constructed, and subjective concept (Locatelli et al., 2022).

Escalation of commitment to ambitious goals increases the likelihood of misconduct and crime (Sleesman et al., 2012, 2018). Escalation of commitment is defined as "decision-making in the face of negative feedback about prior resource allocations, uncertainty surrounding the likelihood of goal attainment, and choice about whether to continue" (Keil et al., 2007: 392).

When an organization develops and maintains a strong systematic socialization program, employees identify not only with the organization but also with its goals. When personal promotion or dismissal, as well as bonuses and benefits link directly and individually to the achievement of goals, then employees identify even stronger with organizational goals. When the socialization process couples tightly to strong accountability systems, employees perceive the pressure from individually oriented regulation to achieve organizational goals. The pursuit of goals therefore does not at all imply the absence of crime. The bottom-line focus within an organizational context might increase the frequency of financial crime on behalf of the organization for profit or enhancement. A strong emphasis on goal attainment might indeed lead organizational members to engage in illegal acts (Kang and Thosuwanchot, 2017).

Incentive systems such as bonus arrangements can lead to white-collar crime such as corruption to meet sales targets or other targets on which bonus payments depend. Alternatively, the offender can pretend having met targets by manipulating accounting (Nichol, 2019: 329):

> Bonus contracts have come under a great deal of criticism in the past few years for creating incentives that encourage managers to manipulate accounting information in order to maximize their pay. Such manipulation can range from subtle earnings manipulation to outright fraud.

When executives perceive high performance goals as invariable, personal desperation for goal achievement can result (Kuvaas et al., 2016: 401):

> Perceiving goals as invariable refers to the extent to which employees believe that the goals in a performance management system represent absolute standards that they must meet without exception, even if they think other factors are more important.

Corporate greed implies that the organization is never satisfied, as it always wants more profit (Goldstraw-White, 2012). Greed reflects needs and desires that are socially constructed, and the needs and desires can never be completely covered or contended. There is a strong preference to maximize wealth for the corporation, possibly at the expense of violating the laws, rules, and guidelines. Economic greed is a strong motive for financial crime (Bucy et al., 2008; Hamilton and Micklethwait, 2006).

Along the threat axis of motive in convenience theory, there is the strain perspective at the individual level and the bankruptcy perspective at the corporate level. Both perspectives require professional skepticism on the part of auditors (Harvin and Killey, 2021; Martinez, 2022; Schuster, 2021; Zager et al., 2016).

The strain perspective emphasizes the frustration of not succeeding with a task, such as the inability to achieve economic prosperity. Strains tend to generate negative emotions, such as anger, depression, and despair. These negative emotions create pressures for corrective action to reduce the gap between the desired and the actual situation, with crime being one possible response. The strain perspective emphasizes strains and stressors that increase the likelihood of crime, the negative emotions (including anger) resulting from those strains that create pressure for corrective action, and the factors that influence or condition the likelihood of criminal coping (Thaxton and Agnew, 2018). Stress is a psychological state that arises from a mismatch between perceived demands and one's ability to meet those demands given available resources (Linder et al., 2021).

The threat of corporate collapse and bankruptcy might cause exploration and exploitation of illegal avenues to survive, where moral panic can occur (Kang and Thosuwanchot, 2017). The survival of the corporation can become so important that no means come across as unacceptable in the current situation (Blickle et al., 2006). Sometimes, fraud and corruption are considered temporary measures to recover from a crisis (Geest et al., 2017), where the measures will be terminated when the crisis is over. A crisis is a fundamental threat to the organization, which is often characterized by ambiguity of cause, effect, and means of resolution (König et al., 2020).

Auditors are charged with the task of identifying and assessing risk factors that exist in and for the companies being audited. Auditors should not accept the concept of ends justifying means when the means represent misconduct or crime. Reaching business objectives by ignoring whether or not means are legitimate or illegitimate should not be acceptable to auditors. Understanding the corporate environment can help auditors reflect on corporate goals and actions. As auditors gain such understanding, they are able to present opinions and consult on crisis measures available in the industry. Auditor advice will aid in the disturbance of motive regarding financial crime. Although auditors cannot directly influence owner decisions, they can nevertheless tell boards and others what increases the risks of misconduct and crime. Working with boards and owners of organizations, often without the presence of executives, auditors can report and provide feedback on targets and strategies. Auditors can alert board members if they think that CEO motives are causing the business to develop in the wrong direction. Auditors have a role of providing advice that is based on their professional knowledge as well as their insights into various client organizations.

Disturbing Opportunity Convenience

Convenience theory suggests that a simple organizational opportunity to commit and conceal wrongdoing is part of the explanation for the phenomenon of white-collar crime occurrence. Some executives have a status implying that they might be "too big to fail and too powerful to jail" (Pontell et al., 2014: 1). Harvin and Killey (2021) suggested that auditor response to this phenomenon should be to ignore the potential superstar status of executives generally and the CEO particularly. One aspect of being professionally skeptical in audit work relates to the frequent high status, sometimes even heroic or superstar status, of CEOs in client organizations (Kakkar et al., 2020; McClean et al., 2018).

Ignoring status includes disregarding strange language and executive humor. Deviant individuals with high social status in privileged positions might not only use language that simply does not make sense to people. White-collar offenders can also use humor to distract attention from their crime. Offender humor distraction as suggested by Yam et al. (2018) implies that potential white-collar offenders can influence the organizational opportunity structure by aggressive humor. Aggressive humor is a negatively directed style of humor that an individual carries out at the expense and detriment of one's relationships with others. It can be teasing with a humorous undertone, or it can be victimization of the receiver. It can be the opposite of self-irony, where the offender makes jokes about others and makes them look ridiculous. The more aggressive an offender's style, the more a sense of humor will signal acceptability of norm violations for the offender. Aggressive humor is a form of hostile behavior. Auditors might observe yet ignore hostile behavior and ask the same professional questions regardless of the behavior of some top managers. While charismatic top executives can override their own organizations and their own controls, auditors have to respond by reporting observations to owner representatives.

According to the theory of convenience, it is the combination of status and access that creates the opportunity structure to commit white-collar crime. Legitimate access to resources can be restricted and monitored based on advice from auditors. For example, auditors can suggest separation of functions and internal controls. As stated by Farrell and Franco (1999), strict internal controls, segregation of duties, as well as separation of functions are needed to combat fraud.

A resource is an enabler applied and used to satisfy human and organizational needs. A resource has utility and limited availability. A white-collar offender has usually access to resources that are valuable (application of the resource provides desired outcome), unique (very few have access to the resource), not imitable (resource cannot be copied), not transferrable (resource cannot be released from context), combinable with other resources (results in better outcome), exploitable (possible to apply in criminal activities), and not substitutable (cannot be replaced by a different resource). According to Petrocelli et al. (2003), access to resources equates access to power. Others are losers in the competition for resources (Wheelock et al., 2011). Auditors need to ensure that segregation of duties and separation of functions regulates access to resources since the resource-based perspective postulates that differences in individuals' opportunities find explanation in the extent of resource access and the ability to combine and exploit those resources.

Disturbing the convenience of concealing financial crime by white-collar offenders is potentially at the core of auditors' efforts as concealment is a matter of lack of oversight and guardianship. Guardianship is supervision that may prevent crime by the presence of individuals who are capable and willing to detect and react to wrongdoing. It is the presence of individuals who may deter crime, informal social control, self-protective or target hardening mechanisms, stakeholder watchdogs such as union leaders, auditing, and other guardianship instruments. However, as argued by Chan and Gibbs (2022), the presence of guardians does not necessarily equate to capability in crime prevention, especially when studied in a dynamic perspective. For example, potential offenders may over time learn how guardians operate and thus how to avoid the attention of guardianship functions.

Even more challenging in the perspective of convenience for potential offenders is the change of role from guardians to offenders where "top managers directly charged with implementing guardianship procedures and protocols were able to leverage their positions/roles to circumvent controls as they acquire motivation to offend" (Chan and Gibbs, 2022: 2). An overlap between corporate guardians and offenders can thus emerge where guardianship becomes non-existent in practice.

Alon et al. (2019) discussed the importance of protecting the owners and shareholders of a firm as opposed to the executives and managers. Owners are interested in ensuring that the board has had instructions for the CEO, and that the CEO follows the instructions. Auditors should ensure that the owners' preferences and risk opinions are manifested in internal controls of executives. By reporting to owners and shareholders, and not protecting executives and managers, auditors might prevent and detect white-collar crime by disturbing the opportunity to conceal illicit activities that could cause decay of organizations from within.

An important initiative by auditors is increased transparency in accounting. The discourse and rituals of transparency, account-giving, and verification are central to corporate governance (Mehrpouya and Salles-Djelic, 2019: 13):

> Transparency has been a normative shell through which financial accounting and audit standards have been pushed around the world. Under the contemporary governance paradigm, financial disclosure regimes are an important dimension of what it means to make organizations, states and individuals transparent and accountable. Champions of transparency, such as

> the former head of the IMF, Michel Camdessus, describe transparency as the "golden rule" of the new international financial system, "absolutely central to the task of civilizing globalization". . . . Transparency implies unhindered access to information for the public. However, the definition of the public, targets and beneficiaries of transparency, along with associated programs and technologies, has been contested and has evolved through time.

Mehrpouya and Salles-Djelic (2019) found that a range of organizations mobilized transparency to champion public accountability. Transparency was also championed to fight corruption and protect customers.

Whistleblowers can be an important source of information for auditors (Alleyne et al., 2013; Bjørkelo et al., 2011; Mpho, 2017). Therefore, auditors should involve themselves in the development and implementation of whistleblowing routines in client organizations. Whistleblowing routines have to be trustworthy for potential whistleblowers as it is important to avoid the fear of retaliation and the fear of conspiracy theories. For example, an approach to executive deviance among cartel members would be to blow the whistle on white-collar crime (Freiberg, 2020; Goncharov and Peter, 2019).

Auditors might emphasize the social license to operate in addition to the legal license to operate when they are communicating their audits in client organizations. Haines et al. (2022: 184) examined "how social control in the form of community pressure might be used to control corporate harm and shape business conduct in a more socially responsible direction". They suggested a social license to civilize, control, or repel corporate activity. They defined a social license as acceptance of a business or business activity within a particular community. The social license adds to the legal license to operate business activities. The social license forms part of a strategy where criminalization becomes social property independent of the criminal justice system. The social license is predominantly centered on social permission for business activity where the media, social movements, and citizen watchdogs exert pressure, demand change, and bring enterprises to account. Similarly, Sale (2021) defined social license as the acceptance of business or organization by the relevant communities and stakeholders.

The extent of oversight and guardianship by auditors is dependent on a number of factors including sufficient funding for the audit work. Suryanto (2014) found that the quality of audits relates to the amount of time that will be spent in the audit process. If an auditor requires more funding, then the auditor can do a more thorough audit and increase the disturbance of potential white-collar crime and increase the likelihood of crime detection. Similarly, Alleyne et al. (2013) expressed concern regarding budget constraints for audits.

Disturbing Willingness Convenience

Convenience theory suggests that a high extent of willingness for deviant behavior is part of the explanation for the phenomenon of white-collar crime occurrence. Willingness is a matter of choice based on identity, rationality, and learning; or it is a matter of innocence based on justification or neutralization.

Narcissistic identity is a special type of narcissism, where the offender sees little or no difference between self and the corporation. The company money is personal money that can be spent whatever way the narcissist prefers (Galvin et al., 2015). Identification with the organization is the process through which an individual's identity becomes entangled with, and imprinted by, the corporation. The person's unique sense of self comes to be understood in reference to that organization, where the organization defines individual self (Toubiana, 2020). Auditors might counter narcissistic identities in their professional skepticism (Zager et al., 2016), where they also might counter potential superstar status of executives (Harvin and Killey, 2021).

Rationality is a consideration of advantages versus disadvantages that are subjectively compared (Müller, 2018; Pratt and Cullen, 2005). If the benefits of crime are less than the costs of crime, then it is not considered rational to commit crime. When auditors successfully improve transparency (Goncharov and Peter, 2019), oversight (Alon et al., 2019), as well as guardianship (Chan and Gibbs, 2022), then the costs of crime increase, thereby reducing the willingness for deviant behavior in client organizations. Specifically, one way in which auditors can disturb willingness is by reviewing, assessing, and arguing for improvements in internal controls in terms of substance rather than formalism. As Farrell and Franco (1999: 4) formulated it, "to combat the problem of fraud, a crucial element in deterring theft is strict internal controls". Similarly, Zager et al. (2016: 699) argued that "the establishment of an appropriate number of internal controls in the company has a significant impact on the prevention of fraud". Furthermore, auditors must make sure that there is no "potential for management override of controls" (Zager et al., 2016: 697). The substance might be illegal funds where offenders attempt to avoid the attention of external and internal control mechanisms, including corporate compliance functions (Gao and Zhang, 2019; Kawasaki, 2020). Rationality is disturbed by increased perceived costs among potential offenders as a result of stronger focus on internal controls as well as by more relevant assessment of management's incentives and opportunities to commit fraud and by modified audit programs away from generic standards given "the fraud cues in the case" (Asare et al., 2015: 90). When auditors develop more relevant understanding and assessment of fraud risks and implement their insights into audit programs and recommendations for internal controls, then actual as well as perceived likelihood of deviance detection increases, which in turn will impact the cost–benefit ratio for potential offenders. Auditors, through their work, aim for the cost of crime significantly to outweigh the benefits of crime.

Learning in the offender mind is a result of personal differential association as suggested by Sutherland (1983). The differential association perspective implies that potential offenders have a preference where they associate with those who agree with them, and distance themselves from those who disagree. This perspective suggests that whether individuals engage in white-collar crime or not depends on their socialization within certain peer groups. The alternative socialization with auditors might reduce the deviant learning effect.

In a justification, the actor admits responsibility for the act in question but denies its pejorative and negative content (Schoen et al., 2021: 730):

> People use justification mechanisms to protect their sense of self. People who sincerely believe that they are a specific kind of person but routinely demonstrate behaviors that indicate otherwise may avoid cognitive dissonance and maintain their sense of self by using justification mechanisms that allow them to "explain away" their behavior.

Martinez (2022) reiterated that auditors must maintain professional skepticism and not accept justification of deviant behavior. Professional skepticism was emphasized by a number of scholars such as Harvin and Killey (2021), Schuster (2021), and Zager et al. (2016). Schuster (2021: 154) concluded that "the continuous use of professional skepticism is needed to promote a high-level audit and to ensure the process's quality".

Neutralization is removal of any potential guilt feelings where the offender does not feel accountable, ashamed, or responsible (Chen and Moosmayer, 2020). Transparency caused by auditors might make it harder for offenders to disclaim responsibility for crime, refuse damage from crime, and refuse victim from crime.

Another innocence perspective in addition to justification and neutralization is sliding on the slippery slope that can make the offender feel innocent, as the offender did not notice ending up on the wrong side of the law (Welsh et al., 2014). Arjoon (2008: 78) explained slippery slope in the following way: "As commonsense experience tells us; it is the small infractions that can lead to the larger ones". A series of small infractions gradually increases over time. Committing small indiscretions over time gradually lead people to complete larger unethical acts that they otherwise would have judged impermissible (Murphy and Dacin, 2011; Pettigrew, 2018). The role of risk assessments by auditors is important in this context as forecasts of sliding on the slippery slope.

Auditing Practice Disturbance Gap

Like certified accountants, certified auditors can give the company legitimacy and can be used to facilitate or commit various forms of financial crime. Økokrim (2021) found that auditors often have chosen to resign from their role at those companies where they have not received sufficient answers to questions. Some auditors are suspected of approving accounts without special control, or they even more actively assist criminals. These auditors are often associated with companies that operate in the gray zone for what is legal. Some auditors accept reporting and being loyal to deviant management (Hurley et al., 2019). In the outside-in perspective on corporate control, the ideal contribution from auditors would be to deny acceptance of accounts where their queries are not satisfactorily answered and report their findings to the board of directors as well as externally to public authorities.

Concealing illegal transactions may result from the failure of auditors to do their job. Alon et al. (2019) argued that accounting and auditing functions have undergone a legitimacy crisis in recent years. Auditors are supposed to serve as gatekeepers to protect shareholders and other stakeholders, but deviant corporate management tends to hire and control auditors instead of letting auditors report to the board of directors or the supervisory board (Hurley et al., 2019). Skeptical auditors tend to be replaced by less skeptical auditors. Reporting fraud to public authorities will also harm auditors (Mohliver, 2019: 316):

> As organizations, audit firms are often severely penalized for client malfeasance. Yet the individual auditors working for these firms are susceptible to "motivated blindness" stemming from conflicts of interest that bias their moral judgment toward choices that help their clients.

The lack of detection by auditors can also be explained by standardization. Herron and Cornell (2021) found that audit work is standardized which harms auditors creativity, thereby preventing recognition of and responses to fraud cues. Standardization harms an improvisational style of thinking, tolerance for unpredictability, and uncertainty, and open-mindedness that is associated with responses to perceived fraud risk cues.

Shadnam and Lawrence (2011) found that morale collapse increases the tendency to financial crime. In fact, repetition of criminal actions might institutionalize such actions. Dion (2008) found that the larger the corporation, the less deterrence effect from laws on financial crime, which may have to do with increased convenience in concealing crime.

A chief financial officer (CFO) in Norway became divorced and his financial motive became stronger. The growing motive caused him to search for opportunity expansion in the organization. One of his actions was to take control over the auditing process, where he succeeded in controlling that what the auditor presented to the CEO and the board of directors. He was thus able to make the organizational opportunity larger. As he noticed that he succeeded in organizational opportunity expansion, his willingness for deviant behavior became greater than it was before.

Hestnes (2017) asked the question in his study of the CFO case: Why did the auditor fail in detecting embezzlement at the company? Normally in a Norwegian context, the auditor is to report annually to the board in the business where the auditor has reviewed accounts. Since the cooperation between the auditor and the CFO went so smoothly, the CEO did not invite the auditor anymore to board meetings. This is where the fourth opportunity expansion occurred. The CFO became the actual person to report external audit results to the board. Mohliver (2019) found that auditor bias toward accepting deviant financial reports increased when there is ambiguity about the appropriateness of a course of action. Financial misreporting that is viewed favorably by the client organization can be recommended by external auditors on the grounds that such reporting is already adopted among companies served by the same auditing firm.

A mechanism for outside-in effects on executive compliance is the threat for both accountants and auditors to be fined and potentially sent to prison. A financial scandal in Norway in a company named Finance Credit caused prison sentences not only for two executives at Finance Credit but also for two auditors from the audit firm KPMG. The auditors were incarcerated because they had helped the white-collar offenders create a non-transparent and complicated corporate structure enabling the offenders to make it look like all subsidiaries were financially sound. A similar case in Norway was the auditor for Sponsor Service, who was reluctant to criticize and question some of the numbers in the accounts. This auditor ended up in prison as well.

Økokrim's (2021) overall assessment regarding auditors was that auditors associate with crime mainly as passive participants. It was considered highly likely that those companies where white-collar crime occur, that both accounting and auditing suffered from shortcomings. The challenge for the criminal justice system is to determine to what extent such professional service providers facilitate crime.

The financial supervisory authority of Norway has revoked the approval as state-authorized public accountants for, among other things, failure to obtain documentation, lack of documentation of performed audits, for not having acted neutrally by having changed the accounts of clients at their requests, and inadequate assessments when entering into client relationships.

In conclusion, the discrepancy between the reluctance of auditors to interfere and the potential benefits from auditors' interference has been evidenced in this chapter. A number of actions based on an attitude of preventing and detecting white-collar offenses have been suggested. Some of the actions require approval by others such as sufficient funding to conduct substance control rather than formal control. Other actions require a state of mind where auditors are not influenced by the heroic status and the humor of chief executives.

References

Alleyne, P., Hudaib, M. and Pike, R. (2013). Towards a conceptual model of whistle-blowing intentions among external auditors, *The British Accounting Review*, 45 (1), 10–23.

Alon, A., Mennicken, A. and Samsonova-Taddei, A. (2019). Dynamics and limits of regulatory privatization: Reorganizing audit oversight in Russia, *Organization Studies*, 40 (8), 1217–1239.

Andrew, A., Candy, C. and Robin, R. (2022). Detecting fraudulent of financial statements using fraud S.C.O.R.E model and financial distress, *International Journal of Economics, Business and Accounting Research*, 6 (1), 211–222.

Arjoon, S. (2008). Slippery when wet: The real risk in business, *Journal of Markets & Morality*, Spring, 11 (1), 77–91.

Asare, S., Wright, A. and Zimbelman, M. (2015). Challenges facing auditors in detecting financial statement fraud: Insights from fraud investigations, *Journal of Forensic & Investigative Accounting*, 7 (2), 63–112.

Asting, C. and Gottschalk, P. (2022). Attorney fraud in the law firm: A case study of crime convenience theory and crime signal detection theory, *Deviant Behavior*, published online doi: 10.1080/01639625.2022.2071657.

Baird, J.E. and Zelin, R.C. (2009). An examination of the impact of obedience pressure on perceptions of fraudulent acts and the likelihood of committing occupational fraud, *Journal of Forensic Studies in Accounting and Business*, 1 (1), 1–14.

Bao, D., Kim, Y., Mian, G.M. and Su, L. (2019). Do managers disclose or withhold bad news? Evidence from short interest, *The Accounting Review*, 94 (3), 1–26.

Benson, M.L. (2021). Theoretical and empirical advances in the study and control of white-collar offenders, *Justice Evaluation Journal*, 4 (1), 1–20.

Berghoff, H. and Spiekermann, U. (2018). Shady business: On the history of white-collar crime, *Business History*, 60 (3), 289–304.

Bishop, D.Y. (2022). *Fraud Risk Management to Detect and Prevent Employee Fraud in Small Rural Businesses*, Dissertation submitted in partial fulfillment of the requirements for the degree of Doctor of Business Administration, Liberty University, School of Business, August, 221 pages.

Bjørkelo, B., Einarsen, S., Nielsen, M.B. and Matthiesen, S.B. (2011). Silence is golden? Characteristics and experiences of self-reported whistleblowers, *European Journal of Work and Organizational Psychology*, 20 (2), 206–238.

Blickle, G., Schlegel, A., Fassbender, P. og Klein, U. (2006). Some personality correlates of business white-collar crime, *Applied Psychology: An International Review*, 55 (2), 220–233.

Braaten, C.N. and Vaughn, M.S. (2019). Convenience theory of cryptocurrency crime: A content analysis of U.S. federal court decisions, *Deviant Behavior*, published online doi: 10.1080/01639625.2019.1706706.

Bucy, P.H., Formby, E.P., Raspanti, M.S. and Rooney, K.E. (2008). Why do they do it? The motives, mores, and character of white collar criminals, *St. John's Law Review*, 82, 401–571.

Chan, F. and Gibbs, C. (2020). Integrated theories of white-collar and corporate crime, in: Rorie, M.L. (editor), *The Handbook of White-Collar Crime*, Wiley & Sons, Hoboken, NJ, chapter 13, pages 191–208.

Chan, F. and Gibbs, C. (2022). When guardians become offenders: Understanding guardian capability through the lens of corporate crime, *Criminology*, 1–21, published online doi: 10.1111/1745-9125.12300.

Chen, Y. and Moosmayer, D.C. (2020). When guilt is not enough: Interdependent self-construal as moderator of the relationship between guilt and ethical consumption in a Confucian context, *Journal of Business Ethics*, 161, 551–572.

Cressey, D. (1972). *Criminal Organization: Its Elementary Forms*, Harper and Row, New York, NY.

Dearden, T.E. and Gottschalk, P. (2020). Gender and white-collar crime: Convenience in target selection, *Deviant Behavior*, 1–9, published online doi: 10.1080/01639625.2020.1756428.

Desmond, S.A., Rorie, M. and Sohoni, T. (2022). Working for God: Religion and occupational crime and deviance, *Deviant Behavior*, published online doi: 10.1080/01639625.2021.2022968.

Dion, M. (2008). Ethical leadership and crime prevention in the organizational setting, *Journal of Financial Crime*, 15 (3), 308–319.

Dodge, M. (2009). *Women and White-Collar Crime*, Prentice Hall, Saddle River, NJ.

Farrell, B.R. and Franco, J.R. (1999). The role of the auditor in the prevention and detection of business fraud: SAS No. 82, *Western Criminology Review*, 2 (1), online www.westerncriminology.org.

Freiberg, A. (2020). Researching white-collar crime: An Australian perspective, in: Rorie, M.L. (editor), *The Handbook of White-Collar Crime*, Wiley & Sons, Hoboken, NJ, chapter 26, pages 418–436.

Friedrichs, D.O., Schoultz, I. and Jordanoska, A. (2018). *Edwin H. Sutherland, Routledge Key Thinkers in Criminology*, Routledge, London, UK.

Friedrichs, D.O. (2020). White collar crime: Definitional debates and the case for a typological approach, in: Rorie, M. (editor), *The Handbook of White-Collar Crime*, Hoboken, NJ: John Wiley & Sons, chapter 2, pages 16–31.

Galvin, B.M., Lange, D. and Ashforth, B.E. (2015). Narcissistic organizational identification: Seeing oneself as central to the organization's identity, *Academy of Management Review*, 40 (2), 163–181.

Galvin, M.A., Loughran, T.A., Simpson, S.S. and Cohen, M.A. (2018). Victim compensation policy and white-collar crime: Public preferences in a national willingness-to-pay survey, *Criminology & Public Policy*, 17, 553–594.

Gao, P. and Zhang, G. (2019). Accounting manipulation, peer pressure, and internal control, *The Accounting Review*, 94 (1), 127–151.

Geest, V.R., Weisburd, D. and Blokland, A.A.J. (2017). Developmental trajectories of offenders convicted of fraud: A follow-up to age 50 in a Dutch conviction cohort, *European Journal of Criminology*, 14 (5), 543–565.

Goldstraw-White, J. (2012). *White-Collar Crime: Accounts of Offending Behavior*, Palgrave Macmillan, London, UK.

Gomulya, D. and Mishina, Y. (2017). Signaler credibility, signal susceptibility, and relative reliance on signals: How stakeholders change their evaluative processes after violation of expectations and rehabilitative efforts, *Academy of Management Journal*, 60 (2), 554–583.

Goncharov, I. and Peter, C.D. (2019). Does reporting transparency affect industry coordination? Evidence from the duration of international cartels, *The Accounting Review*, 94 (3), 149–175.

Gottschalk, P. (2017). Convenience in white-collar crime: Introducing a core concept, *Deviant Behavior*, 38 (5), 605–619.

Gottschalk, P. (2022). Trusted chief executives in convenient white-collar crime, *Crime & Delinquency*, 1–29 doi: 10.1177/00111287221104737.

Haines, F., Bice, S., Einfeld, C. and Sullivan, H. (2022). Countering corporate power through social control: What does a social license offer? *The British Journal of Criminology*, 62, 184–199.

Hamilton, S. and Micklethwait, A. (2006). *Greed and Corporate Failure: The Lessons From Recent Disasters*, Palgrave Macmillan, Basingstoke, UK.

Hansen, L.L. (2020). Review of the book "Convenience triangle in white-collar crime: Case studies of fraud examinations", *Choice Connect*, 57 (5), Association of College and Research Libraries, Middletown, CT.

Harvin, O. and Killey, M. (2021). Do "superstar" CEOs impair auditors' judgment and reduce fraud detection opportunities? *Journal of Forensic and Investigative Accounting*, 13 (3), web.nacva.com, 15 pages.

Herron, E.T. and Cornell, R.M. (2021). Creativity amidst standardization: Is creativity related to auditors' recognition of and responses to fraud risk cues? *Journal of Business Research*, 132, 314–326.

Hestnes, M. (2017). *Hvorfor avdekket ikke revisor underslaget i Hadeland og Ringerike Bredbånd? (Why Did the Auditor Not Detect the Embezzlement at Hadeland and Ringerike Broadband?)*, Master of Science thesis, BI Norwegian Business School, Oslo, Norway.

Hughes, G. (2003). Crime prevention, in: Muncie, J. and McLaughlin, E. (editors), *The Sage Dictionary of Criminology*, Sage, London, UK.

Hurley, P.J., Mayhew, B.W. and Obermire, K.M. (2019). Realigning auditors' accountability: Experimental evidence, *The Accounting Review*, 94 (3), 233–250.

Kakkar, H., Sivanathan, N. and Globel, M.S. (2020). Fall from grace: The role of dominance and prestige in punishment of high-status actors, *Academy of Management Journal*, 63 (2), 530–553.

Kang, E. and Thosuwanchot, N. (2017). An application of Durkheim's four categories of suicide to organizational crimes, *Deviant Behavior*, 38 (5), 493–513.

Karim, K.E. and Siegel, P.H. (1998). A signal detection theory approach to analyzing the efficiency and effectiveness of auditing to detect management fraud, *Managerial Auditing Journal*, 13 (6), 367–375.

Kawasaki, T. (2020). Review of comparative studies on white-collar and corporate crime, in: Rorie, M.L. (editor), *The Handbook of White-Collar Crime*, Wiley & Sons, Hoboken, NJ, chapter 27, pages 437–447.

Keil, M., Depledge, G. and Rai, A. (2007). Escalation: The role of problem recognition and cognitive bias, *Decision Sciences*, 38 (3), 391–421.

Kuvaas, B., Buch, R. and Dysvik, A. (2016). Performance management: Perceiving goals as invariable and implications for perceived job autonomy and work performance, *Human Resource Management*, 55 (3), 401–412.

König, A., Graf-Vlachy, L., Bundy, J. and Little, L.M. (2020). A blessing and a curse: How CEOs' trait empathy affects their management of organizational crisis, *Academy of Management Review*, 45 (1), 130–153.

Linder, S., Leca, B., Zicari, A. and Casarin, V. (2021). Designing ethical management control: Overcoming the harmful effect of management control systems on job-related stress, *Journal of Business Ethics*, 172, 747–764.

Locatelli, G., Mariani, G., Sainati, T. and Greco, M. (2017). Corruption in public projects and megaprojects: There is an elephant in the room! *International Journal of Project Management*, 35 (3), 252–268.

Locatelli, G., Konstantinou, E., Geraldi, J. and Sainati, T. (2022). The dark side of projects: Dimensionality, research methods, and agenda, *Project Management Journal*, 53 (4), 367–381.

Locke, E.A. and Latham, G.P. (2013). Goal setting theory: The current state, in: Locke, E.A. and Latham, G.P. (editors), *New Developments in Goal Setting and Task Performance*, Routledge, New York, NY, pages 623–630.

Lord, N. and Wingerde, K. (2019). Preventing and intervening in white-collar crimes: The role of law enforcement, in: Rorie, M.L. (editor), *The Handbook of White-Collar Crime*, John Wiley & Sons, London, UK, 246–261.

Martinez, D. (2022). How auditors can detect fraud, *New Jersey CPA*, New Jersey Society of CPAs, www.issuu.com/njscpa/.

McClean, E.J., Martin, S.R., Emich, K.J. and Woodruff, T. (2018). The social consequences of voice: An examination of voice type and gender on status and subsequent leader emergence, *Academy of Management Journal*, 61 (5), 1869–1891.

Mehrpouya, A. and Salles-Djelic, M.L. (2019). Seeing like the market; Exploring the mutual rise of transparency and accounting in transnational economic and market governance, *Accounting, Organizations and Society*, 76, 12–31.

Mohliver, A. (2019). How misconduct spreads: Auditors' role in the diffusion of stock-option backdating, *Administrative Science Quarterly*, 64 (2), 310–336.

Moore, C. (2015). Moral disengagement, *Current Opinion in Psychology*, 6, 199–204.

Mpho, B. (2017). Whistleblowing: What do contemporary ethical theories say? *Studies in Business and Economics*, 12 (1), 19–28.

Murphy, P.R. and Dacin, M.T. (2011). Psychological pathways to fraud: Understanding and preventing fraud in organizations, *Journal of Business Ethics*, 101, 601–618.

Müller, S.M. (2018). Corporate behavior and ecological disaster: Dow Chemical and the Great Lakes mercury crisis, 1970–1972, *Business History*, 60 (3), 399–422.

Nichol, J.E. (2019). The effects of contract framing on misconduct and entitlement, *The Accounting Review*, 94 (3), 329–344.

O'Gara, J.D. (2004). *Corporate Fraud: Case Studies in Detection and Prevention*, John Wiley & Sons, London, UK.

Oka, R. (2021). Introducing an anthropology of convenience, *Economic Anthropology*, 8 (2), 188–207.

Økokrim. (2021). *Temarapport: Profesjonelle aktører (Theme Report: Professional Actors)*, Økokrim, Norwegian National Authority for Investigation and Prosecution of Economic and Environmental Crime, Oslo, Norway.

Oyerogba, E.O. (2021). Forensic auditing mechanism and fraud detection: The case of Nigerian public sector, *Journal of Accounting in Emerging Economies*, published online doi: 10.1108/JAEE-04-2020-0072.

Petrocelli, M., Piquero, A.R. and Smith, M.R. (2003). Conflict theory and racial profiling: An empirical analysis of police traffic stop data, *Journal of Criminal Justice*, 31 (1), 1–11.

Pettigrew, W.A. (2018). The changing place of fraud in seventeenth-century public debates about international trading corporations, *Business History*, 60 (3), 305–320.

Piquero, N.L. (2018). White-collar crime is crime: Victims hurt just the same, *Criminology & Public Policy*, 17 (3), 595–600.

Pontell, H.N., Black, W.K. and Geis, G. (2014). Too big to fail, too powerful to jail? On the absence of criminal prosecutions after the 2008 financial meltdown, *Crime, Law and Social Change*, 61 (1), 1–13.

Pratt, T.C. and Cullen, F.T. (2005). Assessing macro-level predictors and theories of crime: A meta-analysis, *Crime and Justice*, 32, 373–450.

Qu, J. (2021). The challenge against economic regulation ethics under the Covid-19 epidemic: An analysis of unethical behavior of convenience, *Converter Magazine*, 2021 (5), 74–79.

Sale, H.A. (2021). The corporate purpose of social license, *Sothern California Law Review*, 94 (4), 785–842.

Schoen, J.L., DeSimone, J.A., Meyer, R.D., Schnure, K.A. and LeBreton, J.M. (2021). Identifying, defining, and measuring justification mechanisms: The implicit biases underlying individual differences, *Journal of Management*, 47 (3), 716–744.

Schuster, T.D. (2021). *Auditor Inability to Use Professional Skepticism*, dissertation submitted in partial fulfillment of the requirements for the degree of Doctor of Business Administration, Virginia, USA, Liberty University, School of Business, December.

Schweitzer, M.E., Ordonez, L. and Douma, B. (2004). Goal setting as a motivator of unethical behavior, *Academy of Management Journal*, 47 (3), 422–432.

Shadnam, M. and Lawrence, T.B. (2011). Understanding widespread misconduct in organizations: An institutional theory of moral collapse, *Business Ethics Quarterly*, 21 (3), 379–407.

Shawver, T. and Clements, L.H. (2019). The impact of value preferences on whistleblowing intentions of accounting professionals, *Journal of Forensic and Investigative Accounting*, 11 (2), 232–247.

Simmons, A. (2018). Why students cheat and what to do about it, *Edutopia*, www.edutopia.org.

Sleesman, D.J., Conlon, D.E., McNamara, G. and Miles, J.E. (2012). Cleaning up the big muddy: A meta-analysis review of the determinants of escalation of commitment, *Academy of Management Journal*, 55 (3), 541–562.

Sleesman, D.J., Lennard, A.C., McNamara, G. and Conlon, D.E. (2018). Putting escalation of commitment in context: A multilevel review and analysis, *Academy of Management Annals*, 12 (1), 178–207.

Sonnier, B.M., Lassar, W.M. and Lassar, S.S. (2015). The influence of source credibility and attribution of blame on juror evaluation of liability of industry specialist auditors, *Journal of Forensic & Investigative Accounting*, 7 (1), 1–37.

Stadler, W.A. and Gottschalk, P. (2022). Testing convenience theory for white-collar crime: Perceptions of potential offenders and non-offenders, *Deviant Behavior*, 43 (7), 804–820.

Sterri, A. and Borge, K. (2022). *How Can an Auditor Prevent and Detect White-Collar Crime? A Convenience Theory Approach*, Master of science in business economics thesis, BI Norwegian Business School, Oslo, Norway, 124 pages.

Suryanto, T. (2014). Determinants of audit fee based on client attribute, auditor attribute, and engagement attribute to control risks and prevent fraud: A study on public accounting firms in Sumatra-Indonesia, *International Journal of Economics and Business Administration*, 2 (3), 27–39.

Sutherland, E.H. (1983). *White Collar Crime – The Uncut Version*, Yale University Press, New Haven, CT.

Szalma, J.L. and Hancock, P.A. (2013). A signal improvement to signal detection analysis: Fuzzy SDT on the ROCs, *Journal of Experimental Psychology: Human Perception and Performance*, 39 (6), 1741–1762.

Thaxton, S. and Agnew, R. (2018). When criminal coping is likely: An examination of conditioning effects in general strain theory, *Journal of Quantitative Criminology*, 34, 887–920.

Theoharakis, V., Voliotis, S. and Pollack, J.M. (2021). Going down the slippery slope of legitimacy lies in early-stage ventures: The role of moral disengagement, *Journal of Business Ethics*, 172, 673–690.

Toubiana, M. (2020). Once in orange always in orange? Identity paralysis and the enduring influence of institutional logics on identity, *Academy of Management Journal*, 63 (6), 1739–1774.

Vasiu, V.I. (2021). Convenience triangle in white-collar crime: Case studies of fraud examinations, *Criminal Law and Criminal Justice Books*, Rutgers, the State University of New Jersey, May, www.clcjbooks.rutgers.edu.

Vasiu, V.I. and Podgor, E.S. (2019). Organizational opportunity and deviant behavior: Convenience in white-collar crime, *Criminal Law and Criminal Justice Books*, Rutgers, the State University of New Jersey, July, www.clcjbooks.rutgers.edu.

Wells, J.T. (1997). *Occupational Fraud and Abuse*, Obsidian Publishing Company, Austin, TX.

Welsh, D.T. and Ordonez, L.D. (2014). The dark side of consecutive high performance goals: Linking goal setting, depletion, and unethical behavior, *Organizational Behavior and Human Decision Processes*, 123, 79–89.

Welsh, D.T., Ordonez, L.D., Snyder, D.G. and Christian, M.S. (2014). The slippery slope: How small ethical transgressions pave the way for larger future transgressions, *Journal of Applied Psychology*, 100 (1), 114–127.

Welsh, D.T., Baer, M.D., Session, H. and Garud, N. (2020). Motivated to disengage: The ethical consequences of goal commitment and moral disengagement in goal setting, *Journal of Organizational Behavior*, 1–15, published online doi: 10.1002/job.2467.

Wheelock, D., Semukhina, O. and Demidov, N.N. (2011). Perceived group threat and punitive attitudes in Russia and the United States, *British Journal of Criminology*, 51, 937–959.

Yam, K.C., Christian, M.S., Wei, W., Liao, Z. and Nai, J. (2018). The mixed blessing of leader sense of humor: Examining costs and benefits, *Academy of Management Journal*, 61 (1), 348–369.

Zager, L., Malis, S.S. and Novak, A. (2016). The role and responsibility of auditors in prevention and detection of fraudulent financial reporting, *Procedia Economics and Finance*, 39, 693–700.

10 Theater of the Courtroom

The concept of language games was introduced by Ludwig Wittgenstein. His philosophy combined with Goffman's theater analogy of performance can be applied to the courtroom as a theater scene. Storytelling by prosecution and defense differ implicitly during examinations, but the underlying stories are never explicitly told. This chapter presents two court cases from Norway, where white-collar offenders were on trial. In the first case, defense performance was concerned with negligence fraud, while prosecution performance was concerned with intentional fraud. In the second case, defense performance was concerned with friendship services, while the prosecution performance was concerned with municipal corruption.

In Norwegian criminal law, an offender guilty of negligent fraud can be sentenced to a maximum of two years in prison. An offender guilty of intentional fraud can be sentenced to a maximum of six years in prison. Negligence is a form of guilt, which means that the offender has acted contrary to how a generally sensible person would have acted in a similar situation. Negligence is a significant deviation in the exhibited behavior – where "a wrong has been committed" (Rodriguez-Blanco, 2021: 2) – from a behavior that can objectively be described as justifiable. Intentionality is a form of guilt, which means that the offender has acted consciously and had the will to perform the act. Intentionality implies a commitment or plan to carry out an action or actions.

A member of parliament in Norway admitted to negligent fraud, but denied intentional fraud. The prosecutor brought her case to the court with the allegation of intentional fraud. While the role of the prosecutor in the storytelling in the courtroom as a theater scene was to convince the court that the fraud was intentional rather than negligent, the role of the defense lawyer in the storytelling in the courtroom as a theater scene was to convince the court that the fraud was negligent rather than intentional (Birkemo, 2021; Ekroll, 2021; Ekroll and Johansen, 2021; Kruger and Haugsbø, 2021; Olaisen, 2021).

The purpose of this study is to examine how prosecutor and defender played their roles in court to convince the judge. The study is framed in the theater of the courtroom, where prosecutor and defender are actors doing their performances within certain rules for behavior in front of the judge (Hjort, 2019; Schoultz and Flyghed, 2021). While the prosecutor waited to present his narrative

DOI: 10.4324/9781003379249-13

of intentional fraud, the defendant presented her narrative of negligent fraud when interviewed in the media ahead of court hearings (Olaisen, 2021: 8):

> I have made mistakes. Made a fool of myself. I don't agree with all the errors. But it is I who has been stupid, and there is no one to blame but myself. I do not resent anyone else, and it is I who eventually has to face the consequences of my mistakes, she says. However, nothing has been done intentionally on my part.

First in this chapter, the offense by the parliament member is presented by application of convenience theory (Asting and Gottschalk, 2022; Braaten and Vaughn, 2019; Dearden and Gottschalk, 2020; Stadler and Gottschalk, 2022). Next, the perspective of the courtroom as a theater scene is introduced (Goffman, 1974; Jordanoska, 2017; Schoultz and Flyghed, 2021). Then, the contrasting storytelling for defense and prosecution is presented.

To further illustrate the courtroom as a theater scene, a second case is introduced in this chapter. The case is concerned with an architect who helped a municipal officer make drawings of the municipal officer's new house for free (Klevstrand and Solem, 2020; Ytreberg, 2018). The municipal officer happened to be in charge of approvals and denials when the architect applied for building permits for his clients. While the defense argued that the architect helped the municipal officer as a friend, the prosecution argued that it was corruption. The case would be dismissed if the judge believed in friendship as the basis for the favor, while the architect would be sentenced to prison for corruption if the judge believed in the favor as a bribe (Brevik, 2021; Brevik and Holmøy, 2021; Holmøy, 2021a, 2021b; Holmøy and Brevik, 2021; Trædal, 2021a, 2021b).

Member of Parliament and Mansion Architect

The parliament member claimed travel expenses to be refunded in excess of her actual expenses in the years 2016, 2017, and 2018. She was not entitled to approximately NOK 115,000 (about US$13,000). Some travel invoices were dated when she must have been to other places than stated, for example, at home, in the family cabin, or on private trips.

The theory of convenience suggests that there is a financial motive, an organizational opportunity, and a personal willingness for financial crime by white-collar offenders (Asting and Gottschalk, 2022; Braaten and Vaughn, 2019; Dearden and Gottschalk, 2020; Stadler and Gottschalk, 2022). The offender belongs to the elite in society who abused her privileged and trusted professional position for personal gain. In the case of the parliament member in Norway, she had messy personal finances and was always late paying bills. Sometimes, she faced formal debt collection (Olaisen, 2021). Therefore, the strain from a potential threat of personal financial collapse seems to have been the motive as illustrated by motive-threats-individual in Figure 10.1. As argued

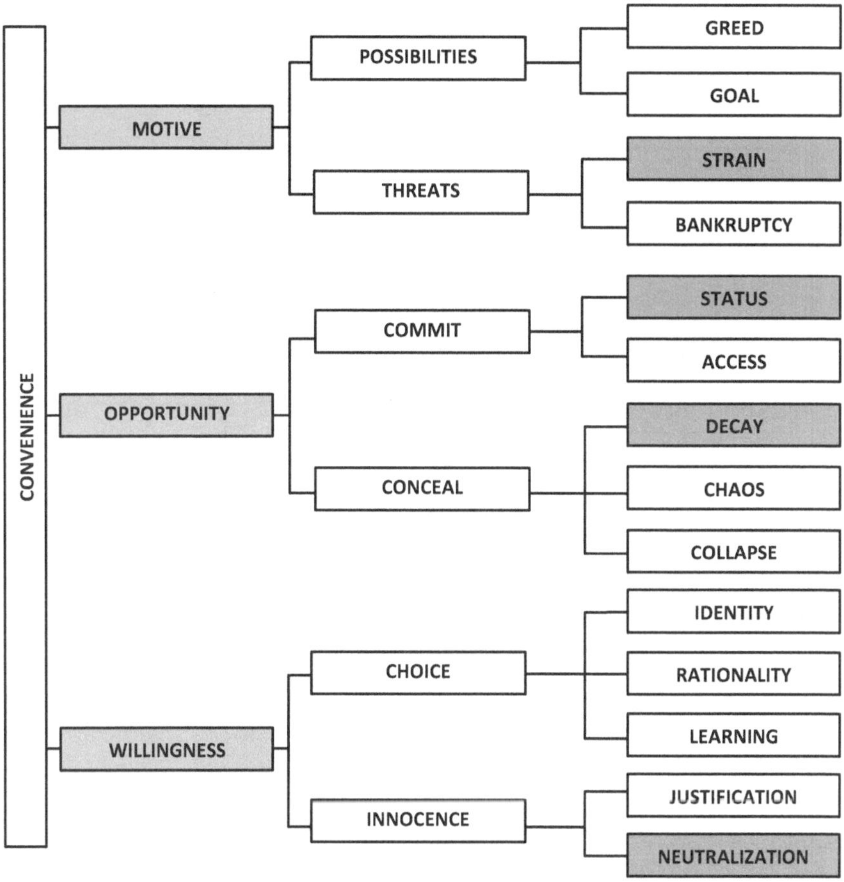

Figure 10.1 Convenience themes in the case of the parliament member

by Thaxton and Agnew (2018), the desire to avoid strain and pain is a frequent motive for financial crime.

The status of a member of parliament is high with no real guardianship or control. It was an investigative journalist who detected the wrongdoing (Birkemo, 2021; Suvatne, 2019). Status makes it convenient to commit crime (Kakkar et al., 2020), while lack of guardianship and control makes it convenient to conceal crime (Kawasaki, 2020), as illustrated in Figure 10.1.

The offender neutralizes guilt feeling by claiming mistake without intention. In addition, she feels sorry for herself becoming a victim of media attention and negative reactions from political figures and neighbors. Neutralization, as illustrated in Figure 10.1, is a frequent explanation of willingness for deviant behavior (Sykes and Matza, 1957).

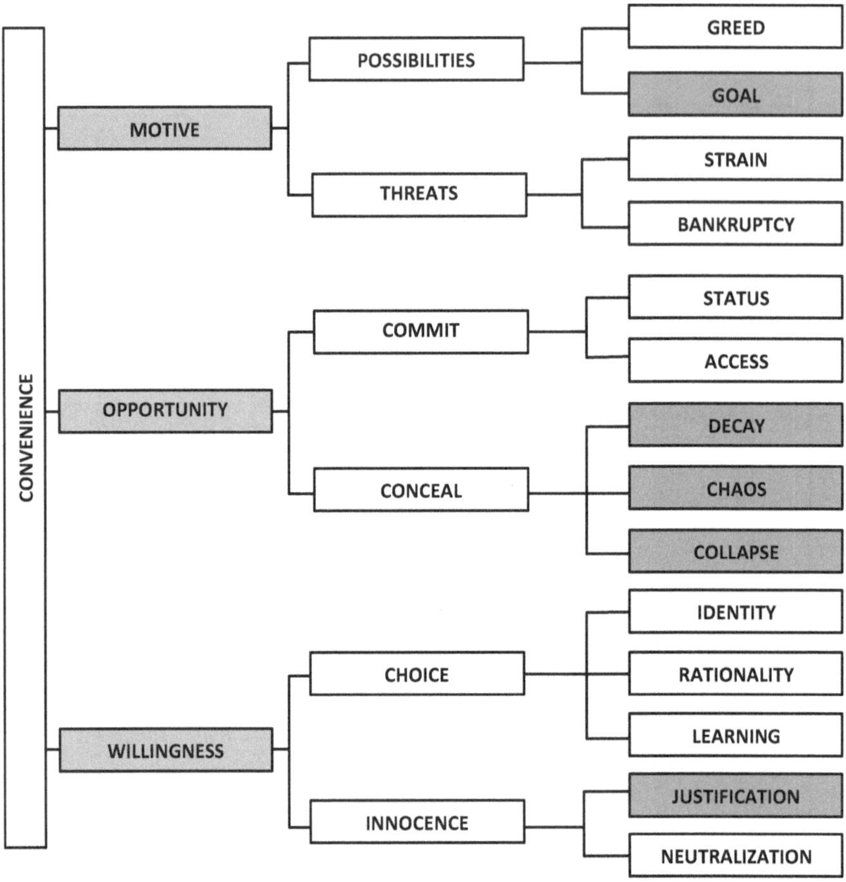

Figure 10.2 Convenience themes in the case of the architect

When assuming corruption, convenience themes for the architect are illustrated in Figure 10.2. It was apparently corporate greed on behalf of his architectural firm that motivated exploiting possibilities. Greed is a frequent motive for financial crime. Goldstraw-White (2012) defined greed as socially constructed needs and desires that can never be completely covered or contended.

He was able to conceal the alleged wrongdoing because of decay in terms of institutional deterioration (Rodriguez et al., 2005), chaos caused by lack of guardianship and oversight (Mohliver, 2019), and collapse from external manipulation (Goncharov and Peter, 2019) in the administration of the municipality. He might justify his actions by arguing that the municipality was in charge of approving all his construction applications on behalf of his rich and mighty clients. In a justification, the actor admits responsibility for the act in question but denies its pejorative and negative content (Schoen et al., 2021).

Storytelling in the Courtroom Theater

Court rooms vary across national legislations. In Norway, the judge sits higher and looks down on the other court participants. On the left side of the judge sits the defendant with his or her defense lawyer. On the right side of the judge sits the prosecutor. At the end of the court room facing the judge are a few benches for spectators. If the case has media attention, then some journalists can be found on a bench. Otherwise, mainly family and friends of the defendant are present, and their presence is often limited to the opening and closing of the court hearings.

Court hearings in minor criminal violence or theft cases last for a day. More serious violence and financial crime cases last for a week or a month. Serious white-collar crime cases with corporations involved tend to last for months. The length of court hearings is a matter of evidence and detail as well as the need for witness statements. The only relevant information for the judge is what the two sides present orally during sessions in court. The procedure is the same in all Scandinavian countries. The American legal system, in contrast to the Scandinavian, is characterized by a plea bargaining culture, not least in white-collar crime cases.

When studying a high-profile transnational corporate bribery case in Sweden, Schoultz and Flyghed (2021) applied the theater analogy to understand the performance in court. They looked at the theater of the courtroom as the stage for performance. The performance of prosecutor, defender, as well as judge serves to influence the others in order to control their impressions of the performers and the situation. In the criminal court, the spatial positioning clarifies who belongs to what side. For example, the defense lawyer sits next to the client. The defendant claims innocence while the prosecutor claims guilt. The defendant claims being a scapegoat for corporate wrongdoing. The prosecutor claims that the indictment is well founded and that it should result in a guilty verdict. The defense lawyer's role is to advance the client's interests and cast doubt upon the prosecutor's statements and evidence.

The court led by the presiding judge tends to be passive during case hearings (Schoultz and Flyghed, 2021: 8):

> The role of the third team, the court, led by the presiding judge, is generally more passive and involves determining whether the arguments presented should lead to a finding of guilty or not guilty. This role also involves being the audience for the performances of the prosecution and defense teams, as they attempt to control impressions of the situation.

In the particular Swedish court case studied by Schoultz and Flyghed (2021: 9), the researchers were interested in the performance of unbelonging by the defense, implying that the defendant did not rightly belong in the court situation:

> The performance of 'unbelonging in court' also includes the defense claim of being scapegoated by the company, as well as their framing of

> the complexity of the case and of the prosecution as unjust, in relation to which they directed accusations against the prosecutor.

The defense strategy had several layers. First, it was to maintain that the events did not violate any law. Next, if the judge decided that the law had been broken, then the client lacked intent. Third, if there was an intention, then it was the corporation rather than the executive that deserved blame attribution. Fourth, the defendant had made no personal gain from the incident and could thus not be convicted of financial crime. Finally, the defendant was already victimized in both personal and professional life. In sum, the defense strategy served to reinforce each of the three defendants' unbelonging in court.

In addition to prosecution, defense, and court, there was also a fourth presence of the corporation involved in the trial studied by Schoultz and Flyghed (2021: 12), where the Swedish corporation already had admitted to wrongdoing and paid millions to resolve charges:

> The passive role of the corporate defense team became apparent when reading through the field notes from the court hearings. The representatives of Telia were rarely mentioned, but when they were, the notes were mostly focused on their absence and passivity. In contrast to the other defense teams, the company's defense team did not question the prosecutor's definition of the situation. On the first day of the trial, when all parties to the case presented their positions, Telia's lawyer asked himself "Does it constitute a crime? The Telia Company has no opinion on this. We leave that to the court to determine". Their lack of defense is quite natural given that the company had nothing to lose during the trial, if the individuals placed on the trial were convicted of criminal offenses, besides the confiscation of profits. And since the Dutch authorities would confiscate this amount anyway in the case of the defendants being acquitted, the company was not at risk of having to make any additional payments. Further, the company was required to keep to the acknowledgement of guilt that had already been made in the American courts, in order to avoid breaking the agreement reached with the American authorities.

The employer Telia did not enter into any argumentative role in favor of their former executives. Rather, the silent approach was to separate corporate interests from individual interests. Gottschalk and Benson (2020) found this to be typical for corporate accounts of scandals at later stages of crisis evolution. In the Swedish case, the defendants found that they had been scapegoated by the corporation (Schoultz and Flyghed, 2021: 12):

> Scapegoating involves the corporation transferring the responsibility for an act or event from the corporation itself to one or a few symbolic figures. It reduces complexity and allows a corporation to avoid scrutiny. This is also what the defense then argued in court when they referred to the

> global settlement: "Telia has had powerful commercial reasons for entering into this contract and it should not be ascribed any evidentiary value. The incentive, we have already said, was 1.4 billion (Swedish Kronor)". During the trial, the defense argued that the only reason for Telia's confession of being guilty of bribery offenses as part of the global settlement was commercial, and that this had no bearing whatsoever on the question of the guilt of the executives. . .. They were not accused of committing crimes against the company, but for the company, and they perceived that they were being scapegoated and sacrificed in order to allow the company to continue doing business.

In the theater of the courtroom, the defendant was not allowed to criticize the prosecutor. The presiding judge did not approve of it and interrupted it by saying that direct accusations against the prosecutor before a sitting court could not be allowed. However, the defendant's lawyer was allowed to criticize the prosecutor with statements such as "there are serious flaws in the prosecutor's conclusions", "the interpretations are often sweeping, unclear and lump groups of people together", "contain many things that are simply incorrect", and "difficult for our client to free himself of the idea that this has been deliberate" (Schoultz and Flyghed, 2021: 13).

In the theater of the court room, Schoultz and Flyghed (2021) interpreted the judge's intervention against the defendant's criticism of the prosecutor as a protective practice in order to help the performers in the theater play their roles. Similarly, Jordanoska (2017) analyzed the efficient management of complex fraud cases in court. She found that judges actively have to manage the trial as well as the cooperative attitude on the part of both prosecution and defense, which thus affects the interactions between the actors in the court.

The court performance research by Schoultz and Flyghed (2021) was based on Flower's (2018a, 2018b) court studies, Goffman's (1959, 1974) frame analysis, Jordanoska's (2017, 2021) trial studies, and Walenta's (2020) courtroom ethnography.

Embezzlement by Member of Parliament

The indictment stated that the member of parliament was charged with violating section 372 of the Norwegian criminal code, conferred with section 371 letter a: Having caused loss or danger of loss to someone. The fraud was considered serious because special emphasis was placed on the fact that it had been committed on several occasions, over a long period of time, and the offender had abused her privileged position as a member of the Norwegian parliament. The indictment concerned 56 travel invoices totaling NOK 117,776 that is approximately US$13,000. Six weeks had been set aside for the trial starting November 2, 2021 (Trædal, 2021a, 2021b). The fraud was detected more than two years earlier by investigative journalists at the Norwegian newspaper Aftenposten (Birkemo, 2021; Suvatne, 2019).

The case against the parliament member from the Labor party was the second case of travel expenses that ended up in court based on Aftenposten's revelations. In 2020, a former parliamentary representative for the Progress party was sentenced to 11 months unconditional imprisonment for fraud. By then, the Norwegian Supreme Court had sharpened the sentence as a result of him having abused the confidence that lies in being elected to the Norwegian parliament. The offender confessed in the district court to what he was accused of (Trædal, 2021a).

The same police investigators who investigated the Progress party member also investigated the Labor party member. The charges against the Labor party member were concerned with 56 fraudulent travel refund bills to the parliament administration. A state prosecutor and a police prosecutor were in charge of prosecution, while two attorneys were defending the Labor party member of parliament (Trædal, 2021a, 2021b). The parliament member's explanation for her wrongdoing could be briefly summarized as follows (Trædal, 2021b): What she did at those various occasions had changed without travel bills being changed accordingly. She forgot to correct them before she handed them in. She explained that she was in the habit of submitting draft travel expenses forms before she left. However, she claimed that all her travels included activities as a parliamentary representative when several of the trips in question took place.

The two competing narratives of the defense performance suggesting negligent fraud and the prosecution performance suggesting intentional fraud are summarized in Table 10.1.

A narrative refers to a way of organizing and speaking the world; it is the way to make sense of meanings that unfold in and through time. "The law, focused on putting facts in the world into coherent form and presenting them persuasively – to make a case – always results in particular narratives that differ between the defense and the prosecution" (Brooks, 1996: 14). If the judge(s) would rely on the defense performance of negligence fraud, then the maximum sentence could be two years in prison. If the judge(s) would believe the prosecution performance of intentional fraud, then the maximum sentence could be six years in prison.

Corruption by Summer Mansion Architect

Many rich and mighty Norwegians have a preference for the island of Tjøme in the southern part of Norway for their summer mansions as vacation resorts. The attractiveness of Tjøme Island might be compared to the attractiveness of Cape Cod in the United States. The mansion owners prefer having their houses close to the ocean with access to private piers and diving boards. However, Norwegian law prohibits buildings in the 100-m belt along the shoreline for two reasons. First, there is wildlife that should be protected. Second, the right of public access shall secure everyone the opportunity to move along the seaside, whether they are rich or poor. Many rich and mighty Norwegians

Table 10.1 Theater performers in the criminal fraud case against a member of parliament

Defense Performance of Negligence Fraud	*Prosecution Performance of Intentional Fraud*
Some of the trips also involved meeting members of my constituency.	Some of the trips were of private character with family and friends.
I have had a routine of posting trips in advance. Sometimes I forgot to withdraw travel refund bills since the trips were cancelled.	Sometimes she issued travel refund bills to get refund for travels that never took place.
I had a hard time keeping an overview over my spending and personal finances.	She was better at making a national budget than a household budget.
It was negligence on my part but no intentional fraud.	It was not just negligence on her part, it was intentional fraud.
I did not act with knowledge and will. I have a hard time remembering numbers.	She acted with knowledge and will.
I was always in the role of parliamentarian, there was no distinction between professional and private life.	Sometimes she was obviously a parliamentarian, other times she was obviously a private citizen.
I am charged because I lack control and am bad at writing travel expense bills.	She is charged because she has deliberately misled the parliament to enrich herself.
The administration in the parliament helped me correct and submit correct travel bills.	The administration in the parliament requested documentation and correction of mistakes.
What I ended up doing on various trips changed a lot of times. Sometimes I forgot to change travel bills accordingly.	She intentionally misled the parliament administration to refunds above the entitled sum.
My mistakes could go both ways, some in my favor and some in my disfavor.	Only once in 56 cases was financial deviance in her disfavor.
It was quite legitimate to create a travel invoice and also submit it before the travel was completed.	It is not the intention of the system to refund a travel before it is completed.
My mistakes are concerned with changes in travels and wrong number of days and kilometers.	Her wrongdoing is concerned with refund for travels that were private, travels that never took place, and overcharge for completed travels.

ignored such laws by hiring an architect who was well connected in the municipality of Tjøme (Klevstrand and Solem, 2020; Ytreberg, 2018).

The architect told in court on November 4, 2021, how he helped the municipal manager (Brevik, 2021):

> In the spring of 2010, I became aware that he had been divorced and had to move from the family home to the new location. I was aware that he had acquired a plot of land and wanted to build a house. These were things we had talked about the times we met. I made the drawings at home on my own Mac. I am pretty sure I sent him the drawings on May 1, 2010, and that I did not help him with the application. He did it himself. I am

Table 10.2 Theater performers in the criminal corruption case against an architect

Defense Performance of Friendship Services	*Prosecution Performance of Municipal Corruption*
I helped him as a friend in a situation where he was going through a private crisis.	He helped him since he was so helpful in approving all his construction applications.
My accountant normally takes care of hours registered on projects for potential invoicing of clients.	He never registered hours that he worked for his so-called friend.
I showed him how I use a computer program for architectural purposes.	He did the computer work all by himself as an architect without involvement from others.
Corruption is a far more serious matter than this case.	This case is a typical matter of serious corruption.
My friendship services did not influence his work in the municipality.	His friendship services influenced the work in the municipality.
There were mutual services, while I helped make architectural drawings; he helped me carpet an outdoor deck.	There was no mutuality but rather a discrepancy in favor of the municipal employee.
I have helped many friends with architectural drawings, free of charge.	The relationship to the municipal employee was professional and no friendship.
My SMS message simply meant that I would look at it upon my return to the office.	His SMS message told that the municipality would have to approve his application.
I was familiar with the code of ethics, but I did not think of it as a gift or benefit to one who has the authority to make decisions.	Ethical guidelines for architects state that architects shall not give commissions, gifts, or other benefits to anyone who has a recommending or deciding authority when awarding contracts or case decisions.

pretty sure I used the firm's templates and library when I drew, and that I removed the firm's logo, since this was no official project.

The architect was accused of bribing municipal officials and became convicted to prison in a district court. He appealed the verdict to a court of appeals, where the defense performance of friendship services versus the prosecution performance of municipal corruption on the court scene took place as listed in Table 10.2. Basically, the defendant claimed to have treated the main municipal official as a friend, while the prosecutor claimed that it was corruption (Brevik, 2021; Brevik and Holmøy, 2021; Holmøy, 2021a, 2021b; Holmøy and Brevik, 2021).

Language Games in Prosecution and Defense

The courtroom as a theater scene represents a perspective where the actors do not communicate with each other for the purpose of exchanging information and opinions among themselves. Rather, the communication serves the purpose of informing and convincing an audience. In the real theater, the audience is people who have paid for tickets to see the performance. In the courtroom, the audience is the judge or judges who are to receive messages tailored to convince. For example, when the prosecutor examines the defendant, the purpose is not for the prosecutor to learn more about the defendant. It is not a conversation with the defendant. The purpose is for the prosecutor to convince the court as the audience that the defendant is guilty. Similarly, the purpose for the defense lawyer is to convince the court that the defendant is innocent. There is no real dialogue between the examiner and the examined, as it is a matter of performance on the scene to guide the communication in a direction of desired replies that the court can listen to. If a desired response does not emerge, then the examiner can either continue or change the subject, depending on the perceived likelihood of getting an outcome of the communication that serves the prosecution or the defense. This is in line with the perspective of research by Hjort (2019: 2) that considered the lingual exchange in the courtroom as language games, when she analyzed a particular murder case in a Norwegian courtroom in her doctoral dissertation:

> In this thesis I seek a better understanding of the defendants' speaking-situation in the courtroom. For this particular purpose I consider the lingual exchange in the courtroom as language games, and I argue this term is able to shed light on central aspects of this specific situation. The concept of language games is introduced by Ludwig Wittgenstein and his philosophy is the chief source of inspiration in this thesis. I try to show that the concept is able to illuminate how the juridical actor's questions is part of ongoing language games performed to advance certain arguments and achieve set goals – usually to underpin or undermine the defendants credibility at specific areas. The defendant's answers must therefore be regarded as a response to the initiated language game. The language games in the courtroom is assigned to promote or challenge different but specific narratives. In this thesis I operate with the term underlying narratives. These narratives are never, or seldom, verbalized explicitly at discourse level. Therefore, we need to regard the defendants' response as a reaction to the narrative that is implied in the specific language game. I claim that these fundamental conditions affect the defendants speaking situation – and that it's crucial to take these into consideration in order to undertake a fair assessment of their credibility, and in the end to sentence or acquit them. The courtroom setting has a very exceptional lingual practice that makes the distinction between game and speaking, introduced by Rush Rhees, relevant. I find that the lingual/legal practice in court is governed by rules, strategies and tactics that makes it resemble a game, and that this constitutes challenging conditions in terms of the defendant's ability to get heard or acknowledged as an individual, without at the same time trying to expand or challenge the conditions that determines the language games.

In this quote, Hjort (2019) tells that the concept of language games was introduced by Ludwig Wittgenstein, and his philosophy was the chief source of inspiration in her PhD thesis. One famous quote from Wittgenstein (1953, 2010) is that "A man will be imprisoned in a room with a door that's unlocked and opens inwards; as long as it does not occur to him to pull rather than push". Hjort (2019) attempted in her thesis to show how the concept of language games is able to explain the performance of juridical actors in the courtroom.

In the quote above, Hjort (2019) further tells that Rush Rhees introduced the distinction between games and speaking that is relevant because of the very exceptional lingual practice in the courtroom setting. Rhees (1970, 1999) explored the work of Wittgenstein and the possibility of discourse.

Just like Schoultz and Flyghed (2021), Hjort (2019) found that the courtroom can be likened to a theater stage. Similar to the fact that the linguistic exchanges between actors in the theater do not take place for the actors' own benefit, but rather for the audience, the exchanges that take place in the courtroom is addressed to the judging court. The competing stories of the prosecution and the defense are told by means of examining the suspect, witnesses, and experts in the field. The criminal procedure act in Norway regulates the language games as a result of the changing premises for various examinations. The head of the court, who is a state appointed judge, is responsible for the initial part of the examination, where the defendant is supposed to be allowed to explain freely in own words and on own terms the incident to which the indictment applies. At this initial stage of the examination, the defendant is empowered to govern own language game. The head of the court is expected to be neutral and has generally not taken a specific view of the case that is up for legal consideration.

In the following examinations, however, the fact that the parties have special and often contradicting views on the matter will influence the language games. The defendant becomes involved in the language games without knowing in what direction the games are heading. The games can create defendant confusion at two levels: First, who is in charge of the examination; second, what the examination is concerned about. The themes of the questioning implicitly indicate what points in the underlying narratives are at stake, but the underlying narratives are never explicitly stated. In a situation where two competing narratives meet – from the prosecutor and the defender, respectively – there will typically be some points where the underlying narratives are consistent and others where the disagreements will be substantial and significant. The conditions of the language games change depending on the extent of coherence in the underlying narratives by opposing parties (Hjort, 2019: 116):

> The conditions of the language games thus change depending on who examines whom and which topics are the subject of the interrogation. The change in conditions is reflected in the language games that are initiated and how the participating actors react to them. A game between two parties involves a response, and the person who starts a language game lays down restrictions on how it is relevant to respond, so that the first move becomes important for how the counter-move can take place. The person

who is to react to a game that has been started, for example in the form of a specific question from one of the legal actors, does not know which language game she is invited into until she is forced to react to it. When the theme of the examination is one where the underlying stories of the participants coincide, we will be able to assume that the accused willingly takes part in the game and reacts with language games that are about confirming, nuancing and enlightening. If the topic of the examination is one where the underlying narratives compete with each other, we can expect the accused to be more reluctant and find it necessary to react with language games that are about correcting, defending, diverting or challenging. In other words, if the defendant is confronted with a theme in which her underlying narrative differs from that of the questioner (who started the game), it characterizes the conditions for the language games. Nevertheless, although it is easier to achieve an interaction between the accused and the defense counsel, the overall practice in the courtroom affects even the most open and friendly language games; defendants are usually forced to act in a game.

Several scholars, such as Moi (2017: 46), have discussed characteristics of language games:

> To learn to recognize and practice language-games, then, is to learn to recognize and practice differences. To be able to distinguish between language games is also to be able to tell the difference between the use of the same word in different language-games.

The language games in the courtroom take place because the various actors introduce different and often contradicting narratives of incidents that are the matter in question. There will always be room for interpretations where storytelling by various parties needs to be interpreted by the audience. When listening to oral presentations and oral examinations, the listeners are hearing information that they themselves turn into knowledge by combining the information with a personal interpretation of the context (Mannucci and Yong, 2018). Therefore, even when everyone in the courtroom is hearing the same thing, they will nevertheless have different knowledge of what was said.

Questioning by Prosecution and Defense

The themes of the questioning by prosecutor and defender implicitly indicate what points in the underlying narratives are at stake, but the underlying narratives are never explicitly stated. The seemingly hidden stories are never told in court. There is an implicit storytelling going on in front of the judge, where the implicit defense story is concerned with innocence, while the implicit prosecution story is concerned with guilt. The stories are not hidden, but they are never explained. This is obvious in our two criminal case studies.

The implicit story by the prosecution is that the member of parliament committed fraud over a long period of time. She intentionally produced and submitted refund sheets with illegitimate numbers to make her overcome her messy private finances. More importantly for the prosecution, she was a trusted person with high social status. She was elected by the people to be a member of the national assembly that makes decisions on what is right and what is wrong in terms of laws and regulations. She belonged to the ruling class in society. How could she violate such laws herself? Why should the ruled class follow laws when individuals in the ruling class ignore their own laws? Here it is important to prosecute to set an example. The ruled class will be reluctant to obey laws if individuals in the ruling class – such as the member of parliament – can avoid prosecution. When setting an example in the exceptional case of prosecuting a member of the elite, it is important to emphasize the violation of national trust by the offender as an elected member of the national assembly.

The implicit story by the defense, however, is a mother of three children who never was very good at keeping track of her personal finances. She often forgot to pay her bills, and she was often short of money. Although she was always able to pay bills in the end, she was often very late. She spent all her time in politics for the Labor party and considered every occasion as an opportunity to influence people to vote for her party. She travelled and visited her constituency to learn about their needs. She never had her head above the waters in money matters. Therefore, she tried to get what she thought she was entitled to, as quickly as possible, so that she could cover bills that were resting on her desk. Rather than being prosecuted, she should receive help from experts on financial matters. Someone should have intervened to help her out of her financial mess. Her party, the parliament administration, her bank, or someone else should have intervened to help her sort out her financial obligations. When she says in court that she was unable to make a household budget, but good at making a national budget, she obviously was in need of help.

Similar to the fraud case against the member of parliament, the corruption case against the architect has underlying narratives that differ between prosecution and defense. The prosecution considers the architect a clever businessperson who sets up his architectural firm on the island of Tjøme with a dozen employees. The firm enabled rich and mighty clients to build fantastic summerhouses along the shoreline on the island that violated environmental laws. The architect succeeded by bribing municipal officials who approved all his construction applications.

The defense, on the other hand, would have an underlying story of a very friendly and helpful architect who considered many on the island as his friends, including people who worked in the municipality. He did architectural favors for people in need, often without charging them for the work. He applied for permits on behalf of his clients, and he was not involved in the way the municipality handled the applications.

The courtroom as a theater scene where language games take place in Norway and Sweden is echoed in a study in Germany where the public entertainment is emphasized. The public is entertained by television transmission from courtrooms as well as direct reporting on the Internet. Middelhoff (2020), a chief executive in Germany convicted to three years in prison, argues that the judge or judges are unable to be impartial or objective when the storm of news coverage reaches everyone on a continuous basis. Therefore, not only defense and prosecution do perform their roles in court with the judge or judges as the audience, but also the general public and the politicians in the country become a relevant audience.

In conclusion, the concept of language games was introduced by Ludwig Wittgenstein. His philosophy combined with Goffman's theater analogy of performance can be applied to the courtroom as a theater scene. Storytelling by prosecution and defense differ implicitly during examinations, but the underlying stories are never explicitly told. This chapter presented two court cases from Norway, where white-collar offenders were on trial. In the first case, defense performance was concerned with negligence fraud, while prosecution performance was concerned with intentional fraud. In the second case, defense performance was concerned with friendship services, while the prosecution performance was concerned with municipal corruption.

This chapter framed defendants' alleged actions within the theory of convenience for white-collar crime, where offenders have a financial motive, an organizational opportunity, and a personal willingness for deviant behavior. An avenue for future research could be to introduce this theory as a contingent approach in the study of the courtroom as a theater scene. Underlying storytelling by prosecution and defense might vary significantly depending on the motive as possibilities or threats, the opportunity as mainly to commit or to conceal, and the willingness mainly based on choice or innocence.

For the parliament member, Figure 10.1 suggests individual threats, status, decay, and neutralization as convenience themes. For the island architect, Figure 10.2 suggests corporate possibilities, decay, chaos, collapse, and justification as convenience themes. In the defense perspective, the parliament offender would then be portrayed as a person in deep trouble, dealing with a parliament without financial control, and without responsibility. The prosecution would then have to identify the opposite perspective. In the defense of the architect, a municipality out of control would be the main issue, where the architect carries no responsibility. Again, the prosecution would have to identify the opposite perspective.

References

Asting, C. and Gottschalk, P. (2022). Attorney fraud in the law firm: A case study of crime convenience theory and crime signal detection theory, *Deviant Behavior*, published online doi: 10.1080/01639625.2022.2071657.

Birkemo, A. (2021). Bedrageritiltalt: Første dag i retten for Liadal, daily Norwegian newspaper *Dagsavisen*, www.dagsavisen.no, retrieved November 11.

Braaten, C.N. and Vaughn, M.S. (2019). Convenience theory of cryptocurrency crime: A content analysis of U.S. federal court decisions, *Deviant Behavior*, published online doi: 10.1080/01639625.2019.1706706.

Brevik, H.C. (2021). Rune Breilis dag i retten: -Jeg har hjulpet mange venner med tegninger (Rune Breili's day in court: -I have helped many friends with drawings), daily local newspaper *Tønsbergs Blad*, Thursday, November 4, page 6.

Brevik, H.C. and Holmøy, E. (2021). Nytt SMS-bevis ble lagt fram i retten (New SMS evidence was presented in court, daily local newspaper *Tønsbergs Blad*, Friday, November 5, page 7.

Brooks, P. (1996). The law as narrative and rhetoric, in: Brooks, P. and Gewirtz, P. (editors), *Law's Stories*, Yale University Press, New Haven, CT.

Dearden, T.E. and Gottschalk, P. (2020). Gender and white-collar crime: Convenience in target selection, *Deviant Behavior*, published online doi: 10.1080/01639625.2020.1756428.

Ekroll, C. (2021). Jeg har dummet meg ut (I have made a fool of myself), daily Norwegian newspaper *Aftenposten*, Sunday, October 24, page 15.

Ekroll, C. and Johansen, I.E.K. (2021). Arbeiderpartiets stortingsrepresentant Hege Haukeland Liadal tiltalt for grovt bedrageri (The Labor Party's parliamentary representative Hege Haukeland Liadal charged with gross fraud), daily Norwegian newspaper *Aftenposten*, www.aftenposten.no, retrieved March 26.

Flower, L. (2018a). Doing loyalty: Defense lawyers' subtle dramas in the courtroom, *Journal of Contemporary Ethnography*, 47 (2), 226–254.

Flower, L. (2018b). *Loyalty Work: Emotional Interactions of Defence Lawyers in Swedish Courtrooms*, Doctoral thesis, Lund University, Sweden.

Goffman, E. (1959). *The Presentation of Self in Everyday Life*, Penguin Books, Cambridge, MA.

Goffman, E. (1974). *Frame Analysis: An Essay on the Organization of Experience*, Harvard University Press, London, UK.

Goldstraw-White, J. (2012). *White-Collar Crime: Accounts of Offending Behavior*, Palgrave Macmillan, London, UK.

Goncharov, I. and Peter, C.D. (2019). Does reporting transparency affect industry coordination? Evidence from the duration of international cartels, *The Accounting Review*, 94 (3), 149–175.

Gottschalk, P. and Benson, M.L. (2020). The evolution of corporate accounts of scandals from exposure to investigation, *British Journal of Criminology*, 60, 949–969.

Hjort, L.N. (2019). *Språk, spill og fortellinger i rettssalen (Language, Games and Stories in the Courtroom)*, doctoral dissertation for the degree of PhD, Norway: University of Bergen.

Holmøy, E. (2021a). -Korrupsjon er langt mer alvorlig enn dette (-Corruption is far more serious than this), daily local newspaper *Tønsbergs Blad*, Wednesday, November 3, page 7.

Holmøy, E. (2021b). Fagdommer i nær relasjon til firmaet i saken (Professional judge in close relation to the company in the case), daily local newspaper *Tønsbergs Blad*, Thursday, November 4, page 6.

Holmøy, E. and Brevik, H.C. (2021). Betalte 1,4 mill. for svart arbeid (Paid 1,4 million for black work), daily local newspaper *Tønsbergs Blad*, Saturday, November 6, page 7.

Jordanoska, A. (2017). Case management in complex fraud trials: Actor and strategies in achieving procedural efficiency, *International Journal of Law in Context*, 13 (3), 336–355.

Jordanoska, A. (2021). Regulatory enforcement against organizational insiders: Interactions in the pursuit of individual accountability, *Regulation & Governance*, 15 (2), 298–316.

Kakkar, H., Sivanathan, N. and Globel, M.S. (2020). Fall from grace: The role of dominance and prestige in punishment of high-status actors, *Academy of Management Journal*, 63 (2), 530–553.

Kawasaki, T. (2020). Review of comparative studies on white-collar and corporate crime, in: Rorie, M.L. (editor), *The Handbook of White-Collar Crime*, Wiley & Sons, Hoboken, NJ, chapter 27, pages 437–447.

Klevstrand, A. and Solem, L.K. (2020). Økokrim undersøker hytteeiere, tiltaler arkitekt (Økokrim investigates cabin owners, charge architect), Norwegian daily business newspaper *Dagens Næringsliv*, Saturday, May 2, pages 12–13.

Kruger, L. and Haugsbø, F. (2021). Hege Haukeland Liadal (Ap) tiltalt for bedrageri (Hege Haukeland Liadal (Labor Party) charged with fraud, daily Norwegian newspaper VG, retrieved March 26.

Mannucci, P.V. and Yong, K. (2018). The differential impact of knowledge depth and knowledge breath on creativity over individual careers, *Academy of Management Journal*, 61 (5), 1741–1763.

Middelhoff, T. (2020). Im Auge des medialen Sturmes – Angeklagt, verurteilt, vernichtet (In the eye of the media storm – Accused, convicted, destroyed), in: Wohlrabe, M. (editor), *Wie Krisenkommunikation im Gerichtssaal der Ôffentlichkeit Funktioniert (How Crisis Communication Works in the Public Courtroom)*, Springer Fachmedien, Springer Nature, Wiesbaden, Germany.

Mohliver, A. (2019). How misconduct spreads: Auditors' role in the diffusion of stock-option backdating, *Administrative Science Quarterly*, 64 (2), 310–336.

Moi, T. (2017). *Revolution of the Ordinary – Literary Studies After Wittgenstein, Austin, and Cavell*, The University of Chicago Press, Ohio, Chicago.

Olaisen, A. (2021). Intervju med Hege Haukeland Liadal: Om hva som har skjedd og hvordan hun har klart å leve med presset (Interview with Hege Haukeland Liadal: About what has happened and how she has managed to live with the pressure, daily Norwegian newspaper *Haugesunds Avis*, Saturday, October 23, pages 8–9.

Rhees, R. (1970). *Discussions of Wittgenstein*, Routledge, London, UK.

Rhees, R. (1999). *Wittgenstein and the Possibility of Discourse*, Cambridge University Press, London, UK.

Rodriguez, P., Uhlenbruck, K. and Eden, L. (2005). Government corruption and the entry strategies of multinationals, *Academy of Management Review*, 30 (2), 383–396.

Rodriguez-Blanco, V. (2021). The law of negligence, blameworthy action and the relationality thesis: A dilemma for Goldberg and Zipursky's civil recourse theory of tort law, *Law and Philosophy*, published online doi.org/10.1007/s10982-021-09430-w.

Schoen, J.L., DeSimone, J.A., Meyer, R.D., Schnure, K.A. and LeBreton, J.M. (2021). Identifying, defining, and measuring justification mechanisms: The implicit biases underlying individual differences, *Journal of Management*, 47 (3), 716–744.

Schoultz, I. and Flyghed, J. (2021). Performing unbelonging in court – Observations from a transnational corporate bribery trial – A dramaturgical approach, *Crime, Law and Social Change*, published online doi: 10.1007/s10611-021-09990-x.

Stadler, W.A. and Gottschalk, P. (2022). Testing convenience theory for white-collar crime: Perceptions of potential offenders and non-offenders, *Deviant Behavior*, 43 (7), 804–820.

Suvatne, S.S. (2019). Ap-topp trekker seg fra alle verv (Labour top resigns from all positions), daily Norwegian newspaper *Dagbladet*, www.dagbladet.no, retrieved April 10.

Sykes, G. and Matza, D. (1957). Techniques of neutralization: A theory of delinquency, *American Sociological Review*, 22 (6), 664–670.

Thaxton, S. and Agnew, R. (2018). When criminal coping is likely: An examination of conditioning effects in general strain theory, *Journal of Quantitative Criminology*, 34, 887–920.

Trædal, T.J. (2021a). Tidligere Ap-politiker erkjenner uaktsomhet, benekter forsettlig bedrageri (Former Labor politician admits negligence, denies intentional fraud), daily Norwegian newspaper *Aftenposten*, Wednesday, November 3, pages 18–19.

Trædal, T.J. (2021b). Bedre på å lage nasjonalbudsjett enn husholdningsbudsjett (Better at making a national budget than a household budget), daily Norwegian newspaper Aftenposten, Thursday, November 4, page 32.

Walenta, J. (2020). Coortroom ethnography: Researching the intersection of law, space, and everyday practices, *The Professional Geographer*, 72 (1), 131–138.
Wittgenstein, L. (1953). *Philosophical Investigations*, Chiron Academic Press, London, UK.
Wittgenstein, L. (2010). *Tractatus Logico-Philosophicus*, Chiron Academic Press, London, UK.
Ytreberg, R. (2018). Kommunen stoppet Breili-prosjekt på Tjøme (The municipality stops Breili project on Tjøme), Norwegian daily business newspaper *Dagens Næringsliv*, Monday, April 30, pages 4–5.

11 Corporate Internal Investigations

When there is suspicion of financial misconduct and crime in public and private organizations, organizations tend to hire corporate investigators to conduct fraud examinations. Fraud examinations by corporate investigators are a form of alternative policing where corporate investigators rather than police detectives work to establish facts in contractual relationships with client organizations that are requesting answers. Corporate investigators normally document their work in fraud examination reports that usually are kept secret for various reasons. The secrecy is a problem, since some reports tend to cause dramatic life events for individuals without any transparency of corporate investigations. The research presented in this chapter is important, as it identifies characteristics of fraud examination reports after corporate investigations. Despite the tendency of secrecy and confidentiality in most corporate investigations, it has nevertheless been possible to detect and retrieve a number of fraud examination reports. The collection of reports started in 2015 and is still going on. Research results in this chapter are based on a sample of 163 reports from many countries. The outcome for suspects might be nothing, unknown, resignation, dismissal, prosecution, fine, or prison, where outcomes such as prosecution or prison in the criminal justice system often occurred independent of fraud examinations by corporate investigators.

Among the Norwegian cases in the sample, 19% of the suspects were found innocent, 14% resigned, and 11% were dismissed. In other countries, 14% were found innocent, 26% resigned, and 11% were dismissed.

Corporate investigators are assigned the task of reconstructing past events and sequences of events. Assignments have a mandate addressing questions such as: What happened or did not happen? When did it happen? Who did what to make it happen or not happen? Why did it happen? Investigators conduct interviews, read documents, and search other information sources for potential answers to the questions (Button et al., 2022; Gottschalk, 2020; King, 2020; Meerts, 2020; Wood, 2020).

Fraud examinations by corporate investigators are a form of alternative policing where corporate investigators rather than police detectives work to establish facts in contractual relationships with client organizations that are requesting answers. It is often not a form of privatization of law enforcement as

DOI: 10.4324/9781003379249-14

corporate investigators take on the task of establishing facts outside the criminal justice system. The perspective of alternative policing is a shift from the public sphere toward the private sphere across the policing landscape (Stenström, 2018; White, 2020). Corporate investigators normally document their work in fraud examination reports.

The business of corporate investigations has become an industry with accounting firms, audit firms, law firms, consulting firms, and independent forensic examiners. Their business model is to apply knowledge to negative client situations to establish answers to questions that they are paid to address. The remuneration for examination work is normally based on time spent and expenses involved in the search for answers (King, 2021).

The outcome of fraud examinations ranges from no consequences at all to dramatic life events for accused individuals. Sometimes suspects suffer harm even when corporate investigators found no evidence of wrongdoing. During fraud examinations, individuals who are subject to scrutiny may experience uncertainty, isolation, and negative media attention. Despite serious consequences for many individuals, corporate investigators are allowed to operate almost whatever way they like as long as clients are happy with the work and pay for it. Private investigators are in an unregulated industry where only statutes from their basic business apply, such as client-attorney privileges and rules for certified accountants. Adding to the problematic role of private examiners as emphasized early by Williams (2005) and Schneider (2006) is the secrecy of corporate investigation reports (Gottschalk and Tcherni-Buzzeo, 2016). The need for research to study the performance of corporate investigators is thus obvious as their potential malpractice can harm innocent individuals and entities in democratic societies that assume fairness.

Researchers in many countries have studied fraud examinations by corporate investigators. In Australia, King (2021) focused on attributes of corporate investigators that might enable successful fraud examinations. In Canada, Schneider (2006) explored the role of private sector investigative agencies in combating money laundering. In the Netherlands, Meerts (2020) studied struggles of cooperation in public–private relations in the investigation of internal financial crime. In Norway, Gottschalk (2020) evaluated fraud examination reports after corporate investigations by application of a maturity model. In the United Kingdom, Button (2020) studied the new private security industry, the private policing of cyberspace, and the regulatory questions.

This research attempts to identify characteristics of fraud examination reports after corporate investigations. The research reported in this chapter is based on two samples of investigation reports identified and retrieved in recent years. The larger sample of 116 reports is concerned with fraud issues in Norway, while the smaller sample of 47 reports is concerned with fraud issues in Austria, Bangladesh, Canada, Congo, Denmark, Germany, Ghana, Iceland, Japan, Moldova, the Netherlands, New Zealand, Nigeria, Russia, Sudan, Sweden, Switzerland, the United States, and Vietnam. The total of 163 reports is a convenience sample for research yet unique to empirical study of work by corporate investigators.

This chapter addresses the following research question: *What characteristics of fraud examination reports can be identified after corporate investigations?* Characteristics include suspicion investigated, the number of pages, the outcome, public audit following private audit, and other issues that can provide insights into the work of corporate investigators in fraud examinations. The outcome for suspects might be nothing, unknown, resignation, dismissal, prosecution, fine, or prison. Case outcomes in the criminal justice system, such as prosecution or prison, often develop independent of the fraud examinations by corporate investigators.

Australian, Dutch, and the UK Research

In his study of what makes a successful corporate investigator in Australia, King (2020) conducted an exploration of private investigators attributes. He identified nine attributes that make a successful corporate investigator. His research method was interviews with 33 corporate investigators in Australia. Data collection was through semi-structured interviews. Sample interview questions were: Can you describe the types of skills you need in corporate investigation? Can you provide up to five skills necessary for corporate investigation work? What characteristics do you think are important for a corporate investigator to possess?

On the basis of interview answers, King (2020: 709) ranked the nine corporate investigator attributes:

> This study found that the corporate investigator needs an array of attributes to effectively work in a complex and challenging environment, identifying nine main attributes. The three most important, as identified by the interviewees, were communication, motivation, and industry experience. Communication was easily considered the most critical attribute (90 per cent). All interviewees discussed communication during the interview, and it was frequently refereed to throughout the entire interview process. This finding is consistent with those of other studies that found communication to be essential for the effectiveness of police detectives, financial investigators, and forensic accountants.

In Australia, there is a requirement of a certificate for the licensing of private investigators. Thirty-two out of 33 corporate investigators in Australia held this certificate. In Norway, there is no such requirement of a certificate to practice as a corporate investigator. It is unknown whether there is such a requirement in countries where this research obtained internal investigation reports.

While the study by Schneider (2006: 285) in Canada dates a while back, it is nevertheless interesting briefly to review the research that explored the role played by private sector financial investigative agencies (FIA) in combating money laundering in Canada and abroad:

> This emergent "anti-money laundering industry" is unique in that it is ultimately concerned with economic, organized, and terrorist crimes. These crimes are much more complex, multi-jurisdictional and threatening to mass society than the "street-level" property crime that is the overwhelming focus of the private policing sector. With the advent and growth of this cottage industry, the focus of the private policing sector now stretches from the most rudimentary disorder and property crime problems all the way to complex, highly-organized and multi-jurisdictional criminal and national security issues. What's more, this anti-money laundering industry has contributed to not only the ongoing fragmentation of policing in society, but with increased attention being paid to detecting terrorist financing, it has perhaps initiated a similar fragmentation of national security enforcement. This study recommends that public policies and programs be developed that nurture an increased and more formal role for FIAs within the context of a partnership with government agencies.

Schneider (2006) expressed skepticism toward the growing industry of corporate investigators. He was at that time in line with others such as Williams (2005) in the United Kingdom, who questioned the legitimacy of private policing of financial crime.

Similar to King (2020) in Australia, Meerts (2020) has done extensive research on corporate investigators in the Netherlands. She interviewed 59 corporate investigators to answer her research question: What is the role of corporate investigators in the investigation and settlement of norm violations within organizations? To answer this question, she examined (1) the legal frameworks within which corporate investigators operate, (2) the investigative methods corporate investigators may use, and (3) the settlements that are possible as a response to the corporate investigations.

Meerts (2018: 6) found that the legal framework is almost non-existent or non-functioning for corporate investigators in the Netherlands:

> Respondents indicate that the state has very little insight into what happens in the corporate security sector. . . . The legal framework that applies is dependent on the label an investigator wears. . . . Although forensic accountants and legal investigators are regulated by a general legal framework, these laws are not constructed to deal with investigative activities – rather, they are focused on traditional accounting activities and the traditional role of the lawyer. . . . The diversification in the corporate investigations arena and in legal frameworks and control create a fragmented field in which the state has very little knowledge about actual activities. Democratic control over the corporate security sector is very limited. Control over corporate investigations is, for an important part, reliant on the ethics of individual

> investigators and on the client. This places much responsibility on organizations using the services of corporate investigators.

Meerts (2018: 9) found that the investigative methods corporate investigators may use derive from a large arsenal of possibilities:

> Apart from (financial) documentation, much information may be derived from the internal systems at place in an organization. . . . Much additional information is, furthermore, provided by desk research into open sources. . . . Interviews with the 'subject' or 'involved person' are usually done only at the end of investigations. . . . Following the widely-used adversarial principle, interviewees are given the opportunity to read their statement and to correct factual errors. . . . Many corporate investigations remain entirely in the private realm, as the investigative possibilities are often enough to provide the necessary information without having to resort to the formal powers of investigation of law enforcement (which could be mobilized through a report to the authorities).

While judges pass verdicts on defendants in court, corporate investigators may arrange settlements in private investigations. Clients often want to settle a matter quietly, for example, by a contract in which parties agree on an amount payable by the involved person. It may also include conditions, such as the termination of the labor contract. Non-disclosure clauses are fairly standard to settlement agreement where parties commit themselves to the confidentiality of the agreement and the circumstances of termination (Meerts, 2018).

In the United Kingdom, Button et al. (2022) studied the outcomes of investigative work. Among 78 in-house investigators in public and private organizations, 31% of cases they investigated led to criminal prosecution. For the 27 forensic investigators, 27% of cases they investigated led to criminal prosecution. The 75 private investigators had similar results with a mean of 24.5% criminal prosecutions.

Button et al. (2022) distinguished three main groups of investigators who are involved in private investigations: In-house investigators are doing reviews in private and public organizations where they are employed, forensic investigators are doing reviews in terms of professional services and are based in the accountancy and legal sectors, while private investigators do reviews and charge fees to clients for investigative services.

The research was based on a questionnaire that was distributed to investigators that could be found on various lists, including the Association of British Investigators, UK Professional Investigators Network, University of Portsmouth database of fraud contacts, and Midlands Fraud Forum. A total of 331 responses were received and applied in descriptive statics analysis.

The demographics of the investigators showed a male-dominated occupation with more than 70% male and less than 30% female. However, for in-house public investigators, the balance was closer to 60% male and 40% female.

Male dominance was highest among private investigators, who charge fees to clients for investigative services where the male fraction was almost 90%. The average age of the respondents was quite high (Button et al., 2022).

Secrecy of Investigation Reports

Despite the tendency of secrecy and confidentiality in most corporate investigations, it has nevertheless been possible to detect and retrieve a number of fraud examination reports. The collection of reports started in 2015 and is still going on. Every year since 2015, students in an elective class on financial crime in a Norwegian business school have had an assignment of evaluating an investigation report of their choice. Over the years, the sample of examination reports from Norway is growing, and now there are 116 reports to be presented in this chapter. Some students in Norway evaluated reports from other countries such as Denmark, Germany, and Sweden. Students in an elective class on financial crime at the department of criminal justice at a university in the United States had a similar assignment in the spring term 2018. The total number of reports from other countries than Norway now adds up to 47 reports. The detection and retrieval of various reports were successfully conducted by both course instructors and class participants.

Despite the large number of 163 reports, there is no way of telling to what extent these reports are representative for all examination reports produced by corporate investigators. The available reports are probably biased in some way. One kind of bias might be that the disclosure of the reports indicates public awareness and public interest where political bodies such as municipalities and governments can be stakeholders. The client organizations might have a motive of improving their reputation by disclosing reports. Therefore, the sum of reports is a convenience sample that does not allow for generalization to the total population of examination reports.

Despite the growing number of reports in the sample, the reports represent only a very small fraction of produced reports. In Norway, it can be estimated that 100 corporate investigators in various firms work full-time on fraud examinations for client organizations. Assuming that they sometimes work in teams and sometimes work alone, it can be estimated that at least 100 reports are produced annually. The oldest Norwegian report in the sample is from 2007 and the newest from 2022. During these 16 years, we might estimate that 1,600 reports were handed over to clients from investigators. Only 116 reports were successfully retrieved in this research that represents only 7% known reports versus 90% unknown reports.

The methodology applied to investigation reports in this book is content analysis (Bell et al., 2018; Braaten and Vaughn, 2019). Content analysis is any methodology or procedure that works to identify characteristics within texts attempting to make valid inferences (Patrucco et al., 2017). Content analysis assumes that language reflects both how people understand their surroundings and their cognitive processes. Therefore, content analysis makes it possible to identify and determine relevant text in a context (McClelland et al., 2010).

If the outcome of an investigation occurred ahead of or during the fraud examination, the outcome is visible in the investigation report. If the outcome occurred after completion of the fraud examination, searches in the media enabled retrieval of outcome to a large extent. However, some outcomes were not possible to find.

Review of 163 Investigation Reports

Appendix A lists the total of 163 reports. The table is organized alphabetically by country, starting with Austria and ending with Vietnam. The first entry is concerned with the investigated client organization of International Biathlon Union (IBU) in Austria. The investigating examination entity was a specially appointed commission. The suspicion of white-collar crime investigated was concerned with the president having received various favors from the Russian biathlon union. Also the secretary general was suspected of reluctance to react to the Russian doping scandal in response to the personal favors granted to the president.

Appendix A is dominated by reports from Norway. The first report listed was concerned with a nursing home operated by Adecco. Investigators from Norwegian law firm Wiersholm were assigned the task of examining whether employees were financially exploited by long working hours, low hourly pay rates, and bad housing conditions. Many of the employees were coming from other countries, and they did not know their rights according to Norwegian labor laws and standards.

An initial coding for analysis of the reports listed in Appendix A is concerned with public versus private client organizations, categories of suspected financial crime, and categories of examination firms. Out of 163 examination reports, there are 87 public client organizations and 76 private client organizations. Typical examples of public client organizations are the Norwegian foreign ministry concerned with fraud in housing rental for diplomats in Vietnam, the tax administration in Washington, D.C. concerned with embezzlement by a trusted employee, and the city of Oslo's concern regarding the chief executive employing family members in public housing administration. Typical examples of private client organizations are the car manufacturer General Motors that kept secret the ignition switch failure on the Cobalt car that could cause substantial financial loss for the company, the Fédération internationale de football association (FIFA) that suspected corruption at the allocation of world cup events, and the Swedish bank Swedbank that was concerned with money laundering in their branch offices in Eastern Europe.

Four main categories of financial crime can be defined (Gottschalk, 2010): fraud, theft, manipulation, and corruption. Fraud is unlawful and intentional making of a misrepresentation, which causes actual prejudice, or which is potentially prejudicial to another. Fraud is to create a misjudgment or maintain an existing misjudgment to induce somebody to do something that the person or organization otherwise would not do. Theft refers to the illegal taking of another person's, a group's, or an organization's property without the victim's consent. For example, identity theft combined with identity fraud is the unlawful use of another's personal identifying information. Manipulation can be defined as a means of gaining illegal control or influence over others' activities, means, and results. Managers can withhold bad news by accounting misrepresentation, since financial statements are a substantive component of a firm's communications with its stakeholders. Corruption is defined as the giving, requesting, receiving, or accepting of an improper advantage related to a position, office, or assignment. The improper advantage does not have to be connected to a specific action or to not doing this action. It will be sufficient if the advantage can be linked to a person's position, office, or assignment. Corruption covers a wide range of illegal activity such as kickbacks, embezzlement, and extortion. While fraud is one out of four crime categories, fraud is elsewhere in this book used as a general term for financial crime.

In the sample of 163 reports, there are 56 fraud suspicion cases, 29 theft suspicion cases, 45 manipulation suspicion cases, and 33 corruption suspicion cases. In the Norwegian subsample of 116 reports, there are 45 cases of fraud suspicion, 21 cases of theft suspicion, 27 cases of manipulation suspicion, and 23 cases of corruption suspicion.

The latter findings can be compared to conviction statistics regarding white-collar offenders convicted to prison in Norway. In the database of 405 convicts from 2009 to 2015, there are 171 fraud cases, 17 theft cases, 142 manipulation cases, and 75 corruption cases (Gottschalk, 2022). There are thus some similarities with the reports in terms of frequency of offenses, where there are more fraud cases and manipulation cases than there are theft cases and corruption cases.

If returning here for a moment to the public versus private client organizations where the Norwegian part of the sample has 71 public and 45 private clients, respectively, the 405 convicts have a different distribution. Among the 405 convicted white-collar offenders in Norway, 32 convicts worked in the public sector while 373 convicts worked in the private sector. The discrepancy between the fraction of fraud examinations in the public sector and the fraction of convicts in the public sector is interesting. The fraction of fraud examinations is 61% for public and 39% for private, respectively, while the fraction of convicted offenders is 8% for public and 92% for private, respectively. Several possible explanations emerge here. First, it might be more common to conduct fraud investigations in public than in private organizations. Second, it might be more common to make investigation reports known more frequently from the public than from the private sector. Furthermore, the detection rate for offenders might be lower in the public compared to the private sector.

In addition to the coding of public versus private client organizations and categories of suspected financial crime, there are categories of examination firms where corporate investigators work for their clients. The first category is law firms. Examples of law firms include Kammeradvokaten in Denmark, Wiersholm in Norway, Mannheimer Swartling in Sweden, Wilmer Cutler Pickering in the United States, and Duane Morris in Vietnam. Out of 163 examination reports, 50 reports were written by law firms (31%). Then there is the category of accounting and audit firms that also might have legal departments such as BDO, Deloitte, Ernst & Young, KPMG, and PwC. Sixty-eight reports out of 163 reports were written by such firms (42%). The third and final category of investigative entities is various other forms of units such as public audit functions (e.g., State Auditor, Kommunerevisjon), special task forces (e.g., Brookings, Commission, Council, Freeh, Garcia, McLaren), and various public agencies (e.g., Finansinspektionen, Finanstilsynet).

Some investigations result in several examination reports. For example, in Moldova where banks were depleted of funds that disappeared abroad, Kroll wrote several reports. Another example is Ferde toll collection in Norway that was first investigated by Kluge and the following year by Deloitte.

Many of the public audit investigations (e.g., State Auditor, Kommunerevisjon) were conducted long after wrongdoing was committed and prosecuted. Those examination reports typically contribute less to detection and more to recommendations regarding the prevention of similar incidence in the future. For example, suspected corruption in public procurement in the city of Oslo was first investigated by BDO and then Deloitte, before the municipal audit Kommunerevisjon looked into the wrongdoing and made several recommendations for the future.

Outcomes for Crime Suspects

In the following appendices, the large Norwegian sample is in Appendix B while it was separated from other countries in Appendix C. Furthermore, the tables only include investigation reports where explicit suspicion of white-collar crime was the case in terms of named individuals. The purpose of including named individuals is to be able to identify the cases of white-collar crime suspicion rather than discussing the persons' potential innocence or guilt. On the basis of this procedure, there are 103 examination reports from Norway listed in Appendix B and 38 examination reports from other countries listed in Appendix C. The Norwegian sample was thus reduced by 11% from 116 to 103, and the global sample was reduced by 19% from 47 to 38, by excluding 13 reports and 9 reports, respectively.

The first column in Appendix B for the Norwegian sample lists client organizations that hired corporate investigators to conduct fraud examinations. The examination firms, where corporate investigators work, are listed in the second column. The third column in the table shows the number of pages in each examination report. The fourth column lists the last name of the suspects. The fifth and final column lists the outcome for each suspect. If the outcome occurred ahead of or during the fraud examination, the outcome is visible in the investigation report. If the outcome occurred after completion of the fraud examination, searches in the media enabled retrieval to a large extent. However, some outcomes were not possible to find, and they are marked "Unknown" in the right-hand column in Appendix B.

Some suspects are mentioned twice as there were two investigation reports. For example, CEO Juvik at Ferde toll collection was subject to attention by both Kluge and Deloitte. None of them found any evidence of wrongdoing on the part of the chief executive. Therefore, the first entry is "Nothing" while the second is a repetition in terms of "(Noting)". To avoid double counting when looking at the number of various outcomes, only the first entry is considered.

There are unknown outcomes for 29 suspects in Appendix B, and there are 17 outcomes of nothing. Some voluntarily left their positions shortly after occurrence of relevant incidents that were examined, and those outcomes are labeled "Resignation". There are 12 resignations. Some suspects were forced to leave, and those outcomes are labeled "Dismissal". There are ten dismissals. Some suspects ended up in the criminal justice system without any known final outcome. They are labeled "Prosecution", and there are three prosecutions in the table. The most serious outcome for a suspect is incarceration labeled "Prison", and there are 19 imprisonments in the table.

All these groups are interesting for various reasons. The unknown group makes up 32% of the sample of suspects. The nothing group is interesting because innocent individuals become subject to scrutiny that was unjustified. While found innocent in the end, they certainly suffered during the investigation. The nothing group makes up 19% of the sample of suspects. The resignation group is interesting as it is unclear why they left their positions without being blamed for any wrongdoing. The resignation group makes up 14% of the sample of suspects. The dismissal group has suspects that were somehow blamed for negative events and forced to leave their positions. The dismissal group makes up 11% of the sample of suspects. The prosecution group makes up 3% of the sample. The final group has 19 suspects that were sentenced to prison. The prison group makes up 21% of the sample of suspects.

The largest group of those known outcomes is the group of 19 prisoners. It is not obvious whether corporate investigators by their examination reports had any influence on the final outcome of incarceration for those suspects since police detectives, state prosecutors, and court judges are the three actors in the criminal justice system who determined the destiny for this group of suspects. However, in most of the cases, pieces of information in fraud examination reports contributed to work in the criminal justice system. For example in the Betanien case, BDO found evidence of more money embezzled than the suspect initially had confessed. CEO Blomhoff was in charge of establishing a nursing home for the Betanien foundation in Spain, and his privileged role allowed him both to trigger transfer of money from Norway and to allocate that money for property development and construction work in Spain. He diverged some of the funds to buy his own apartment in Spain and to cover other personal expenses. Fraud examiners were able to identify more misappropriation of funds where the final amount became the basis for sentencing the chief executive in Norwegian court.

Appendix C lists examination reports from other countries in alphabetical order by client organizations. The first column lists each client organization, and second column lists the national location of each organization. The next column lists the investigation firm, and then follows the number of pages in each examination report. The fifth column lists the last name of suspects. The sixth and final column lists the outcome for each suspect. If the outcome occurred ahead of or during the fraud examination, the outcome is visible in the investigation report. If the outcome occurred after completion of the fraud examination, searches in the media enabled retrieval to a large extent. However, some outcomes were not possible to find, and they are marked "Unknown" in the right-hand column in Appendix C.

There are unknown outcomes for four suspects in Appendix C, and there are five outcomes of nothing. Some voluntarily left their positions shortly after occurrence of relevant incidents that were examined, and those outcomes are labeled "Resignation". There are nine resignations. Some suspects were forced to leave, and those outcomes are labeled "Dismissal". There are four dismissals. Some suspects ended up in the criminal justice systems without any known final outcome. They are labeled "Prosecution", and there are two prosecutions in the table. The most serious outcome for a suspect is incarceration labeled "Prison", and there are 11 imprisonments in the table.

All these groups are again interesting for various reasons. The unknown group makes up 11% of the sample of suspects. The nothing group is interesting because innocent individuals become subject to scrutiny that was unjustified. While found innocent in the end, they certainly suffered during the investigation. The nothing group makes up 14% of the sample of suspects. The resignation group is interesting as it is unclear why they left their positions without being blamed for wrongdoing. The resignation group makes up 26% of the sample of suspects. The dismissal group has suspects that were somehow blamed for negative events and forced to leave their positions. The dismissal group makes up 11% of the sample of suspects. The prosecution group makes up 6% of the sample. The final group has 11 suspects who were sentenced to prison. The prison group makes up 32% of the sample of suspects.

The largest group of those known outcomes is the group of 11 prisoners. It is again not obvious whether corporate investigators by their examination reports had any influence on the final outcome of incarceration for those suspects since police detectives, state prosecutors, and court judges are the three actors in the criminal justice system who determine the destiny for this group of suspects. However, in most of the cases, pieces of information in fraud examination reports contributed to work in the criminal justice system.

Some examination reports have a different conclusion than the criminal justice system. One example from Germany might illustrate this phenomenon. When KPMG investigated Wirecard, they found no evidence of wrongdoing. This was in the spring of 2020. It was the newspaper *Financial Times* that had suggested fictitious customer relationships and accounting manipulation. A few months after the publication of the KPMG report, Wirecard collapsed and CEO Braun was prosecuted in the German criminal justice system.

A comparison of the sample from Norway with the sample from other countries indicates some differences as listed in Appendix D. There are many more unknown outcomes in the Norwegian sample. There are far more resignations in other countries, and there are far more incarcerations in other countries.

In conclusion and in comparison to the reviewed literature of research in Australia, it is interesting to reflect on the attribute of communication among corporate investigators. One indication of poor communication skills is the inability to contact and gain access to relevant persons for interviews. For example, the Commission that examined alleged corruption at IBU in Austria failed in their communication with two suspects. Both suspects declined the opportunity to comment on the allegations and evidence set out in the examination report. Another example is concerned with information from whistleblowers. Communicating with whistleblowers is not easy as there is frequent noise and uncertainty in whistleblowing messages regarding observed or assumed wrongdoing. Whistleblowers are often the initial source of information that can direct examiners in their efforts. Bruun Hjejle relied successfully on their communication with a whistleblower at Danske Bank, McLaren relied successfully on communication with a whistleblower regarding doping of Russian athletes in Sochi, and Duane Morris communicated successfully with a whistleblower in Vietnam.

In comparison to the reviewed literature of research in the Netherlands, the sample of examination reports supports the finding that corporate investigators tend to have a much wider focus than police detectives. While the criminal justice system is only interested in persons who might have violated laws and thus potentially interested in prosecuting and sentencing such individuals, corporate investigations might have a focus of avoiding similar incidents in the future. For example, the State Auditor was interested in detecting and preventing admission processes at the University of California that make corruption convenient. Both Shearman Sterling and Waters in their review of the Wells Fargo scandal were interested in the decision-making culture within the bank that caused wrongdoing. Yet another example are the investigations by Clifford Chance at Swedbank as well as Bruun Hjejle at Danske Bank that went beyond potential money laundering incidents and recommended improved anti-money laundering routines at the banks.

In comparison to the reviewed literature of research in the United Kingdom, the Norwegian sample of examination reports has 24% prosecution, which is the sum of prosecution (3%) and conviction (21%). The sample of other countries has 38% prosecution, which is again the sum of prosecution (6%) and conviction (32%). As mentioned in the literature review, the UK research studied the outcomes of investigative work. Among 78 in-house investigators in public and private organizations, 31% of cases they investigated led to criminal prosecution. For the 27 forensic investigators, 27% of cases they investigated led to criminal prosecution. The 75 private investigators had similar results with a mean of 24.5% criminal prosecutions. So on average, it might be argued that one-third or one-fourth of privately investigated suspects end up in the criminal justice system before, during, or after alternative policing in corporate investigations.

References

Bell, E., Bryman, A. and Harley, B. (2018). *Business Research Methods*, Second Edition, Oxford University Press, New York, NY.

Braaten, C.N. and Vaughn, M.S. (2019). Convenience theory of cryptocurrency crime: A content analysis of U.S. federal court decisions, *Deviant Behavior*, published online https://doi.org/10.1080/01639625.2019.1706706.

Button, M. (2020). The "new" private security industry, the private policing of cyberspace and the regulatory questions, *Journal of Contemporary Criminal Justice*, 36 (1), 39–55.

Button, M., Kapend, R. and Stiernsted, P. (2022). Investigative private policing beyond the police: An exploratory study, *Policing & Society*, published online doi: 10.109/10439463.2022.2071894.

Gottschalk, P. (2010). Categories of financial crime, *Journal of Financial Crime*, 17 (4), 441–458.

Gottschalk, P. (2020). Filling the gap in white-collar crime detection between government and governance: The role of investigative journalists and fraud examiners, *Journal of White Collar and Corporate Crime*, 2 (1), 36–46.

Gottschalk, P. (2022). *The Convenience of Corporate Crime: Financial Motive – Organizational Opportunity – Executive Willingness*, De Gruyter Verlag, Germany, Berlin.

Gottschalk, P. and Tcherni-Buzzeo, M. (2016). Reasons for gaps in crime reporting: The case of white-collar criminals investigated by private fraud examiners in Norway, *Deviant Behavior*, 38 (3), 267–281.

King, M. (2020). What makes a successful corporate investigator: An exploration of private investigators attributes, *Journal of Financial Crime*, 27 (3), 701–714.

King, M. (2021). Profiting form a tainted trade: Private investigators' views on the popular culture glamorization of their trade, *Journal of Criminological Research Policy and Practice*, published online doi: 10.1108/JCRPP-07-2020-0050.

McClelland, P.L., Liang, X. and Barker, V.L. (2010). CEO commitment to the status quo: Replication and extension using content analysis, *Journal of Management*, 36 (5), 1251–1277.

Meerts, C.A. (2018). The organization as the cure for its own ailments: Corporate investigators in the Netherlands, *Administrative Sciences*, 8 (25), 1–15.

Meerts, C.A. (2020). Corporate investigations: Beyond notions of public-private relations, *Journal of Contemporary Criminal Justice*, 36 (1), 86–100.

Patrucco, A.S., Luzzini, D. and Ronchi, S. (2017). Research perspectives on public procurement: Content analysis of 14 years of publications in the Journal of Public Procurement, *Journal of Public Procurement*, 16 (2), 229–269.

Schneider, S. (2006). Privatizing economic crime enforcement: Exploring the role of private sector investigative agencies in combating money laundering, *Policing and Society*, 16 (3), 285–312.

Stenström, A. (2018). The private policing of insurance claims: Power, profit and private justice, *British Journal of Criminology*, 58 (2), 478–496.

White, A. (2020). What is the privatization of policing? *Policing: A Journal of Policy and Practice*, 14 (3), 766–777.

Williams, J.W. (2005). Governability matters: The private policing of economic crime and the challenge of democratic governance, *Policing & Society*, 15 (2), 187–211.

Wood, J.D. (2020). Private policing and public health: A neglected relationship, *Journal of Contemporary Criminal Justice*, 36 (1), 19–38.

Appendix A

Characteristics at Suspicion

Investigated client organization	*Investigating examination firm*	*Suspicion of white-collar crime investigated*
AUSTRIA		
International Biathlon Union	Commission (2021) by appointment	*President received various favors from the Russian biathlon union*
BANGLADESH		
Padakhep Save the Children NGO	Inspector General (2012) in the United States	*Embezzlement of funds to fight disease*
CANADA		
Niagara Falls municipality	Ombudsman (2022) of Ontario	*Improper hiring of chief administrative officer*
Pelham town	KPMG (2017) audit and law firm	*Development project manipulation in accounting*
CONGO		
Mercy Corps humanitarian aid	Smith (2020) investigation service	*Corruption in local procurement of goods and services*
DENMARK		
Banedanmark public railroad	Kammeradvokaten (2020a) law firm	*Corruption by vendor to procurement executives*
Bestseller garment store chain	Offersen Christoffersen (2021) law firm	*Violating sanctions against Myanmar for production of clothes*
Danske Bank banking in Estonia	Bruun Hjejle (2018) law firm	*Money laundering in Estonian branch*
Danske Bank banking in Denmark	Plesner (2020) law firm	*Fraud by system of expired bank deposits*
Ejendomsstyrelse property management	Kammeradvokaten (2020b) law firm	*Corruption in procurement of property services*
Region Syddanmark public authority	Kromann Reumert (2015) law firm	*Fraud by abuse of public position*
Socialstyrelsen social security	PwC (2019c) audit and law firm	*Embezzlement by trusted employee*
Socialstyrelsen social security	Kammeradvokaten (2019) law firm	*Executive lack of control and guardianship*
GERMANY		
Wirecard digital financial services	KPMG (2020) audit and law firm	*Fictitious customer relationships, accounting manipulation*

Investigated client organization	*Investigating examination firm*	*Suspicion of white-collar crime investigated*
GHANA		
BioFuel bioenergy production	Kluge (2009) law firm	*Corruption in Ghana to obtain licenses*
ICELAND		
Samherji fishing industries	Kleinfeld (2019) at Al Jazeera	*Corruption for fishing rights in Namibia*
JAPAN		
Olympus digital equipment provider	Deloitte (2011b) audit and law firm	*Accounting manipulation and fraud*
Toshiba digital equipment provider	Deloitte (2015) audit and firm	*Accounting manipulation and fraud*
MOLDOVA		
Moldova Banca de Economii Sociala	Kroll (2017) forensic investigation firm	*Bank fraud by loans transferred abroad for money laundering*
THE NETHERLANDS		
Oceanteam offshore services	Sands (2019) law firm	*Abuse of company money by majority shareholder*
NEW ZEALAND		
Fujifilm digital equipment leasing	Deloitte (2017e) audit and law firm 2017	*Accounting fraud by charging customers ahead of time*
NIGERIA		
Nigerian National Petroleum Corporation	PwC (2015b) audit and law firm	*Embezzlement and corruption in oil exploration*
NORWAY		
Adecco nursing home	Wiersholm (2011) law firm	*Fraud in employment contracts for hourly overtime rates*
Agder fengsel prison and probation	BDO (2021) accounting and audit firm	*Illegal benefits achieved by the assistant prison executive*
Ahus public hospital	PwC (2013a) audit and law firm	*Fraud when charging mapping services*
Alver municipality	Nordhordland (2019) public audit	*Family member favored in cost arrangement*
Andebu municipality	BDO (2014a) accounting and audit firm	*Abuse of mayor position in procurement*
Arendal public traffic station	Traffic (2017) internal audit function	*Corruption for illegal vehicle permits*
Askøy municipality	BDO (2018) accounting and audit firm	*Public procurement from family members*
Bergensklinikkene private health clinic	Ernst & Young (2019a) audit and law firm	*Subsidy fraud by false number of addicts hospitalized*
Betanien Methodist foundation	BDO (2014) accounting and audit firm	*Embezzlement by chief executive (CEO)*
Bodø municipality	Salten (2020) municipal audit	*Stamina health overcharged services to the municipality*
Briskeby public sports arena	Lynx (2011) law firm	*Fraud in public construction funds*

(*Continued*)

(Continued)

Investigated client organization	*Investigating examination firm*	*Suspicion of white-collar crime investigated*
BTS Utvikling property development	Schjødt (2021) law firm	*Conflict of interest between public and private business activities*
Bærum municipality	G-partner (2007) law firm	*Corruption at public procurement among family members*
Caverion subcontractor services	Wiersholm (2019) law firm	*Substandard wages and working hours*
Dale property development	Rogaland revisjon (2015) public audit	*Public funds spent on private vacations*
Demokratene political party	Partirevisjon (2016) internal control function	*Illegitimate government subsidy*
DNB banking	Hjort (2016) law firm	*Tax evasion in wealth management revealed by Panama Papers*
DNB banking	Finanstilsyn (2020) inspection authority	*Helped Samherji launder money for corruption in Namibia*
DNB banking	Finanstilsyn (2021) inspection authority	*Helped Samherji and others launder money*
Drammen municipality	Deloitte (2017a) audit and law firm	*Corruption in building permits*
DSS security service in government ministries	Arntzen de Besche (2021) law firm	*Ignorance toward union leaders regarding misconduct*
Eckbo foundations	Thommessen (2009) law firm	*Chairperson fraud in foundation funds*
Fadderbarna foundation	BDO (2011) accounting and audit firm	*Fake documents hiding fraud abroad*
Ferde road toll collection	Kluge (2019) law firm	*Conflict of interest for chief executive at procurement*
Ferde road toll collection	Deloitte (2020) audit and law firm	*Abuse of position at mergers*
FilmCamp public fund for productions	Kommunerevisjon (2016b) public audit	*Fraud by abuse of public funding*
Fjell municipality	Deloitte (2017b) audit and law firm	*Corruption in construction permits*
Flyktningtjenesten public refugee funding	Kommunerevisjon (2015c) public audit	*Embezzlement by refugee services manager*
Forsvaret military contracts	Dalseide (2006) special public committee	*Corruption in military computer contracts*
Forsvaret military logistics	PwC (2014a) audit and law firm	*Corruption in military sales unit*
Forsvaret department of defense routines	PwC (2015a) audit and law firm	*Illegal profits from sale of discarded equipment*
Fredrikstad municipality	PwC (2018a) audit and law firm	*VAT fraud by public company*
Fredrikstad municipality	Simonsen (2018) law firm	*VAT fraud by public company*
Fretex Salvation Army	Grette (2017) law firm 2017	*Financial targets to remove executive*

Investigated client organization	*Investigating examination firm*	*Suspicion of white-collar crime investigated*
Furuheim foundation nursing home	Hald (2006) law firm	*Fraud in foundation construction*
Fyrlykta foundation childcare	Deloitte (2017c) audit and law firm	*Fraud of public funds for excessive salaries*
Fyrlykta foundation childcare	Stiftelsestilsyn (2018) public inquiry	*Fraud of public funds for excessive salaries*
Født Fri minority organization	Ernst & Young (2020) audit and law firm	*Abuse of public funds for private expenses in foundation*
Gartnerhallen fruits and vegetables	Wiersholm (2018) law firm	*Fraud by farmers demanding repay from distributor*
Gassnova public projects	BDO (2013a) accounting and audit firm	*Corruption in public procurement*
Grimstad municipality	BDO (2016) accounting and audit firm	*Manipulation and corruption in public procurement*
Grimstad municipality	Hjort (2018) law firm	*Manipulation and corruption in public procurement*
Hadeland broadband mobile company	PwC (2014b) audit and law firm	*Embezzlement by chief financial officer (CFO)*
Hadeland energy supply company	PwC (2014c) audit and law firm	*Embezzlement by chief financial officer (CFO)*
Halden municipality skating hall	KPMG (2012) audit and law firm	*Fraud in construction project*
Halden municipality buildings	Hjort (2013) law firm	*Corruption in building permits*
Helse Nord hospital	PwC (2018b) audit and law firm	*Fraud at executive removal from position*
Hugaas entrepreneur firm	Arntzen de Besche (2022) law firm	*Bankruptcy fraud by board and management*
Hurtigruten cruises	Wiersholm (2020) law firm	*Lack of disclosure of* COVID-*19 outbreak onboard*
Jondal municipality	SBDL (2018) law firm	*Corruption and private enterprise praxis*
Kragerø shipping	Deloitte (2011a) audit and law firm	*Compensation for leader without contract*
Kristiansand municipality	Kommunerevisjon (2016a) public audit	*Private property developer abused political position*
Kvam Auto car dealer	Wikborg Rein (2015) law firm	*Majority shareholder fraudulent behavior*
Kvinnherad municipality	Deloitte (2019a) audit and law firm	*Fraud in chief executive retirement compensation*
Langemyhr building company	PwC (2008a) audit and law firm	*Fraudulent working hours invoicing*
Leksvik municipality	Kommunerevisjon (2017) public audit	*Illegal benefits to chief executive*
Lunde transportation company	Vierdal (2012) law firm	*Bankruptcy fraud*
Moscow school by Norway	Ernst & Young (2013a) audit and law firm	*Paid teachers without teaching*
NAV public welfare administration	NOU (2020)	*Fraudulent attacks on legitimate social security recipients*

(*Continued*)

(Continued)

Investigated client organization	*Investigating examination firm*	*Suspicion of white-collar crime investigated*
NDLA public learning software	Deloitte (2015a) audit and law firm	*Private abuse of public funds*
NFF football players association	Lynx (2012) law firm	*Fraud in player transfers*
Nittedal municipality	Grimstad (2020) law firm	*Abuse of position by mayor in property development*
Nittedal municipality	PwC (2022) audit and law firm	*Reluctance to report notification to politicians*
Norfund foreign aid	PwC (2020b)	*Threat actor applied business email compromise method*
Norsk Tipping public betting company	Deloitte (2010) audit and law firm	*CEO private property served by company facilities*
Næringsdepartement department of industry	PwC (2016) audit and law firm	*Corruption in state-owned enterprises*
Næringsdepartement department of industry	Ernst & Young (2018) audit and law firm	*Embezzlement by executive in aid program*
Obos housing construction	KPMG (2021a)	*Sold housing blocks to friend without involvement of members*
Obos housing construction	Committee (2022)	*Development of member democracy to prevent fraud*
Orange health services provider	Bergen kommune (2016) municipal audit function	*Fraud by executive compensation*
Oslo Boligbygg municipal housing	BDO (2017b) accounting and audit firm	*Corruption in public procurement*
Oslo Boligbygg municipal housing	Deloitte (2018) audit and law firm	*Corruption in public procurement*
Oslo Boligbygg municipal housing	Kommunerevisjon (2018a) public audit	*Corruption at procurement of facilities*
Oslo Boligbygg municipal housing	Deloitte (2019b) audit and law firm	*Fraud at over-priced procurement*
Oslo Bymiljø municipal parks	Ernst & Young (2019b) audit and law firm	*Fraud by fake invoicing of park works*
Oslo Energigjenvinning public recycling	PwC (2019a) audit and law firm	*Fraud by abuse of working hours*
Oslo Omsorgsbygg *housing administration*	PwC (2009) audit and law firm	*Abuse of Norwegian public funds in Spain*
Oslo Omsorgsbygg housing administration	Kommunerevisjon (2018b) public audit	*Chief executive employed family members*
Oslo Omsorgsbygg housing administration	PwC (2019b) audit and law firm	*Chief executive employed family members*
Oslo Renovasjon public garbage collection	Deloitte (2017d) audit and law firm	*Fraud in employment contracts*
Oslo Undervisning educational buildings	Kommunerevisjon (2006a) public audit	*Project manager bribed in corruption*
Oslo Undervisning educational buildings	Kommunerevisjon (2006b) public audit	*Property manager bribed in corruption*
Oslo Unibuss public transportation	Wiersholm (2012) law firm	*Corruption in public procurement*

Investigated client organization	*Investigating examination firm*	*Suspicion of white-collar crime investigated*
Oslo Vei public road construction	Kvale (2013) law firm	*Bankruptcy fraud*
Oslopolitiet Oslo police district	Committee (2021) appointed by the police	*Ignorance toward corrupt police officers*
Politiets Utlending police department	KPMG (2016) audit and law firm	*Executive abuse of overtime compensation*
Rana municipality	PwC (2008a) audit and law firm	*Corruption in public investment fund*
Revac garbage recycling	Kommunerevisjon (2015a) public audit	*Insurance fraud by putting a building on fire*
Rogaland road projects by municipality	PwC (2020c)	*Abuse of government funding of roads in the municipality*
Rogstad law firm	VG Skup (2020) investigative journalists	*Managed law firm from his prison cell*
Romanifolk minority foundation	Stiftelsestilsyn (2017) public authority	*Fraud in abuse of public subsidies*
Romerike Vannverk public waterworks	Distriktsrevisjon 2007 public audit	*Fraud in privatization of public property*
Siva state funding of industries	Wikborg Rein (2018) law firm	*Chief executive funded his own company*
Skjervøy municipality	Kommunerevisjon (2015b) public audit	*Public funds allocated to personal property*
Stangeskovene forest company	Ernst & Young (2013b) audit and law firm	*Private stock exchange excluding bidders*
Stavanger municipality	PwC (2013) audit and law firm	*Kidnapping fraud in public childcare*
Tana municipality	Kommunerevisjon (2021) municipal audit	*Embezzlement by trusted municipal manager*
Telenor VimpelCom mobile phone company	Deloitte (2016a) audit and law firm	*Corruption to obtain licenses in Uzbekistan*
Tidal music streaming service	NTNU (2018) research group	*Fraudulent manipulation of streaming accounting*
Tjøme municipality	BDO (2017a) accounting and audit firm	*Corruption in building permits at the seaside*
TrendTech investment securities	Finanstilsyn (2016) public authority	*Misrepresentation of investor figures*
Troms Kraft energy company	Nergaard (2013) at Norscan consulting firm	*Fraudulent abuse of company funds*
Universitetet i Bergen state university	PwC (2021) audit and law firm	*Rector helped friend finance a project with university funding*
Utenriksdepartement foreign ministry	Kontrollenhet (2016) internal audit	*Fraud in financing of development project*
Utenriksdepartement foreign ministry	Kontrollenhet (2017) internal audit	*Fraud in financing of development project*
Utlendingsdirektoratet foreign affairs	Deloitte (2016b) audit and law firm	*Subsidy fraud at return of refugees*
Vestfold and Telemark county municipality	Wiersholm (2022) law firm	*Reluctance to handle notification regarding misconduct*

(*Continued*)

(Continued)

Investigated client organization	*Investigating examination firm*	*Suspicion of white-collar crime investigated*
Vestre Toten municipality	Ernst & Young (2022) audit and law firm	*Reluctance to handle notification regarding wrongdoing*
Vestre Viken hospital	PwC (2018c) audit and law firm	*Fraudulent diagnoses to obtain more state funding*
Videoforhandlere series production	BDO (2013b) accounting and audit firm	*Abuse of state subsidies*
Vistamar rehabilitation center	Kommunerevisjon (2018c) public audit	*Embezzlement by chief executive*
Vitalegruppen private nursing	BDO (2017c) accounting and audit firm	*Fraud in municipal subsidies*
XXL sports store chain	DLA Piper (2019) law firm	*Price fixing for market manipulation*
Zachariasbryggen property development	Selmer (2014) law firm	*Fraud in transfer of property rights*
Ørland municipality	Simonsen (2020) law firm	*Abuse of position as mayor to influence resource allocation*
Østre Toten municipality	KPMG (2021b)	*Data virus attack to gain financially from reopening systems*
RUSSIA		
Moscow anti-doping laboratory	McLaren (2016) independent investigator	*Manipulation of doping test results in the laboratory*
SUDAN		
South Sudan human rights in republic	Council (2021) conference room paper	*Human rights violations and related economic crime*
SWEDEN		
Kraft & Kultur energy enterprise	Ernst & Young (2012) audit and law firm	*Accounting fraud by misrepresentation*
Kraft & Kultur energy enterprise	Deloitte (2013) audit and law firm	*Accounting fraud by misrepresentation*
Nasdaq Clearing securities market	Finansinspektion (2021) public inspection	*Declaration of default by clearing member*
Nordea banking	Mannheimer Swartling (2016) law firm	*Tax evasion in wealth management*
Swedbank banking	Clifford Chance (2020) law firm	*Money laundering in Baltic states*
SWITZERLAND		
FIFA football association	Garcia (2014) special committee	*Corruption at allocation of world cup*
THE UNITED STATES		
Apollo Global Management finance	Dechert (2021) law firm	*Financial misconduct between Leon Black and Jeffrey Epstein*
British Petroleum offshore oil	Freeh (2013) special committee	*Fraud in settlement program after deepwater accident*

Investigated client organization	*Investigating examination firm*	*Suspicion of white-collar crime investigated*
Coatesville school district	BDO (2015) accounting and audit firm	*Embezzlement of income from athletic activities*
CTO Washington technology office	Sidley Austin (2010) law firm	*Corruption in software procurement*
Enron energy company	Wilmer Cutler Pickering (2002) law firm	*Accounting fraud*
Equinor onshore oil exploration	PwC (2020a) audit and law firm	*Personal luxury expenses charged to the company*
General Motors car manufacturer	Jenner Block (2014) law firm	*Ignition switch failure fraud*
Lehman Brothers bankruptcy	Jenner Block (2010) law firm	*Executive deviance in securities*
Tax Administration Washington, D.C.	Wilmer Cutler Pickering (2008) law firm	*Embezzlement of property tax refunds*
Trump Organization	Brookings (2021) governance studies	*Falsifying business records and tax fraud*
Trump Organization	Supreme Court (2022) attorney general petition	*Fraudulent conduct by misleading financial statements*
University of California at several campuses	State Auditor (2020) in California	*Corruption in university admission process by sport coaches*
University of Texas Medical Center	Hastings (2012) law firm	*Abuse of university funds for private travels*
Wells Fargo's Community bank	Shearman Sterling (2017) law firm	*Deviant sales practices at the bank defrauding customers*
Wells Fargo's Community bank	Waters (2020) House representative	*Deviant sales practices at the bank defrauding customers*
WorldCom communications	Wilmer Cutler Pickering (2003) law firm	*Fraudulent accounting influencing share prices*
VIETNAM		
Utenriksdepartement foreign ministry	Duane Morris (2016) law firm	*Fraud in housing rental for diplomats*

Appendix B

Characteristics of Suspects in Norway

Organization	*Examiner*	*Pages*	*Suspect*	*Outcome*
Adecco private nursing home	Wiersholm (2011)	23	Kristiansen	Unknown
Agder fengsel prison	BDO (2021)	40	Klemmetsen	Nothing
Ahus public hospital	PwC (2013a)	15	Mjeldheim	Unknown
Alver municipality	Nordhordland (2019)	32	Dale	Unknown
Andebu municipality	BDO (2014a)	23	Sommerstad	Unknown
Arendal public traffic station	Traffic (2017)	20	Olsen	Prison
Askøy island municipality	BDO (2018)	39	Ådlandsvik	Unknown
Bergensklinikkene health clinic	Ernst & Young (2019a)	59	Lossius	Dismissal
Betanien foundation	BDO (2014)	10	Blomhoff	Prison
Bodø municipality services	Salten (2020)	80	Øksenvåg	Nothing
Breili local architects	BDO (2017a)	39	Breili	Prosecution
Briskeby athletic stadium	Lynx (2011)	267	Stensrud	Unknown
BTS property development	Schjødt (2021)	25	Thomassen	Resignation
Bærum municipality	G-partner (2007)	43	Ramstad	Prison
City taxi operating	PwC (2007)	88	Clausen	Prison
DNB bank offshore	Hjort (2016)	18	Bjerke	Resignation
DNB bank client account	Finanstilsyn (2020)	36	Bjerke	Resignation
DNB bank client accounts	Finanstilsyn (2021)	40	Bjerke	Resignation
Drammen municipality	Deloitte (2017a)	53	Cranner	Prison
DSS ministry security service	Arntzen de Besche (2021)	116	Hope	Nothing
Eckbo foundation	Thommessen (2009)	119	Eckbo	Nothing
Ferde toll collection	Deloitte (2020)	88	Juvik	Nothing

Organization	*Examiner*	*Pages*	*Suspect*	*Outcome*
Ferde toll collection	Kluge (2019)	40	Juvik	(Nothing)
Fjell Bergen municipality	Deloitte (2017b)	33	Bjørndal	Unknown
Forsvaret military logistics	PwC (2014a)	35	Stavrum	Prison
Forsvaret military routines	PwC (2015a)	50	Stavrum	(Prison)
Fredrikstad municipality	PwC (2018a)	78	Finess	Dismissal
Fredrikstad municipality	Simonsen (2018)	100	Finess	(Dismissal)
Fretex salvation army	Grette (2017)	132	Vestre	Nothing
Furuheim foundation	Hald (2006)	164	Walle	Prison
Fyrlykta foundation	Deloitte (2017c)	70	Sahlström-Leyh	Unknown
Fyrlykta foundation	Stiftelsestilsyn (2018)	28	Sahlström-Leyh	(Unknown)
Født Fri foundation	Ernst & Young (2020)	36	Rehman	Dismissal
Gartnerhallen fruits	Wiersholm (2018)	32	Hansen	Prison
Grimstad municipality	BDO (2016)	64	Lyngstad	Resignation
Grimstad municipality	Hjort (2018)	8	Lyngstad	(Resignation)
Hadeland broadband	PwC (2014b)	32	Brorson	Prison
Hadeland energy supplier	PwC (2014c)	25	Brorson	(Prison)
Halden skating ice hall	KPMG (2012)	121	Montelius	Unknown
Halden municipality	Hjort (2013)	46	Montelius	(Unknown)
Helse Nord hospital	PwC (2018b)	40	Ingebrigtsen	Nothing
Hugaas entrepreneur	Arntzen de Besche (2021)	66	Aarhaug	Dismissal
Hurtigruten cruises	Wiersholm (2020)	51	Skjeldam	Nothing
Jondal municipality	SBDL (2018)	71	Isdal	Unknown
Kragerø fjord boats	Deloitte (2011a)	109	Rognli	Resignation
Kristiansand municipality	Kommunerevisjon (2016a)	25	Ugland	Nothing
Kvam Auto cars	Wikborg Rein (2015)	93	Vikør	Unknown
Kvinnherad municipality	Deloitte (2019a)	86	Øvregård	Unknown
Langemyhr construction	PwC (2008a)	27	Langemyhr	Dismissal
Leksvik municipality	Kommunerevisjon (2017)	36	Dretvik	Unknown
Lunde Group transport	Vierdal (2012)	86	Lunde	Prison

(*Continued*)

(Continued)

Organization	*Examiner*	*Pages*	*Suspect*	*Outcome*
Moscow school	Ernst & Young (2013a)	52	Grahn	Dismissal
NAV public welfare	NOU (2020)	328	Monland	Resignation
NDLA learning arena	Deloitte (2015a)	57	Høines	Dismissal
NFF player transfers	Lynx (2012)	50	Haakonsen	Unknown
Nittedal municipality	Grimstad (2020)	29	Thorkildsen	Prosecution
Nittedal municipality	PwC (2022)	92	Solli	Nothing
Norfund foreign aid	PwC (2020b)	34	Threat Actor	Nothing
Norsk Tipping betting	Deloitte (2010)	61	Nordby	Dismissal
Nærings ministry	Ernst & Young (2018)	49	Williams	Unknown
Obos housing construction	KPMG (2021a)	42	Siraj	Nothing
Orange health	Bergen kommune (2016)	60	Paulsen	Unknown
Oslo Boligbygg social housing	BDO (2017b)	79	Fredriksen	Prison
Oslo Boligbygg social housing	Deloitte (2018)	593	Fredriksen	(Prison)
Oslo Boligbygg social housing	Kommunerevisjon (2018a)	88	Fredriksen	(Prison)
Oslo Boligbygg social housing	Deloitte (2019b)	82	Fredriksen	(Prison)
Oslo Bymiljø environment	Ernst & Young (2019b)	28	Skjaker	Prison
Oslo Energigjenvinning	PwC (2019a)	154	Kristiansen	Dismissal
Oslo Omsorgsbygg	PwC (2009)	92	Clausen	Unknown
Oslo Omsorgsbygg	PwC (2019b)	21	Johansen	Resignation
Oslo Omsorgsbygg	Kommunerevisjon (2018b)	76	(Johansen)	(Resignation)
Oslo Renovasjon garbage collection	Deloitte (2017d)	93	Enger	Prison
Oslo Undervisning	Kommunerevisjon (2006a)	44	Murud	Prison
Oslo Undervisning	Kommunerevisjon (2006b)	30	Nettli	Prison
Oslo Unibuss transportation	Wiersholm (2012)	23	Leite	Prison
Oslo Vei road construction	Kvale (2013)	53	Staff	Unknown
Politiets Utlending police unit	KPMG (2016)	74	Kvigne	Nothing
Rana north municipality	PwC (2008b)	52	Reithaug	Unknown

Organization	*Examiner*	*Pages*	*Suspect*	*Outcome*
Revac garbage recycling	Kommunerevisjon (2015a)	81	Aas	Prison
Rogaland road projects	PwC (2020c)	50	Heinzerling	Unknown
Rogstad law firm of inmates	VG Skup (2020)	180	Ghauri	Nothing
Romanifolk foundation	Stiftelsestilsyn (2017)	36	Gustavsen	Unknown
Romerike water works	Distriktsrevisjon (2007)	555	Henriksen	Prison
Siemens technology	Dalseide (2006)	184	Moestue	(Fine)
Siva industrial growth	Wikborg Rein (2018)	74	Susegg	Unknown
Skjervøy fisheries	Kommunerevisjon (2015b)	138	Waage	Nothing
Stangeskovene forests	Ernst & Young (2013b)	103	Schweigaard	Nothing
Stavanger municipality	PwC (2013)	14	Thune	Nothing
Tana municipality	Kommunerevisjon (2021)	48	Unknown	Prosecution
Telenor VimpelCom	Deloitte (2016a)	54	Espen	Dismissal
Tidal music streaming	NTNU (2018)	78	Sanders	Unknown
TrendTech brokerage	Finanstilsyn (2016)	29	Jensen	Unknown
Troms Kraft energy	Nergaard (2013)	38	Schei	Unknown
Tromsø municipality	Kommunerevisjon (2015c)	30	Engdahl	Prison
Universitetet i Bergen	PwC (2021)	68	Olsen	Resignation
Utenriksdep. foreign ministry	Kontrollenhet (2016)	48	Nystuen	Unknown
Utenriksdep. foreign ministry	Kontrollenhet (2017)	48	Nystuen	(Unknown)
Vestre Viken hospital	PwC (2018c)	30	Jacobsen	Unknown
Vistamar rehabilitation	Kommunerevisjon (2018c)	92	Ruiz	Unknown
XXL sports store chain	DLA Piper (2019)	41	Grøterud	Resignation
Vitalegruppen private nursing	BDO (2017c)	50	Andersson	Unknown
Zachariasbryggen property	Selmer (2014)	52	Hauge	Resignation
Ørland municipality	Simonsen (2020)	36	Myrvold	Resignation

Appendix C

Characteristics of Other Suspects

Organization	*Country*	*Examiner*	*Pages*	*Suspect*	*Outcome*
Apollo Global Management	USA	Dechert (2021)	12	Black	Unknown
Bestseller clothing	Denmark	Offersen Christoff. (2021)	122	Povlsen	Nothing
British Petroleum	USA	Freeh (2013)	93	Sutton	Unknown
Coatesville school district	USA	BDO (2015)	54	Como	Unknown
CTO Washington	USA	Sidley Austin (2010)	60	Acar	Prison
Danske Bank	Denmark	Bruun Hjejle (2018)	87	Borgen	Dismissal
Enron energy	USA	Wilmer Cutler Pickering (2002)	218	Lay	Prison
Equinor energy	USA	PwC (2020a)	53	Maloney	Resignation
FIFA World Cup 2018/2022	Switzerland	Garcia (2014)	359	Blatter	Resignation
Fujifilm technology	New Zealand	Deloitte (2017e)	89	Whittaker	Prison
General Motors	USA	Jenner Block (2014)	325	Barra	Nothing
International Biathlon	Austria	Commission (2021)	220	Besseberg	Dismissal
Kraft & Kultur	Sweden	Ernst & Young (2012)	31	Benulic	Prison
Kraft & Kultur	Sweden	Deloitte (2013)	136	Benulic	(Prison)
Lehman Brothers bank	USA	Jenner Block (2010)	239	Fuld	Resignation
Moldova banking sector	Moldova	Kroll (2017)	58	Shor	Resignation

Organization	*Country*	*Examiner*	*Pages*	*Suspect*	*Outcome*
Nasdaq Clearing	Sweden	Finansinspektion (2021)	46	Aas	Resignation
NNPC petroleum	Nigeria	PwC (2015b)	199	Kachikwu	Nothing
Nordea bank	Sweden	Mannheimer Swartling (2016)	42	Wærsted	Resignation
Oceanteam offshore	The Netherlands	Sands (2019)	256	Halbesma	Nothing
Olympus technology	Japan	Deloitte (2011b)	243	Kikukawa	Prison
Pelham public project	Canada	KPMG (2017)	100	Pupo	Unknown
Samherji fishing	Iceland	Kleinfeld (2019)	10	Stefansson	Resignation
Social security	Denmark	Kammeradvokaten (2019)	163	Nielsen	Prison
Social security Socialstyrelsen	Denmark	PwC (2019c)	80	Nielsen	(Prison)
Swedbank banking	Sweden	Clifford Chance (2020)	218	Bonnesen	Dismissal
Syddanmark region	Denmark	Kromann Reumert (2015)	27+media	Holst	Resignation
Tax Washington	USA	Wilmer Cutler Pickering (2008)	126	Walters	Prison
Toshiba technology	Japan	Deloitte (2015b)	90	Tanaka	Prison
Trump Organization	USA	Brookings (2021)	60	Trump	Prosecution
Trump Organization	USA	Supreme Court (2022)	115	Trump	Prosecution
University of California	USA	State Auditor (2020)	82	Salcedo	Prison
University of Texas	USA	Hastings (2012)	365	Wildenthal	Nothing
Utenriksdep. Ministry	Vietnam	Duane Morris (2016)	172	Trang	Dismissal
Wells Fargo bank	USA	Shearman Sterling (2017)	113	Tolstedt	Resignation
Wells Fargo bank	USA	Waters (2020)	74	Tolstedt	(Resignation)
Wirecard financial	Germany	KPMG (2020)	74	Braun	Prison
WorldCom technology	USA	Wilmer Cutler Pickering (2003)	345	Ebbers	Prison

Appendix D

Comparison of Outcomes for Suspects

Outcome	*Norway*	*Others*
Unknown	32%	11%
Nothing	19%	14%
Resignation	14%	26%
Dismissal	11%	11%
Prosecution	3%	6%
Prison	21%	32%
TOTAL	100%	100%

12 Characteristics of Corporate Investigators

Rather than the traditional view of corporate investigations as a form of privatization of public policing, this chapter applies the perspective of alternative policing where there is a shift from the public sphere toward the private sphere across the policing landscape. The chapter addresses the following research question: What characteristics can be identified among corporate investigators who conduct alternative policing of financial crime? This research attempts to answer the research question by review of research on corporate investigators in Australia, Canada, the Netherlands, Norway, and the United Kingdom. The typical corporate investigator has policing or security background and is in his second or third career. In most countries, the corporate investigator is employed in a firm that conducts accounting, auditing, legal, or security services. The typical outcome of a corporate investigation is a report to the client organization that paid for the work.

The corporate investigator is a detective in the private policing business undertaking internal examinations in client organizations. The corporate investigator conducts commercial inquiries by undertaking factual reviews of documents, interviews with suspects, and other investigative steps. The client expectation is that corporate investigators will uncover and verify the facts of the case, reconstruct past events and sequences of events, allowing the client to make informed decisions to either litigate or resolve matters on a commercial basis. The corporate investigator is hired by both private and public corporations to find answers to questions (What happened? When did it happen? How did it happen? Who did what to make it happen or not happen? Why did it happen?), when there is suspicion of misconduct and potential financial crime by white-collar offenders (Button et al., 2022; Gottschalk, 2020; King, 2020d; Meerts, 2020).

The lack of disclosure of reports (Gottschalk and Tcherni-Buzzeo, 2017) and the anonymity of corporate investigators (King, 2020a) is a problematic matter in democratic societies where transparency is a requirement for democratic control. For example, criminal courts are open to visit to attend court proceedings. In contrast, corporate internal investigations are typically closed, even when the corporate investigator takes on all three roles of detective, prosecutor, and judge (Gottschalk, 2019). While these three roles are separated in

DOI: 10.4324/9781003379249-15

the criminal justice system in democratic societies, some corporate investigators first examine the matter, then prosecute the suspect, and then convict the suspect. For example, the suspect can be fired from the job in the client organization, where the conclusion from the corporate investigator is the foundation for the dismissal of the person. As emphasized by Button et al. (2022: 1), corporate investigators "have escaped extensive academic scrutiny".

Therefore, this chapter addresses the following research question: *What characteristics can be identified among corporate investigators who conduct alternative policing of financial crime?* The chapter attempts to answer this question by review of research from Australia, Canada, the Netherlands, Norway, and the United Kingdom.

Alternative Policing of Economic Crime

Corporate investigators perform alternative policing of financial crime when they are hired by private and public organizations to conduct internal examinations. Research on corporate investigator performance has been conducted in Australia, Canada, the Netherlands, Norway, and the United Kingdom. In Australia, King (2012, 2020a, 2020b, 2020c, 2020d, 2021a, 2021b) has done extensive research on corporate investigators regarding their own professional image. In Canada, Schneider (2006) explored the role of private sector investigative agencies in combating money laundering. Meerts (2014, 2018, 2019, 2020, 2021) has done extensive research on corporate investigators in the Netherlands regarding their roles. In Norway, Gottschalk (2016, 2020, 2021) has done extensive studies of the outcome of corporate investigations in the form of investigation reports. In the United Kingdom, Brooks et al. (2009), Button (2020), Button and Gee (2013), Button and Stiernstedt (2017, 2018), Button et al. (2007a, 2007b, 2015, 2022), Johnston et al. (2008), Williams (2005a, 2005b), and Wood (2020) have examined private policing of fraud by the security industry and found, among other things, older men in their second careers.

The traditional perspective of privatization was applied by Schneider (2006) regarding privatizing economic crime enforcement in Canada, while this chapter applies the perspective of alternative policing that is a parallel activity to the criminal justice system. Privatization would imply that the state has left certain tasks to business enterprises, which law enforcement agencies have not done. Privatization could also imply that the business sector has taken over tasks from public agencies with or without state consent, which the corporate investigation industry has certainly not done. Therefore, a more relevant and fruitful research perspective is to study corporate investigators as operating in parallel and as an alternative to the criminal justice system. The perspective of parallel and alternative investigations is thus dominating this chapter, which Johnston et al. (2008) labeled corporate-anchored policing in contrast to state-anchored policing.

Australia: Professional Image

Corporate investigators in Australia provide a wide specter of services such as corporate and financial investigations, risk advisory, and cyber and misconduct investigations. According to King (2020b), most corporate investigators in Australia work for lawyers, accountants, and government agencies. Law firms were the most likely to use the services according to his interviews of 33 investigators. King (2021a: 11) asked questions about corporate investigators' views regarding the professional image of their work:

> The private investigators who participated in this study took pride in the services they provided to clients and noted the challenges involved in undertaking private investigation without recourse to a police badge or coercive authority. Rather, they found that the meticulous application of their technical and professional skills allowed them to resolve complex and diverse issues, including employment law disputes and insurance and corporate fraud. Interviewees refuted that their occupation used deception, stating that much of their cases involved potential litigation and the use of deception could compromise the case. The occupation involves briefing clients, managing client investigations and liaising with claims managers, lawyers, accountants, police and the public. For all the interviewees, private investigation was a second or third career choice, with many being former police officers. Others had deliberately chosen the career after successfully working in finance or law.

In Australia, there is a requirement of a certificate for the licensing of private investigators. Thirty-two out of 33 corporate investigators in Australia held this certificate.

Canada: Role of Private Sector

While the study by Schneider (2006: 285) dates a while back, it is nevertheless interesting briefly to review the research that explored the role played by private sector financial investigative agencies (FIA) in combating money laundering in Canada and abroad:

> This emergent "anti-money laundering industry" is unique in that it is ultimately concerned with economic, organized, and terrorist crimes. These crimes are much more complex, multi-jurisdictional and threatening to mass society than the "street-level" property crime that is the overwhelming focus of the private policing sector. With the advent and growth of this cottage industry, the focus of the private policing sector now stretches from the most rudimentary disorder and property crime problems all the way to complex, highly-organized and multi-jurisdictional criminal and national security issues. What's more, this anti-money laundering industry

> has contributed to not only the ongoing fragmentation of policing in society, but with increased attention being paid to detecting terrorist financing, it has perhaps initiated a similar fragmentation of national security enforcement. This study recommends that public policies and programs be developed that nurture an increased and more formal role for FIAs within the context of a partnership with government agencies.

Schneider (2006) expressed skepticism toward the growing industry of corporate investigators. He was at that time in line with others such as Williams (2005a, 2005b) in the United Kingdom who questioned the legitimacy of private policing of financial crime.

The Netherlands: Professional Roles

Similar to King (2012, 2020a, 2020b, 2020c, 2020d, 2021a, 2021b) in Australia, Meerts (2014, 2018, 2019, 2020, 2021) has done extensive research on corporate investigators in the Netherlands. She interviewed 59 corporate investigators to answer her research question: What is the role of corporate investigators in the investigation and settlement of norm violations within organizations? To answer this question, she examined (1) the legal frameworks within which corporate investigators operate, (2) the investigative methods corporate investigators may use, and (3) the settlements that are possible as a response to the corporate investigations.

Meerts (2018: 6) found that the legal framework is almost non-existent or non-functioning for corporate investigators in the Netherlands:

> Respondents indicate that the state has very little insight into what happens in the corporate security sector. . . . The legal framework that applies is dependent on the label an investigator wears. . . . Although forensic accountants and legal investigators are regulated by a general legal framework, these laws are not constructed to deal with investigative activities – rather, they are focused on traditional accounting activities and the traditional role of the lawyer. . . . The diversification in the corporate investigations arena and in legal frameworks and control create a fragmented field in which the state has very little knowledge about actual activities. Democratic control over the corporate security sector is very limited. Control over corporate investigations is, for an important part, reliant on the ethics of individual investigators and on the client. This places much responsibility on organizations using the services of corporate investigators.

Meerts (2018: 9) found that the investigative methods corporate investigators may use derive from a large arsenal of possibilities:

> Apart from (financial) documentation, much information may be derived from the internal systems at place in an organization. . . . Much additional

> information is, furthermore, provided by desk research into open sources. . . . Interviews with the 'subject' or 'involved person' are usually done only at the end of investigations. . . . Following the widely-used adversarial principle, interviewees are given the opportunity to read their statement and to correct factual errors. . . . Many corporate investigations remain entirely in the private realm, as the investigative possibilities are often enough to provide the necessary information without having to resort to the formal powers of investigation of law enforcement (which could be mobilized through a report to the authorities).

While judges pass verdicts on defendants in court, corporate investigators may arrange settlements in private investigations. Clients often want to settle a matter quietly, for example, by a contract in which parties agree on an amount payable by the involved person. It may also include conditions, such as the termination of the labor contract. Non-disclosure clauses are fairly standard to settlements agreement where parties commit themselves to the confidentiality of the agreement and the circumstances of termination (Meerts, 2018).

Norway: Outcome of Investigations

Gottschalk (2016, 2020, 2021) has done extensive studies on the outcome of corporate investigations that result in investigation reports. The list of private policing reports in Table 12.1 includes only reports where a white-collar suspect could be identified. The table lists a total of 80 reports from Norway. The first column tells the name of the organizations where suspected wrongdoing occurred. Some organizations are public organizations such as municipalities in Norway. Other organizations are banks and business enterprises. The second column shows fraud examiner firms such as global audit firms and local law firms.

The list in Table 12.1 does not include reports that are shorter than 30 pages, as less than 30 pages make it hard to identify convenience themes and maturity levels. However, for some investigations, it was possible to access additional information elsewhere, such as verdicts, media reports, and several examination reports about the same case. Those are included in the list by Gottschalk (2020).

The last names of the suspects are listed in the fourth column. The purpose of listing names is to enable readers easily to find case stories in the media. As listed in the fifth and final column, most suspects were innocent based on the presumptions of innocence in democratic nations. When brackets are applied in the final column, then it is repetition of the above. For example, PwC (2014b) and PwC (2014c) are concerned with Hadeland broadband and Hadeland energy, respectively, where both investigations focus on Brorson as the suspect.

In Norway, 18 out of 80 individuals were sentenced to prison and incarcerated, which represents a conviction rate of 23% among those investigated by private fraud examiners. The convictions were not necessarily a result of work by fraud examiners. Convictions occurred in some cases before fraud

Table 12.1 Characteristics of fraud examinations with white-collar suspects in Norway

Organization	*Examiner*	*Pages*	*Suspect*	*Verdict*
Askøy municipality	BDO (2018)	39	Ådlandsvik	None
Bergensklinikkene health	Ernst & Young (2019a)	59	Lossius	None
Betanien foundation	BDO (2014)	10+verdict	Blomhoff	Prison
Breili architects	BDO (2017a)	39	Breili	None
Briskeby sports stadium	Lynx (2011)	267	Stensrud	None
Bærum municipality	G-partner (2007)	43	Ramstad	Prison
City Taxi	PwC (2007)	88	Clausen	Prison
DNB bank	Hjort (2016)	18+media	Bjerke	None
Drammen municipality	Deloitte (2017a)	53	Cranner	Prison
Eckbo foundation	Thommessen (2009)	119	Eckbo	None
Ferde toll collection	Deloitte (2020)	88	Juvik	None
Ferde toll collection	Kluge (2019)	40	Juvik	None
Fjell municipality	Deloitte (2017b)	33	Bjørndal	None
Forsvaret military logistics	PwC (2014a)	35	Stavrum	Prison
Forsvaret military routines	PwC (2015a)	50	Stavrum	(Prison)
Fredrikstad municipality	PwC (2018a)	78	Finess	None
Fredrikstad municipality	Simonsen (2018)	100	Finess	(None)
Fretex salvation army	Grette (2017)	132	Vestre	None
Furuheim foundation	Hald (2006)	164	Walle	Prison
Fyrlykta foundation	Deloitte (2017c)	70	Sahlström	None
Gartnerhallen fruits	Wiersholm (2018)	32	Hansen	Prison
Grimstad municipality	BDO (2016)	64	Lyngstad	None
Hadeland broadband	PwC (2014b)	32	Brorson	Prison
Hadeland energy	PwC (2014c)	25+broad	Brorson	(Prison)
Halden ice hall	KPMG (2012)	121	Montelius	None
Halden municipality	Hjort (2013)	46	Montelius	(None)
Helse Nord hospital	PwC (2018b)	40	Ingebrigtsen	None
Jondal municipality	SBDL (2018)	71	Isdal	None
Kraft & Kultur energy	Deloitte (2013)	136	Benulic	Prison
Kraft & Kultur energy	Ernst & Young (2012)	31	Benulic	(Prison)
Kragerø fjord boats	Deloitte (2011a)	109	Rognli	None
Kristiansand municipality	Kommunerevisjon (2016)	25+media	Ugland	None

Organization	*Examiner*	*Pages*	*Suspect*	*Verdict*
Kvam Auto cars	Wikborg Rein (2015)	93	Vikør	None
Kvinnherad municipality	Deloitte (2019a)	86	Øvregård	None
Langemyhr construction	PwC (2008a)	27+dismissal	Langemyhr	None
Leksvik municipality	Kommunerevisjon (2017)	36	Dretvik	None
Lenvik municipality	Kommunerevisjon (2018a)	104	Hagerupsen	None
Lunde Group transport	Vierdal (2012)	86	Lunde	Prison
Moscow school	Ernst & Young (2013a)	52	Grahn	None
NDLA learning arena	Deloitte (2015a)	57	Høines	None
NFF player transfers	Lynx (2012)	50	Haakonsen	None
Norsk Tipping betting	Deloitte (2010)	61	Nordby	None
Nærings ministry	Ernst & Young (2018)	49	Williams	None
Oceanteam offshore	Sands (2019)	256	Halbesma	None
Orange health	Bergen kommune (2016)	60	Paulsen	None
Oslo housing	BDO (2017b)	79	Fredriksen	None
Oslo housing	Deloitte (2018)	593	Fredriksen	(None)
Oslo housing	Deloitte (2019b)	82	Fredriksen	(None)
Oslo urban environment	Ernst & Young (2019b)	28+verdict	Skjaker	Prison
Oslo energy recycling	PwC (2019a)	154	Kristiansen	None
Oslo care buildings	PwC (2009)	92	Clausen	None
Oslo care buildings	PwC (2019b)	21+media	Johansen	None
Oslo renovation	Deloitte (2017d)	93	Enger	Prison
Oslo educational buildings	Kommunerevisjon (2006a)	44	Murud	Prison
Oslo educational buildings	Kommunerevisjon (2006b)	30	Nettli	Prison
Oslo unibuss transportation	Wiersholm (2012)	23+verdicts	Leite	Prison
Oslo road construction	Kvale (2013)	53	Staff	None
Politiets police unit	KPMG (2016)	74	Kvigne	None
Rana municipality	PwC (2008b)	52	Reithaug	None
Revac garbage recycling	Kommunerevisjon (2015a)	81	Aas	Prison

(*Continued*)

Table 12.1 (Continued)

Organization	*Examiner*	*Pages*	*Suspect*	*Verdict*
Romerike water works	Distriktsrevisjon (2007)	555	Henriksen	Prison
Siemens technology	Dalseide (2006)	184	Moestue	Fine
Siva industrial growth	Wikborg Rein (2018)	74	Susegg	None
Skjervøy fisheries	Kommunerevisjon (2015b)	138	Waage	None
Stangeskovene forests	Ernst & Young (2013b)	103	Schweigaard	None
Stavanger municipality	PwC (2013)	14+media	Thune	None
Taters association	Stiftelsestilsyn (2017)	36	Gustavsen	None
Telenor VimpelCom	Deloitte (2016)	54	Espen	None
Tidal streaming	NTNU (2018)	78	Sanders	None
TrendTech brokerage	Finanstilsynet (2016)	29+media	Jensen	None
Troms Kraft energy	Nergaard (2013)	38	Schei	None
Tromsø municipality	Kommunerevisjon (2015c)	30	Engdahl	Prison
Utenriks ministry	Duane Morris (2016)	172	Trang	None
Utenriks ministry	Kontrollenhet (2016)	23 + 25	Nystuen	None
Utenriks ministry	Kontrollenhet (2017)	25 + 23	Nystuen	(None)
Vestre Viken hospital	PwC (2018c)	30	Jacobsen	None
Vistamar nursing home	Kommunerevisjon (2018b)	92	Ruiz	None
XXL sports stores	DLA Piper (2019)	41	Grøterud	None
Vitale Group health	BDO (2017c)	50	Andersson	None
Zachariasbryggen property	Selmer (2014)	52	Hauge	None

examinations, while other convictions occurred during or after fraud examinations were completed.

The United Kingdom: Second Careers

Button et al. (2022) studied the outcomes of investigative work. Among 78 in-house investigators in public and private organizations, 31% of cases they investigated led to criminal prosecution. For the 27 forensic investigators, 27% of cases they investigated led to criminal prosecution. The 75 private investigators had similar results with a mean of 24.5% criminal prosecutions.

Button et al. (2022) distinguished three main groups of investigators that are involved in private investigations: In-house investigators are doing reviews in private and public organizations where they are employed, forensic investigators are doing reviews in terms of professional services and are based in the accountancy and legal sectors, while private investigators do reviews and charge fees to clients for investigative services.

The research was based on a questionnaire that was distributed to investigators that could be found on various lists, including the Association of British Investigators, UK Professional Investigators Network, University of Portsmouth database of fraud contacts, and Midlands Fraud Forum. A total of 331 responses were received and applied in descriptive statics analysis.

The demographics of the investigators showed a male-dominated occupation with more than 70% male and less than 30% female. However, for in-house public investigators, the balance was closer to 60% male and 40% female. Male dominance was highest among private investigators who charge fees to clients for investigative services where the male fraction was almost 90%. The average age of the respondents was quite high (Button et al., 2022: 6):

> Those same male-dominated private investigators were also older too, with around 86.3%, 41 years or over, and almost three-quarters 51 and over. Also, 37% of private investigators were 61+, which was under 9% for the other three main categories. Across the whole sample of investigators, an older profile was the norm with just under 80% being 41 and over. The youngest profile was among forensic accountant-based investigators with almost 45% being 40 or under. In-house private investigators also had around a third in this age category. For the in-house public investigators, the age profile was dominated by the 41–60 with almost three quarters in this age group.

Button et al.'s (2022) exploratory study of investigative private policing beyond the police was yet another important research endeavor in the United Kingdom. Previous studies of private policing in the United Kingdom included work by Brooks et al. (2009), Button (2020), Button and Gee (2013), Button and Stiernstedt (2017, 2018), Button et al. (2007a, 2007b), Button et al. (2015), Johnston et al. 2008), Williams (2005a, 2005b), and Wood (2020) who have all examined private policing of fraud by the security industry.

Among the 331 respondents, there was a dominance of older men in their second careers. The respondents included a large number of former police officers as 73 had served as uniformed police officers and 80 as police detectives. Twenty-six respondents had military background. The sample also included 18 former security services (MI5, MI6, etc.) employees.

Evaluation of Investigation Reports

Similar to the study by Gottschalk (2020) in Norway, Button et al. (2022) studied the outcomes of investigative work in the United Kingdom. One finding in the United Kingdom was that 31% of cases led to criminal prosecution, while a similar finding in Norway was that 23% of the cases led to criminal conviction. Like in Norway, it might be that some of the criminal prosecutions and trials in the United Kingdom took place before or during the private policing, so the term "led to" might be a little misleading. However, it is interesting to note that three out of four suspects were found or considered innocent after the completion of internal examinations by fraud examiners.

This large fraction of innocence in the sample is important, as all countries studied here have a criminal justice system where the benefit of the doubt should always belong to the accused. A person should only be convicted when criminal wrongdoing by that person is evidenced beyond any reasonable doubt.

Apart from Australia, there is no requirement of any training, education, certificate, or degree for the licensing of corporate investigators. Anyone can take on the role of a corporate investigator in Canada, the Netherlands, Norway, and the United Kingdom. In the United States, there are voluntary organizations for corporate investigators such as the Association of Certified Fraud Examiners that offer simple exams to receive a certification. In Norway, one business school has offered a course on corporate investigations to both regular students and executive students.

The business school students in Norway evaluated a number of investigation reports by corporate investigators. Their evaluations are interesting in the perspective of assessing work by corporate investigators at firms such as BDO, EY, PwC, Deloitte, and KPMG. Students were asked to grade investigation reports on a scale from 1 (grade A) to 6 (grade Failure). In the sample from the last two years, there were 23 student grades for EY work, 41 for PwC work, 22 for Deloitte work, six for BDO work, and one for KPMG work.

The average score for Y was 2.8, for PwC 3.4, for Deloitte 2.5, for BDO 3.7, and for KPMG 4.0. Thus, business school students found the best work among Deloitte reports, followed by reports from EY and PwC, ending with KPMG at the bottom. Of course, this is by no means sufficient material to judge the various auditing firms when they conduct fraud examinations for their clients. Nevertheless, it is an interesting avenue for future research.

Two decades have soon passed since Schneider (2006) and Williams (2005b) emphasized the problematic role of fraud examiners in internal investigations, as examiners conduct private policing of economic crime. In the meantime, the business of fraud examinations has grown substantially in forensic departments in auditing firms and in consulting departments in law firms.

The large fraction of confirmed innocents requires corporate investigators to practice professionalism similar to the criminal justice system. Suspects need defense that is paid for by their employers. Gottschalk (2019) made several recommendations to individuals who become subject to fact-finding examinations by fraud examiners, where these statements are a few examples of recommendations:

- Find yourself a lawyer and require that your employer pays for the lawyer, who will assist you before, during and after the fact-finding.
- Require that the client for the fact-finding is included as a topic in the mandate.

- Require access to documentation of the investigator's competence within organizational behavior and management.
- Reject an accusation or conclusion that is based on the preponderance of probability, because it must be documented that allegations are valid beyond any reasonable doubt.

Ideally, corporate investigators should conduct value-oriented examinations where the benefits of their work exceed the costs of their work. Each investigation should focus on the value created by the examination, where the investigation is an investment by the client with an expectation of benefits exceeding costs.

In conclusion, corporate investigators operate on a market where there is demand for and supply of fraud examination services. The demand comes from public and private organizations where there is suspicion of white-collar crime. Corporate investigators from different firms are competitors when offering their services to client organizations. The market for corporate investigations seems to grow globally without any serious attempts to regulate such markets by governments.

This chapter has taken a step back from the general debate regarding alternative policing of financial crime by addressing the research question of what characteristics can be identified among corporate investigators who conduct alternative policing of financial crime. With this background information regarding the current situation, future researchers can extend the study of potential roles and regulations of corporate investigators.

References

Brooks, G., Button, M. and Frimpong, K. (2009). Policing fraud in the private sector: A survey of the FTSE 100 companies in the UK, *International Journal of Police Science & Management*, 11 (4), 493–504.

Button, M. (2020). The "new" private security industry, the private policing of cyberspace and the regulatory questions, *Journal of Contemporary Criminal Justice*, 36 (1), 39–55.

Button, M., Frimpong, K., Smith, G. and Johnston, L. (2007a). Professionalizing counter fraud specialists in the UK: Assessing progress and recommendations for reform, *Crime Prevention and Community Safety*, 9, 92–101.

Button, M. and Gee, J. (2013). *Countering Fraud for Competitive Advantage – The Professional Approach to Reducing the Last Great Hidden Cost*, John Wiley & Sons, Chichester, UK.

Button, M., Johnston, L., Frimpong, K. and Smith, G. (2007b). New directions in policing fraud: The emergence of the counter fraud specialists in the United Kingdom, *International Journal of the Sociology of Law*, 35, 192–208.

Button, M., Kapend, R. and Stiernstedt, P. (2022). Investigative private policing beyond the police: An exploratory study, *Policing and Society*, published online doi: 10.1080/10439463.2022.2071894.

Button, M., Nicholls, C.M., Kerr, J. and Owen, R. (2015). Online fraud victims in England and Wales: Victims' views on sentencing and the opportunity for restorative justice, *The Howard Journal of Criminal Justice*, 54 (2), 193–211.

Button, M. and Stiernstedt, P. (2017). The evolution of security industry regulation in the European Union, *International Journal of Comparative and Applied Criminal Justice*, 41 (4), 245–257.

Button, M. and Stiernstedt, P. (2018). Comparing private security regulation in the European Union, *Policing and Society*, 28 (4), 398–414.

Gottschalk, P. (2016). Private policing of financial crime: Key issues in the investigation business in Norway, *European Journal of Policing Studies*, 3 (3), 292–314.

Gottschalk, P. (2019). Dersom du blir utsatt for faktaundersøkelse: 17 råd om faktaundersøkelse (If you are subjected to fact-finding: 17 advices on fact-finding), web-based university journal *Khrono*, www.khrono.no, retrieved July 13.

Gottschalk, P. (2020). Private policing of white-collar crime: Case studies of internal investigations by fraud examiners, *Police Practice and Research*, 21 (6), 717–738.

Gottschalk, P. (2021). *Private Policing of Economic Crime – Case Studies of Internal Investigations by Fraud Examiners*, Routledge, London, UK.

Gottschalk, P. and Tcherni-Buzzeo, M. (2017). Reasons for gaps in crime reporting: The case of white-collar criminals investigated by private fraud examiners in Norway, *Deviant Behavior*, 38 (3), 267–281.

Johnston, L., Button, M. and Williamson, T. (2008). Police, governance and the private finance initiative, *Policing & Society*, 18 (3), 225–244.

King, M. (2012). The contemporary role of private investigators in Australia, *Criminal Justice Matters*, 89 (1), 12–14.

King, M. (2020a). What makes a successful corporate investigator: An exploration of private investigators attributes, *Journal of Financial Crime*, 27 (3), 701–714.

King, M. (2020b). Out of obscurity: The contemporary private investigator in Australia, *International Journal of Police Science & Management*, 22 (3), 285–296.

King, M. (2020c). Private investigation into economic crime: Regulation of a multidisciplinary field, *Journal of Applied Security Research*, published online doi: 10.1080/19361610.2020.1832018.

King, M. (2020d). Financial fraud investigative interviewing – Corporate investigators' beliefs and practices: A qualitative inquiry, *Journal of Financial Crime*, published online doi: 10.1108/JFC-08-2020-0158.

King, M. (2021a). Profiting from a tainted trade: Private investigators' views on the popular culture glamorization of their trade, *Journal of Criminological Research Policy and Practice*, published online doi: 10.1108/JCRPP-07-2020-0050.

King, M. (2021b). *Pathways and Partnerships: A Study of Private Policing Economic Crime in Australia*, dissertation submitted in fulfilment of the requirements for the degree of doctor of philosophy, School of Justice, Faculty of Law, Queensland University of Technology, Australia.

Meerts, C.A. (2014). Empirical case studies of corporate security in international perspective, in: Walby, K. and Lippert, R.K. (editors), *Corporate Security in the 21st Century – Theory and Practice in International Perspective*, Palgrave Macmillan, Hampshire, Houndmills, pages 97–115.

Meerts, C.A. (2018). The organization as the cure for its own ailments: Corporate investigators in the Netherlands, *Administrative Sciences*, 8 (25), 1–15.

Meerts, C.A. (2019). *Corporate Investigations, Corporate Justice and Public-Private Relations: Towards a New Conceptualisation*, Springer Nature, Palgrave Macmillan, Switzerland.

Meerts, C.A. (2020). Corporate investigations: Beyond notions of public-private relations, *Journal of Contemporary Criminal Justice*, 36 (1), 86–100.

Meerts, C.A. (2021). Struggles in cooperation: Public-private relations in the investigation of internal financial crime in the Netherlands, in: Lord, N., Inzelt, E., Huisman, W. and Faria, R. (editors), *European White-Collar Crime: Exploring the Nature of European Realities*, Bristol University Press, Bristol, UK.

Schneider, S. (2006). Privatizing economic crime enforcement: Exploring the role of private sector investigative agencies in combating money laundering, *Policing & Society*, 16 (3), 285–312.

Williams, J.W. (2005a). Reflections on the private versus public policing of economic crime, *British Journal of Criminology*, 45, 316–339.

Williams, J.W. (2005b). Governability matters: The private policing of economic crime and the challenge of democratic governance, *Policing & Society*, 15 (2), 187–211.

Wood, J.D. (2020). Private policing and public health: A neglected relationship, *Journal of Contemporary Criminal Justice*, 36 (1), 19–38.

Conclusion

Traditionally, control in organizations is concerned with top-down approaches, where executives attempt to direct their employees' attention, behaviors, and performance to align with the organization's goals and objectives. This book took a new approach by turning the problem of control upside down as it focuses on control of executives who find white-collar crime convenient. The bottom-up approach to executive compliance and conformance focuses on organizational measures to make white-collar crime less convenient for potential offenders.

The significance of the bottom-up approach lies in the failure of traditional approaches to prevention and detection of executive deviance. At the top of organizations, trust rather than control is the main attitude toward other privileged individuals. Not surprisingly then, deviance is more convenient at the top than further down in the organization. When scandals emerge after detection of executive wrongdoing, people tend to be surprised as scandals reach newsmaking criminology. The bottom-up approach can be efficient and effective to prevent and detect white-collar crime, as skepticism of management actions creates a motivation to correct the situation. People in the organization want to preserve and improve the reputation and survival of the business and avoid organizational mourning after organizational collapse.

Rather than focusing on the regulatory formalities and staged procedures of compliance and audits, this book emphasized the organizational challenges involved in compliance and conformity work when trusted corporate officials exhibit deviant behavior, refining and advancing knowledge in this field by reference to contemporary international case studies and associated original evaluative research. The themes and cases in this book were carefully selected to provide the reader with an insight into professional conduct and procedural practice – the organization of corporate compliance and conformity against failure, fraud, and corruption – with the theory of convenience placed at the fore. It is the bottom-up approach by application of convenience theory and the challenges from the social license to operate that contributed to the book's uniqueness.

The book has focused on executives' offending behavior not employees. At its core, bottom-up control refers to the manner in which organizational members can use different types of control mechanisms – such as whistleblowing, transparency, resource access, or culture – to monitor, measure, and evaluate executives' avoidance of deviant behaviors and influence them toward achieving the organization's goals in efficient and effective ways. While the hierarchical structure remains with executives at the top of the organization in charge of the business, bottom-up control is a matter of stakeholder involvement in compliance and conformance. While top-down control is often a formal and rigid system, bottom-up control can be an informal and flexible system as discussed in this book.

Index